Thinking the ...

THINKING THE OLYMPICS

The Classical Tradition and the Modern Games

Edited by
Barbara Goff
&
Michael Simpson

Bristol Classical Press

First published in 2011 by
Bristol Classical Press
an imprint of
Bloomsbury Academic
Bloomsbury Publishing Plc
50 Bedford Square
London WC1B 3DP

Editorial arrangement © 2011 by
Barbara Goff and Michael Simpson
The contributors retain copyright in
their individual contributions

CIP records for this book are available from the
British Library and the Library of Congress

ISBN 978-0-7156-3930-6

Typeset by Ray Davies
Printed and bound in Great Britain by
CPI Group Ltd, Croydon, Surrey

Contents

Contents

Acknowledgements

This volume derives from a conference held at the Institute of Classical Studies, University of London, in September 2008. We should like to thank all those who facilitated the conference, especially Mike Edwards and Olga Krzyszkowska of the Institute, Nina Aitken of the University of Reading, Maria Wyke, Peter Dunwoodie, and Lorna Hardwick who delivered the closing remarks. We would also like to acknowledge the financial support offered to the conference by the Department of Classics at the University of Reading, the Department of English and Comparative Literature at Goldsmiths, University of London, the Hellenic Society, and the Classical Association.

We would also like to thank the IT help desk at the University of Reading and Mira Vogel at Goldsmiths, University of London, for invaluable help with images. Finally we would like to express our gratitude to our editor, Deborah Blake, for her commitment and encouragement throughout the publication process.

List of Contributors

Stephen Brunet is Associate Professor of Classics and Affiliate Faculty in Kinesiology at the University of New Hampshire. His scholarly work focuses on such topics as the use of dwarf athletes in the Roman games and the careers of young athletes during the Roman Empire. He is the co-author, along with Stephen Trzaskoma and R. Scott Smith, of the *Anthology of Classical Myth*.

Debbie Challis is Audience Development Officer at the Petrie Museum of Egyptian Archaeology and has worked in museums and archives for over ten years. Her research includes current practice in museums relating to the display of antiquity, the reception of the classical world and archaeology in visual culture during the nineteenth century and the impact of racial science on ideas about the past. She has curated the exhibition *Typecast: The 'racial types' of Francis Galton and Flinders Petrie* at the Petrie Museum (29 March-22 December 2011). Publications include *From the Harpy Tombs to the Wonders of Ephesus: British Archaeologists in the Ottoman Empire* (Duckworth, 2008).

Armand D'Angour is Fellow and Tutor in Classics at Jesus College, Oxford. His publications include articles on ancient Greek music and on Greek and Roman poetry. His book *The Greeks and the New: Novelty in Ancient Greek Imagination and Experience* is due to be published shortly by Cambridge University Press. He was commissioned by the International Olympic Committee to compose a Pindaric Ode to Athens for the 2004 Olympic Games, and is considering a similar commission from the Mayor of London for the London Olympics 2012.

Barbara Goff is Professor of Classics at the University of Reading. She has published extensively on Greek tragedy and its reception, and is currently developing a research focus on the role of the classical tradition in the formation of modernity, of which this edited collection is the first fruit. She is due to publish a volume in the Classical Diaspora series, titled *Your Secret Language: the cultural politics of classics in the British colonies of West Africa* (Bristol Classical Press, 2013).

List of Contributors

Ann Keen is an architectural historian currently in the dissertation phase of her doctoral studies at Rutgers. Her dissertation focuses on the changing ideals of modern architecture after World War II by examining sports facilities designed for the Summer Olympic Games, 1960-1976. Her professional experience includes architectural investigations with a particular emphasis on twentieth-century resources. In this capacity, she has authored National Register of Historic Places nominations, Historic American Buildings Survey documentation, and numerous cultural resource reports on behalf of the military, government agencies, and private organisations. Recent research on architect Richard Neutra resulted in a small book on his work at Mountain Home Air Force Base in Idaho.

The Rt. Hon. Tessa Jowell MP is currently Shadow Minister for the Olympics. She was Secretary of State for Culture, Media and Sport 2001-07, and Minister for the Olympics 2007-10.

Hugh M. Lee is Professor of Classics at the University of Maryland, College Park. He is the author of *The Program and Schedule of the Ancient Olympic Games* (Hildesheim 2001), and articles and book chapters on Greek and Roman sports. His current research interests lie in the history of the scholarship of Greek and Roman sport, in particular, the contributions of Girolamo Mercuriale, Petrus Faber, and Gilbert West. Since 1988, Lee has served on the editorial board of *Nikephoros. Zeitschrift für Sport und Kultur im Altertum.*

William L. Pressly is a Professor in the Department of Art History and Archaeology at the University of Maryland. In addition to numerous articles and essays on British art, he has published five books, including two on James Barry: *The Life and Art of James Barry* (Yale University Press, 1981) and *James Barry: The Artist as Hero* (Tate Gallery, 1983). His last book was *The Artist as Original Genius: Shakespeare's 'Fine Frenzy' in Late-Eighteenth-Century British Art* (University of Delaware Press, 2007). The painting discussed in his essay in this volume will form part of his next book devoted just to Barry's murals at the Royal Society of Arts in London.

David Gilman Romano is Director of Greek Archaeological Projects at the University of Pennsylvania Museum of Archaeology and Anthropology and Adjunct Professor of Classical Studies at the University of Pennsylvania. His interests include Greek and Roman cities and sanctuaries, Greek and Roman athletics including the ancient Olympic Games, Roman centuriation and land planning and computer applications in archaeology. Since 2004 he has been Co-Director and Field Director of the Mt. Lykaion Excavation and Survey Project in Arcadia, Greece. His publications include *Mapping Augustan Rome* (2002) in collaboration with Lothar

Haselberger and *Athletics and Mathematics in Archaic Corinth: The Origins of the Greek Stadion* (1993) as well as a series of publications on the city and landscape planning of the Roman colony of Corinth.

Michael Simpson is Senior Lecturer in the Department of English and Comparative Literature at Goldsmiths, University of London. His research interests are divided between British Romantic literature and classical reception, especially in certain postcolonial contexts. He is the author of *Closet Performances: Political Exhibition and Prohibition in the Dramas of Byron and Shelley* (Stanford University Press, 1998) and co-author of *Crossroads in the Black Aegean: Oedipus, Antigone, and Dramas of the African Diaspora* (Oxford University Press, 2007). With Barbara Goff he is currently co-writing a book about Classics and the British Labour Movement.

Nigel Spivey is Senior Lecturer in Classical Art and Archaeology in the Faculty of Classics, Cambridge University. Among his publications are *The Micali Painter and his Followers* (Oxford University Press 1987), *Looking at Greek Vases* (co-edited with Tom Rasmussen: Cambridge University Press 1990), *Greek Art* (Phaidon 1996), *Etruscan Art* (Thames & Hudson 1997), *Enduring Creation* (Thames & Hudson 2001), and *How Art Made The World* (BBC/PBS 2005). His research interests cover Greek, Etruscan and Roman topics, as well as the broader prehistory of art, and the 'afterlife' of Classical images. Current projects include a compendious 'interpretative handbook' of Greek sculpture (Cambridge University Press), and a second edition of his 2004 monograph, *The Ancient Olympics* (Oxford University Press).

Damian Stocking is Assistant Professor of English and Comparative Literature at Occidental College, in Los Angeles, California. His primary research interest is the relation between ancient literature and Continental philosophy. He has published work on the Homeric sense of self, the communal work of Greek tragedy, and the ontological implications of style in Archaic and Classical art and literature. He is currently at work on an analysis of Aristophanes' response to Greek philosophy in the *Clouds*.

Eleni Volonaki is a Lecturer in Ancient Greek Literature in the School of Humanities, University of Peloponnese. Her thesis: *A Commentary on Lysias'* Against Agoratos *(13) and* Against Nikomachos *(30)* (University of London) is forthcoming in Papazisis editions (Athens). She has published extensively on Greek Law and Rhetoric, and her forthcoming publications include a commentary on Lycurgus *Against Leokrates*.

List of Illustrations

Other sources of the illustrations are given in the captions. The publishers are grateful to all who have provided illustrations and given permission for their reproduction.

Introduction: Game Plan

Barbara Goff

Every four years a sporting event unfolds distinguished not only by its unparalleled global reach and resonance, but also by its deliberate invocation of ancient Greece. One of the biggest, most lavish shows on earth persists in tracing a lineage from the ancient civilisation of a small, poor country – well in advance of the London Olympics of 2012, official webpages were busy proclaiming the descent of certain sports from their classical counterparts.[1] During its complex history the modern Olympics has managed many contradictions, but surely the persistence of its genuflection to classical antiquity, in the midst of its commercial and technical modernity, invites some comment. Yet to date, there has been very little discussion of the modern Games' relation to the classical tradition.[2] This book hopes to examine some of the aspects of the Olympic claim to continuity between ancient and modern, and thus to contribute to the growing field of research in classical reception studies as well as to the well-established field of Olympic history. This Introduction provides a larger context for individual chapters' investigations.

Some elements of the context do not need discussion; for instance, this book does not have to note that ancient Greece was innocent of any such ritual as the torch relay, or any such race as the marathon, because this has been spelled out in previous studies.[3] What I hope to do instead is to trace some of the ideological work that ancient Greece has been called upon to do, in the service of the modern Olympics. 'Ancient Greece' or 'the classical tradition' does not here denote a pre-existing edifice, but comprises a shifting repertoire of roles, props and scenes which can be articulated as metonyms assembling a familiar but fashioned whole. So an authoritative tradition, answering particular needs, is conjured from discrete and largely theatrical elements. I shall propose that ancient Greece offers an ideal which is always compromised in performance, so that the rhythm of aspiration and instantiation provides a dynamic restlessness that helps to capture the public imagination and drive the development of the Games as an institution. To make this argument I shall first consider the various versions of ancient Greece in the writings of Pierre de Coubertin, and secondly examine some of the other repre-

1

sentations of ancient Greece in more contemporary Olympic rhetoric. I shall suggest that classical antiquity is invoked to elaborate on the very idea of tradition itself, to mediate between past and future, and to address ideological contradictions. Since it is only an idealised version of ancient Greece that could accomplish all these tasks, however, the tasks themselves help to expose the fissures in the ideal; conversely, the fissures help to keep the ideal vigorously productive.

Ancient Greece has also provided the revived Games with a stable and widely recognised iconography. If we analyse medals, posters and opening ceremonies, we can discern a certain temporal arc; while the iconography is robustly Hellenic in the first 50 years or so of the modern Games, the visual identity then relinquishes Hellenic motifs, only to revive ancient Greece with the centenary of the Games and the 'return to Athens' in 2004. Once the Games moved to Beijing in 2008, the discourse could be seen to draw attention to the very different antiquity of China, but also to proclaim certain continuities and significant contrasts. Ancient Greece remains important to modern Olympic ideology, moreover, insofar as the institution of the torch relay proclaims a role for ancient Greece as the sign of peace. The Introduction will close by considering whether in order to retain this role, ancient Greece has to yield to a further idealising representation that arguably robs it of dynamism and descends into kitsch.

A question of origins

The conventional history of the Olympic revival is often rehearsed.[4] Baron Pierre de Coubertin, scion of minor aristocracy, grew up in the shadows of France's defeat in the Franco-Prussian war, despaired over the state of French education, travelled in England and was convinced by the athletic education and muscular Christianity prescribed by Arnold at Rugby. Visiting William Penny Brookes and the Much Wenlock Olympian Class, he conceived of a grander project, the revival of the Olympic Games 'on a basis suited to the conditions of modern life' ((1892) 2000: 297).[5] He proposed the revival in a lecture at the Sorbonne, but his words met with 'total, absolute lack of comprehension' ((1932) 2000: 314). In 1894 he tried again, organising a congress on amateurism at which the last item on the agenda was restoration of the Olympic Games, and here he carried the day ('Preliminary Programme', 2000: 302). The Olympic project, its history and significances, occupy at least one third of the 15,000 pages he published of books, articles, journalism, autobiography, speeches, addresses, and memoranda (Müller 2000: 20).

The story of the Olympics in this version is thus the very specific one of Coubertin's vision. After the success of Athens 1896, which Coubertin celebrates in his 1897 report ((1897) 2000: 350-60), the next two Olympic Games, at Paris and St Louis, are sometimes disrespected, because Coubertin did not approve of them; London 1908 was considered an improvement (Kent 2008: 215), and redemption came to the Olympic movement with Stockholm 1912, with which Coubertin was well pleased. No sooner have the Games proved their viability, however, than war breaks out, forcing the Olympics into abeyance until Antwerp 1920. The 'Golden Age' (Senn 1999: 3) of successful and relatively uncontroversial Games supervenes, terminated by Berlin 1936 and the next wartime suspension. When the Games recommence, in London in 1948, they quickly establish themselves as among the most important international events, but along with their success, begin to suffer from the competing claims of modernity. In the contemporary period, while they have become ever bigger and more impressive, they have also mutated under various contradictory pressures including women's demands, the struggles over apartheid, encroaching professionalism, drugs, terrorism, the Cold War and its reciprocal boycotts, economic tension, corruption scandals in the International Olympic Committee (IOC) itself,[6] and the exactions of global media. How has ancient Greece survived as an object of reverence amid all this change?

We may first note that versions of ancient Greece have stood in for the very ideas of tradition and origin themselves. Commentators describe how the revived Olympics quickly surrounded itself with traditions and rituals, many of which persist (Senn 1999: 3, Müller 2000: 43). Like many institutions, the Olympic Games prefers to present itself as unchanging and inevitable, but since the Games occupy the world stage periodically, they come to be marked by the huge shifts in global politics that can emerge within four years. The notion of a tradition originating in classical antiquity offers a counterpoint to this story of dynamic response to changing circumstances. The IOC's documents repeatedly celebrate an origin in a single man and in the idealised version of ancient Greece that he purveyed, implicitly disallowing any more complex notion of descent and tradition. In this, the IOC may be seen to follow Coubertin's own claim to be sole founder, as in his report on the Athens Olympics ((1897) 2000: 311). Yet elsewhere, Coubertin gave a very different account of origins, siting his activity within a series of initiatives which cannot be attributed to any individual, and acknowledging the crucial contribution of William Penny Brookes ((1890) 2000: 281-6), who was then omitted from the report on Athens. He also noted a number of related late-nineteenth-century developments, such as improved communications, greater opportunity for travel, increased leisure, the development of national organisations in sports, and the popular phenomenon of the World's Fair and great Exhibitions ((1896) 2000: 308).[7] Add to this mix the attraction of archaeological discoveries in Greece itself,[8] and something like the revived Olympics can seem almost inevitable, rather than attributable to individual genius (Mandell 1971: 16).

Recent historians have complicated the story of origins further by rediscovering the role of Greek figures such as Vikelas, the first President of the IOC, and the various Olympic revivals of the mid-nineteenth century, in Greece and elsewhere, which precede Coubertin's initiative.[9] Furthermore, Coubertin himself offers different accounts of the transmission of the athletic ideal from ancient Greece, including or excluding Rome, or the Middle Ages, as the context requires. The 'tradition' of the revived Olympics, then, is quite unlike a straight line from past to present, but the inspirational biography of Coubertin, itself inspired by antiquity, is both easier to grasp, and more like the 'heroic' outcomes required from the Games themselves, than a more complex version.

Ancient solutions to modern ills

The revived Olympics thus came about in the context of several other developments characteristic of modernity.[10] Despite the recognised improvements in transportation, leisure and communications, however, the Games are conscious of themselves, in the writings of Coubertin, as a new solution to an established difficulty rather than as a celebration of positive new trends. Coubertin himself adverts early on to the problems of the French educational system, which aimed at producing examination results rather than rounded individuals ((1889) 2000: 122-7), and was quick to point to the demoralising effects of the defeat by Germany, which had convinced Frenchmen that they were inadequate to the physical demands of contemporary life ((1892) 2000: 288). How ancient Greece is deployed to address these issues is by providing a convenient patina of antique respectability to what might otherwise be seen as brute physical exercise. Thus Coubertin claims that 'the *Manual* of Epictetus is a manual of sport. The *Meditations* of Marcus Aurelius are the thoughts of a sportsman' ((1889) 2000: 129), mobilising ancient Greece to perform the special task of representing a blend of physical with spiritual or artistic endeavour. What enabled ancient Greece to work this way was its still unquestioned prestige throughout European culture, which included the notion that Greece had attained a balance between the physical and the spiritual or artistic. This notion Coubertin illustrated by reference to the combination of religious, artistic and athletic culture at Olympia itself.[11] Freely admitting the need to place 'these meetings under the only patronage which could throw over them a halo of greatness and glory: "The patronage of Classical Antiquity"!' ((1896) 2000: 309), Coubertin deploys the acknowledged transcendence of 'Classical Antiquity' to surmount what might otherwise be a challenging disjunction between physical and spiritual.

That it was an idealised version of ancient Greece that was invoked to revive the Olympics goes without saying, for the nineteenth century knew hardly any other. It is as an ideal that ancient Greece supplies the remedies for various contemporary ills, which in Coubertin's writings include not only the shortcomings of education and physical fitness but also the depredations of industrialisation, alcohol, and social inequality.[12]

4

Introduction: Game Plan

The remedies correspondingly consist not simply in the revived Olympic Games but in the whole vision of balance and harmony that pervades Coubertin's discourse. This vision was shared with some contemporaries, but Coubertin's particular agenda was idiosyncratic as well as representative, so that his expositions repay detailed reading. His descriptions of the ideal would rarely be understood, in themselves, as referring to anything so specific as athletic competitions, and they appear instead as a late efflorescence of the Victorian Hellenism discussed by Jenkyns 1980, Turner 1981 and Clarke 1989. Although not mentioned in these studies, Coubertin exemplifies their findings to a remarkable degree. For instance, how would one identify this description as relating to athleticism? 'It was Hellenism, above all, that advocated measure and proper proportion, co-creators of beauty, grace, and strength. We must return to these Greek concepts to offset the appalling ugliness of the industrial age through which we have just lived.' The idealised Hellenism in Coubertin's writings is a highly flexible instrument, implicitly putting past and present into opposition, but then rescuing both by looking to the future, as in the next part of the quotation: 'Hellenism again! We used to believe that Hellenism was a thing of the past, a dead notion, impossible to revive and inapplicable to current conditions. This is wrong. Hellenism is part of the future. Its philosophy of life is suitable for and adaptable to modern existence' ((1938) 2000: 202). The Hellenism deployed in the Olympic revival thus shows itself as supremely modern, at home with international travel, leisure and national institutions, and oriented towards social justice, yet simultaneously deployed to rescue the world from modernity. As Fischer-Lichte (2005: 85) and others have shown, this contradiction, far from being a liability, works as a guarantee of the revived Olympics' success.

Despite the virtuous combination of physical effort with spiritual uplift, however, and the orientation towards the future of idealised Hellenism, ancient Greece must necessarily be found wanting in relation to the huge task, that of repairing industrial modernity and its ills, with which it is confronted. Coubertin's writings about Greece are encomiastic, but interrupted by some quite critical moments. He compares ancient Greek civic planning, and Greek sporting facilities, unfavourably with modern equivalents ((1909) 2000: 257, (1918) 2000: 276, (1897) 2000: 352), and castigates ancient society for slavery, although he does so largely in order to compare the 'scourge of modern times', alcohol ((1918) 2000: 277). Considering the possibility of legislation to prevent people from abusing their bodies, e.g. with alcohol, he ruminates, not entirely positively, on ancient Greek ethics and sporting spirit ((1910) 2000: 167):

> ... no law of this kind has ever been enforced. It would be futile to turn to Hellenic civilization to find any traces of it. The level attained by the Greeks in this regard was not very high ... The culture of sports in Greece, moreover, was never as widespread as we have believed ... Many authors convey

5

widespread notions of long-standing hostility on the part of public opinion with regard to physical exercises. Besides, those who engaged in exercise were not at all seen as models of virtue and continence.[13]

Coubertin also notes that the ancient Games, far from being always ideal, had succumbed to corruption, albeit 'after long and valiant resistance' ((1920b) 2000: 223). To the extent that the ancient Games were ideal, that very quality threatened them ((1908) 2000: 543): 'At Olympia, vulgar competition was transformed, and in a sense sanctified, by contact with national sentiment superbly excited. Over-excited, I might even say; for it was excess that in the end ruined and corrupted ancient athleticism.' The familiar contours of the ideal here guarantee that the ancient Greeks will 'transform' base emotions and experiences, but the enthusiasm with which they do this leads eventually to a decline. Crucially, the Games' non-ideal nature can be represented as key to their success ((1922) 2000: 209): 'without the religion, the spectacle, the hubbub, and the advertising that prolonged its existence, Ancient Olympia would never have thrived for so many centuries'.

The revived Olympic Games are, then, represented as a solution to the problems of modernity, which ancient Greece can heal by means of being an idealised combination of mind and body. But since such difficulties are too much for any one institution to solve, and since ancient Greece cannot always be presented as the ideal, the representation of the Games is troubled by contradiction. In Coubertin's writings, moreover, the Games are not enough; although there is much celebration of his achievement, there is also a repeated impression that the Games are not satisfactory and must themselves be replaced, or at least supplemented, by new improved institutions. In this rhythm of unachieved ideal and non-ideal instantiation can be read not only Coubertin's negotiation with recalcitrant reality, but also the pattern of how the revived Olympics will play out over the next century, always holding out the possibility of a pure uncorrupted ideal, and always failing to deliver. As some commentators note, this busy dialectic, coordinating past and present, is part of how the modern Olympics capture the general imagination.[14]

The 'failure' of the revived Olympics, in Coubertin's account, does not only involve the inclusion of team sports and of women's events, which he hated; nor does it refer only to the increased commercialism of the revived Olympics, about which he was at best equivocal. Instead, his writings express dissatisfaction even with the 1896 Olympics: 'In Athens, all efforts had been concentrated on the sporting side of the venture in an historical context; there had been no congress, no conference, no sign of any moral or educational purpose' ((1932) 2000: 369). He therefore produces plans for several other institutions, based in notional Greek traditions, to supply this lack. Although he initially agreed that Athens, which had wanted to keep the Games, could host instead a parallel series ((1909b) 2000: 349), the 1906 Games, which were meant to herald this, were hardly mentioned by him, and bore no fruit.[15] Instead, Coubertin elaborates plans for a permanent Olympic home in 'A Modern Olympia' ((1909-10) 2000: 256-68), in which he resists the developments of the actual revived Games by stipulating a modest number of spectators and a moral qualification for participants. Later, he moves in a different direction with a new institution, the restored 'Panathenaea', that will supplement and correct the Olympics ((1927) 2000: 279-80):

> It must be acknowledged that there was something lacking about the celebration of modern Olympiads ... A solution was found ... the restoration of the famous 'Panathenaea', in their amplification and transformation ... They will consist of three parts: athletic contests in the stadium, an historical procession from the stadium to the foot of the Acropolis, and finally a music festival in the theatre of Herod Atticus ... The athletic contests will not last more than two or three days at most, for they will be strictly limited to the ancient trials of strength and skill ... all according to the ancient methods which differ widely from ours.

This institution too came to nothing.

Despite the actual success of the revived Olympics, then, they sometimes seem in Coubertin's discourse almost to be a problem in themselves. The construction of stadiums, for instance, is a betrayal of the Olympic ideal and a means to corrupt athletics ((1928) 2000: 184):

> Stadiums are being built unwisely all over the place ... once seats for forty thousand spectators are built, you have to fill them, and that means drawing a crowd. To draw that crowd, you will need a publicity campaign, and to justify the publicity campaign you will have to draw sensational numbers ... Almost all the stadiums built in recent years are the result of local and, too often, commercial interests, not Olympic interests at all. Now ... people are on the attack against the athletes, accusing them of the corruption that has been forced on them for the past twenty years. ... In my view, these oversized showcases are the source of corruption at the root of the evil.

The success of the revived Olympics has in this account led directly to its failure. What sometimes appears able to replace the modern Olympics, as the renewed expression of the Hellenic ideal, is the revived gymnasium. Coubertin insists that 'Olympic pedagogy ... is not sufficiently served by being glorified before the world once every four years in the Olympic Games. It needs permanent factories. The Olympic factory of the ancient world was the gymnasium. The Olympiads have been renewed, but the gymnasium of antiquity has not – as yet. It must be' ((1918b) 2000: 217). Later he enlarges: 'I wish to see a revival in an extended and modernized form of the municipal gymnasium of antiquity. I should like a place where petitions and records are forbidden, but where any adult at any convenient moment, and without risk of being spied upon and criticized, may practice the simplest forms of exercise' ((1927b) 2000: 235). The ideal, as is the nature of an ideal, is always instantiated somewhere else rather than in the intractable present of the actual revived Games. The orientation within Coubertin's Hellenism towards the future seems to guarantee a kind of febrile vigour which ensures the failure of any one version of the ideal, and consequently a proliferation of forms of it.[16] It is precisely this kind of paradoxical structure that has helped the modern Games to develop in modern circumstances, while claiming a persistence rooted in tradition.

The arts of Hellenism

Coubertin's imaginative Hellenism provides this productive instability, but has not always achieved other kinds of prominence in the revived Olympics. For instance, Coubertin's conception of the Games always included an element of artistic competition, in parallel with the sporting events, in order to promote the Greek idea of balance between physical and mental activity. But lacking the potential inherent in the athletic events for excitement, corruption, gambling, or, more recently, television coverage, the artistic contests did not take off until Stockholm 1912, were never especially popular, and lapsed after London 1948. While the more recent arts festivals often accompanying the Olympics have rarely seemed successful (Garcia 2000), the re-launch of the Cultural Olympiad by Athens in 2004, which was heralded in official sources as a renewed statement of the universality of Greek values, may have inaugurated a new tradition.[17] Although the Cultural Olympiad was also an integrated part of Beijing's 2008 self-representation (Garcia 2008), however, and is energetically promoted by the London Olympic Games Organising Committee as part of its emphasis on 'inclusivity',[18] these last two contexts have less interest in the 'Greekness' of the values that they promote.

While the arts festivals of the revived Olympics have not systematically invoked ancient Greece, the medals, posters, and opening ceremonies frequently do so. In the case of the medals, which regularly express the 'prevailing Zeitgeist' (Van Alfen 2004: 2) the persistence of the classical themes is perhaps quite surprising.[19] Van Alfen suggests that the medals of the revived Olympics consistently invoke a Hellenic vision up until approximately 1932, after which Hellenism is a much more muted theme until it ceases to be influential in mid-century; then with the centenary in 1996, the Hellenic motifs re-emerge. While this is broadly convincing, Van Alfen also notes that the design on the winner's medal remained the same from 1928 till 2004, so that the most important medal always displayed a highly classicising design. On the obverse was a figure of Nike with palm and crown, and on the reverse, a triumphal athlete carried shoulder-high by a crowd, with a version of a classical building in the background. The reverse was modified in 1984 in order to show people in the crowd who were not exclusively white and male (Van Alfen 2004: 24), and in fact different reverses were used at several Olympic Games before then, although the obverse remained the same. The overall design of the medal thus sums up the IOC's winning combination of conservatism and creativity. In 1996, for the centenary, the reverse showed a stylised olive wreath, and 2004, for the 'return to Greece', the entire medal was redesigned by Elena Votsi. The IOC underscores the development: 'The main feature of the medals is the Greek character shown on both sides, since their basic side has been changed for the first time since the Amsterdam Olympic Games in 1928. This is of particular importance, as from now on all Olympic medals will reflect the Greek character of the Games as regards both their origin and their revival.'[20] The obverse of the new medal shows Nike flying into the stadium in Athens where the revived Games of 1896 were first held. On the reverse is the first line from Pindar's *Olympian* VIII. This forcing of the modern into the ancient mould seems to speak less to invocation of Greece than to the IOC's consciousness of its own traditions.

Although the Olympic winner's medal stabilised from 1928 until 2004, there was considerable variety in the early years of the century. The medal of the first Olympics showed a huge head of Zeus on the obverse and a view of the Acropolis on the reverse. As Van Alfen remarks, subsequent medals struggle with the Hellenic dimension, since they display athletes who are Greekly nude, but who sport modern hairstyles and shield their genitals with strategic, if uncomfortable, wreaths and branches.[21] They thus fly in the face of Coubertin's frequently articulated wish that the revived Olympics should conform to the conditions of modern life rather than providing moribund simulacra of antiquity.

The narrative that can be constructed about the Hellenism of Olympic posters is similar; Timmers (2008) finds that Hellenic motifs, such as nude athletes, wreaths, and olive branches, dominate until approximately mid-century. Other classicising images included the head of a crowned athlete for Berlin 1936, the Discobolus of Myron in London 1948, a classical horseman in Melbourne 1956, elements of ancient Roman architecture in Rome 1960. After a hiatus, Atlanta 1996 showed a white silhouette of a figure with a remarkably straight nose, suggesting classical antecedents, while Athens 2004 offered the 'kotinos' or olive wreath as graffito. Again we can read the classicising motifs on the posters as shorthand for the claim to longevity and tradition, while noting that the changing visual identity of the Olympics interrupts any tradition with many other concerns as well.

The appeal of ancient Greece as iconographic shorthand for effort and grace, as well as tradition and origin, can be seen in the fact that the Hellenic symbols did not die out after their use by the Nazi regime in 1936. Although the Berlin Olympics have been much discussed, their particular invocation of ancient Greece makes it appropriate to revisit them here. Initially sceptical about the Games' avowed commitment to international-

9

ism, the Nazi administration subsequently realised that hosting the Olympics could afford them a major propaganda coup, and indeed Hitler planned to retain the Games in Germany forever (Mandell 1971: 293). With their deadly flair for organising mass events, the Nazis were able to tap into the legacy of 'the tyranny of Greece over Germany'[22] and deployed classicising iconography on a scale not paralleled before (Large 2007: 147), or probably since – obtaining incidentally the approval of the aged Coubertin (Gold and Gold 2005: 173). Under Hitler's personal supervision, the architecture of the new stadium was made more classicising than first planned, an open-air theatre was created on the model of Epidaurus (Meyer-Kunzel 2007: 171-2), buildings were decorated with classicising sculpture (roundly criticised by Large 2007: 157), the posters featured a golden Greek athlete's head, the opening night a performance of Aeschylus' *Oresteia* (Fischer-Lichte 2008),[23] and the opening night reception, held in the Pergamon Museum, included a performance of the Hymn to Apollo which had graced Coubertin's initial Sorbonne conference (Mandell 1971: 156). In the run-up to the Games, ordinary Germans were encouraged to identify with the Olympic effort (Large 2007: 163-4) by a special bus which toured the rural districts offering a travelling exhibition on the modern Olympics, with some classical trappings (Mandell 1971: 123-4), and by a Berlin-based exhibition on 'Sport in Hellenic Times' (Gold and Gold 2007: 68). A further initiative was the effort of Nazi intellectuals to prove a racial connection between the Greeks, especially the Dorians or Spartans, and the northern Aryans from whom Germans allegedly descended (Gold and Gold 2005: 167, 170).

Perhaps more significantly, the Nazi administration tried to co-opt the academic establishment by promising to fund, and indeed funding, renewed excavations at Olympia (Mandell 1971: 240, Large 2007: 192). Mandell suggests that Carl Diem, the Secretary of the Berlin Olympic Committee, believed that Hitler and his acolytes were genuinely turning to the classics as a source of good rather than as further justification for their noxious policies. He also claims that the classics appeared as a 'refuge' for those Germans who were not enchanted by the Nazis (Mandell 1971: 240, 283). Berlin 1936 thus suggests the uneasy coexistence of two versions of ancient Greece: one, idolised by Coubertin and his follower Diem, which foregrounded balance and harmony, and was identified with an older tradition of German patriotism; the other deployed by the Nazis, inculcating endurance and rugged collectivity, serving the new nationalist agenda, and focussed on Sparta. Negotiation between the two versions of ancient Greece perhaps permitted the political establishment and the sporting establishment to work together, each in willed ignorance of the other side's fundamental commitments.

Ancient Greece was perhaps most directly invoked in Diem's invention of the torch relay, with its iconic moment of lighting the torch at Olympia. This stroke of ceremonial genius ensured that the Berlin Olympics were seen to descend directly from Greece, while also binding together the countries through which the torch passed, in a foreshadowing of the rather more violent unification to come (Large 2007: 5). Leni Riefenstahl's 1938 film *Olympia* played even more emphatically on the birth of Germany from the spirit of Greece. The twelve-minute prologue of the film moves from titles displayed as inscriptions, through temples seen in clouds and mist, to a series of famous classical statues that culminate in Myron's Discobolus. The statue then becomes a human athlete, and there follows a sequence of naked males throwing the discus, shotput or javelin, and of naked women exercising and dancing, silhouetted against beautiful skies and seascapes. After the final scene dissolves into flames which become those of the torch relay, the torch bearers set off on their journey through south-eastern Europe, to arrive eventually at the Berlin stadium. Geography and history are both telescoped so that the dreamy ideal of Greece can be instantiated in the muscular realities of the Nazi body.[24]

Although the torch relay might be thought irremediably compromised by its Nazi origins, it has been retained. Perhaps its affiliation with Greece overcomes that with Hitler, or perhaps the notions of origins and history are more malleable in Olympic rhetoric than they might at first appear. Since the first postwar Olympics, London 1948, prominently featured the Discobolus, combined on posters with an image of Big Ben, it is possible that this use of the symbolic statue was designed to correct Riefenstahl's earlier emphatic use. In Rome in 1960 the athletic events were set in ancient sites that might also have been thought contaminated by earlier Fascist exploitation, but the sites were represented as defiantly classical rather than mid-century, and the signs of antiquity were again pressed into the service of a celebration of modernity.[25] Moreover, at both Berlin and Rome, athletes of African descent were able consummately to disprove Fascist tenets, upholding the validity of actual sporting performance against political dogma.[26] While the Hellenic ideal can be damaged by its instantiation in historical events, performance can equally well interrupt other ideological formations, to positive effect.

Within the regularly scheduled celebrations of the Olympics, the torch relay and the opening ceremonies, ancient Greece is repeatedly invoked, with sometimes mixed effect. Even in their latest Beijing incarnation, the opening ceremonies have elements of nineteenth-century pageant about them, and while the torch relay has gone high-tech, global, and security-conscious in recent years, the ritual of lighting the torch at Olympia is stubbornly archaising. Although Coubertin railed against 'a procession of Panathenians all dressed up in costume, ascending an artificial rock to a cardboard Propylaea, fake incense burning in painted wooden tripods while ancient hymns are sung to dead gods' ((1894c) 2000: 534), such activities persist. A brief survey of opening ceremonies shows repeated invocation of ancient Greece, but in a context of other quite different tactics, and considerations far removed from simply those of tradition.

Parading the nations

The opening ceremonies of the Olympics are officially celebrated as in some ways the most important part of the Games. Responsible for advertising the host city and of course the Games themselves, they also have the task of convening a global television audience, setting a positive tone for the events to follow, selling more tickets and thus making more money than those events, and demonstrating the authority of the IOC (MacAloon 1996). That their contribution to advertising the 'values of Olympism', as in sporting behaviour, friendship and peace, is not as visible as these less idealised tasks, is sometimes ruefully conceded even in official IOC publications.[27] The opening ceremonies are required to contain certain elements including the parade of athletes, speeches of welcome, oaths by athletes and judges, Olympic hymn and flag, and lighting of the Olympic cauldron (Hogan 2009: 100). In the last few decades, host cities and nations have expanded the ceremony to include artistic programmes in which to represent favoured versions of themselves. Although the opening ceremonies have involved musical programmes, with choirs and marching bands, since the earliest times, the associated activities have arguably become more nationalistic, as well as more grandiose and more spectacular.

This change might be dated to Moscow 1980, which seems to be the first Games explicitly to divide the ceremony into 'protocol' and 'pageant' (Novikov 1980 vol. 2 part 1: 280), and as part of the pageant, to celebrate the nation by means of folkloristic dances (Novikov 1980 vol. 2 part 1: 297). In the face of the American boycott of these Games, this is an understandable gesture, and it may not be coincidence either that Moscow stages elements of a classical tradition, thereby staking a claim to the heart of Europe and its past. 'The parade was preceded by a colourful procession in which youths and girls in ancient Greek costumes rode around the arena in three chariots, symbolising continuity of the Olympic ideals of antiquity with those of the modern Games' (Novikov 1980 vol. 2 part 1: 283). Women in Greek garb re-emerged at the closing ceremony to surround the Olympic flame in a tableau vivant (Novikov 1980 vol. 2 part 1: 300, 305). There were no such references in Los Angeles 1984, even though the organisers acknowledged that they were competing directly with the artistry and skill displayed four years earlier (Los Angeles Olympic Organising Committee 1984 vol. 1 part 1: 200-2). In Seoul 1988, the artistic part of the programme concentrated on the goals of peace and harmony, foregrounding the relevance of the eastern tradition to such ideals, but involved 'Greek maidens' as well as 'Korean nymphs' in a dance around the 'World Tree' (Seoul Olympic Organising Committee 1988 vol. 1 part 2: 393). With Barcelona 1992, the official report draws attention to the need to appeal to the television audience (Cujàs 1992 vol. 4: 42), and the opening ceremonies correspondingly take on an extra dramatic dimension, performing the voyage of Herakles from Greece to the edge of the western world (what is now Spain). For what seems to be the first time, the opening ceremonies display a fully narrative component, which links the host country firmly to the Greek origin of the Games, harnessing the classical tradition to its self-representation. The story of Herakles' voyage, culminating in the building of a temple, takes up many pages of the official report (Cujàs 1992 vol. 4: 56-91).

In Atlanta, in the centenary year 1996, the building of a temple took a central role, and commentators were impressed by the way that silhouettes of ancient sports were projected onto the fabric walls of the 'temple of Zeus' (Atlanta Committee for the Olympic Games 1996 vol. 2 part 2: 61-2). In Sydney, the millennium ceremonies dispensed with any such invocation, but ancient Greece returned with a vengeance in Athens 2004. Celebrating the status of ancient Greek sculpture, the opening ceremony offered a pageant of Greek history dramatised through art, from a Cycladic head which opened to reveal first an archaic kouros and then a classical figure, through representations of Minoan friezes and Pheidian statues, to the arts of the Byzantine, 'Traditional' and Modern Greek periods. What was perhaps most impressive, however, was that all the artworks were played by human participants, dressed and made up like marble or painted wood, often preserving a sculptural stillness as the pageant moved past on giant floats (Athens Committee for the Olympic Games 2004 vol. 2: 166-87). In the case of the Parthenon frieze particularly, it was hard to tell if the sculptures were coming alive or if the performers were turning into marble. While the official report suggests that the story of Greece leads the 'journey of humankind from myth to logic' (Athens Committee for the Olympic Games 2004 vol. 2: 164), the ceremony ensured that Greece connected to all humanity by featuring the double helix, 'formed via lasers on a wall of water' (Athens Committee for the Olympic Games 2004 vol. 2: 184). One commentator remarked on the ceremony's 'simplicity and elegance' (Panagiotopoulou 2008) but this is perhaps not the only possible reaction; the opening ceremony might also suggest a mismatch between the evocation of a specific past and the ambitious claims to universal relevance via DNA, while also registering that to evoke that past can entail a certain petrification into a limited range of attitudes.[28]

The opening ceremony of Beijing 2008 may be understood in part as a riposte to Athens 2004. Even though the award to Beijing had been immensely controversial, and media and academic reports in the run-up to the 2008 Games were equivocal at least, the sheer scale of the Beijing achievement, in terms of technical mastery and ability to mobilise breathtaking numbers of people, generated very favourable media coverage of the opening ceremony. But academic responses to the opening ceremony, contrasting it with Athens, recognised that it threw down a gauntlet to the western humanist tradition for which 'ancient Greece' remains a potent shorthand. Dramatising the invention of the printing press and the compass, as well as replaying epic Chinese voyages of discovery, Beijing 2008 seemed quite pointedly to demonstrate that some well-known contours of western civilisation are in fact eastern. The rhetoric of the 2008 Games repeated that China is the only civilisation that can boast a direct connection to her ancient heritage (unlike Greece which was conquered by the Ottoman Empire) and made it quite clear that here was a whole other tradition which should be recognised and honoured. Furthermore, the hallmark of the proceedings, spectacularly synchronised movements of immense masses of people, implicitly questioned the western obsession with the individual. One commentator ties this element precisely to the Athens opening ceremony: 'Special commentaries and comparisons were dedicated to the 2008 percussionists with a perfect military line-up and synchronization to the single percussionist in Athens and the other percussionists moving freely in the stadium' (Panagiotopoulou 2008). Similarly, where Athens had used people as artworks, Beijing used people as technology, as in the astonishing performance of the human printing press.[29] Panagiotopoulou goes on to conclude that: 'If the Athens 2004 opening ceremony referred to the birth of Western civilization (philosophy and sciences as the ground for western thought and achievements), the Beijing ceremony invited the Western civilization as spectator to admire its own achievements by adopting westernized ways of performance for the sake of television and the global audience.' This view is unconvincing, since the performances were by no means fully westernised, and discussion around the rehearsals for the opening ceremony suggested that the west could never have achieved such standards, precisely because of its allegiance to the values of the individual and his/her health and safety.[30]

Other elements of the rhetoric surrounding the Beijing Olympics were more accommodating, and while these sources are not nearly as prominent as those which concentrate on China and indigenous Chinese tradition, they may be significant in the overall story of the Olympics' relation to ancient Greece. The Humanistic Olympics Studies Centre, an independent research centre of Renmin University in China, produced articles in which ancient Greece and ancient Asia were brought into either comparison or significant contrast. Jin Yuanpu 2004 compares Chinese and Aristotelian theories of language, and Kang Shin Pyo 2005 uses contrast with ancient Greece to discuss the cultural grammar of the Seoul ceremonies. The ritual invocation of ancient Greece may perhaps be thought to perform the function of including China in the Eurocentric community of nations usually assumed by the Olympics. In direct contrast to any such gesture were the Tibetan protests that surrounded the torch relay of 2008, which aimed at excluding China from the community of nations by drawing attention to its record of abuse of human rights. Although the protests accompanied the torch relay throughout its global route, causing significant disruption and reorganisation (including in 2009 an IOC ban on further international relays), it seems likely that the first protests at

Olympia, iconic location of numerous reverent torch-lighting ceremonies, implicitly mobilised the notion of ancient Greece as birthplace of freedom and democracy. Insofar as the location at Olympia also speaks to history and continuity, the protesters can be seen to mount a parodic metonym of the Olympic dynamic that I have suggested in this introduction, interrupting an idealised Hellenic tradition with their own, impassioned performances.

Peace?

The Tibetan protests are the latest in a long history of protests against aspects of the Olympics, but they remind us that the Games persist in invoking the descent from ancient Greece as guarantee of their essentially benign influence on the global scene. While ancient Greece served Coubertin and his supporters as a sign of balance and harmony, it has more recently become shorthand also for 'peace', via the idea of the 'Olympic Truce'.[31] With its message of peace taken around the world, the relay is said to invoke the announcement of the Truce:

> The tradition of the 'Truce' or 'Ekecheiria' was established in ancient Greece in the 9th century BCE by the signature of a treaty between three kings. During the Truce period, the athletes, artists and their families, as well as ordinary pilgrims, could travel in total safety to participate in or attend the Olympic Games and return afterwards to their respective countries. As the opening of the Games approached, the sacred truce was proclaimed and announced by citizens of Elis who travelled throughout Greece to pass on the message.[32]

Although the very limited ambitions of the historical 'truce' have been frequently documented by ancient historians (e.g. Golden 2008: 133-6), the rhetoric of the Olympic establishment is undeterred. Whereas the IOC once promulgated the relatively modest notion that athletes can form friendships in competition which transcend boundaries of nation and ideology, it now claims world peace as a natural outcome of sport. As ancient Greece was mobilised by Coubertin's writings to provide a solution to nineteenth century problems, so in the contemporary period ancient Greece is moulded to the new requirements of the Olympic establishment, here chiefly to give a patina of high cultural respectability to what is in many ways a global commercial enterprise. Indeed, since Jacques Rogge's 1996 statement that the Olympics are primarily about television, commentators might be forgiven for concluding that the IOC harnesses any genuine, constructive anti-war sentiments to its own commercial well-being.[33]

The lighting of the relay torch at Olympia is perhaps the chief moment at which a full-dress version of ancient Greece is invoked by the contemporary Olympics. No official report is complete without a shot of the 'holy high priestess' capturing the sun's rays in the special parabolic mirror, according to the 'traditional ritual', and then bearing the 'sacred' flame to the 'sacred' grove where Coubertin's heart is buried, and where the 'priestess' passes the flame to the first runner. The iconography has not changed since its inception in 1936, and the reverend prose of official reports hardly changes either; it is only very rarely, for instance, that the women participating are described as 'actresses'.[34] From the perspective of this Introduction, the torch relay is highly symbolic of the Olympic movement as a whole: an invented tradition which has captured the public imagination, it literally begins in Greece but then, on its ambitious trajectory, moves through whatever minefields are currently prepared for it by global politics. Yet as the one part of the Olympics that is traditionally free and open to all, the relay remains available, even while embroiled in disputes, as a sign of peace and friendship.[35] In these complex negotiations, the torch relay perhaps signifies that ancient Greece can still be called upon to address the contradictions of modernity.

*

As they seek to make sense of the traditions of the Games, the essays in this volume together reflect the diversity of their common object. Proceeding from numerous disciplinary perspectives, the essays constitute a complex manifold, because they are responding to the inherent complexity of the Games as a loose ensemble, or congeries, of numerous forms – economic, political, historical, cultural, and, within the latter, artistic, literary, dramatic, theatrical and musical – all overlapping differentially in a kind of crowded Venn diagram. Together the essays interrogate the notion of the Games' classical tradition, investigating the active construction of it at different historical junctures, for varying audiences, and in relation to competing demands. The essays address the theme of tradition and the Olympic ideal by analysing different moments of continuity or disjunction, and suggest some of the ways in which an idealising tradition can be interrupted by specific interests.

Some of the shared concerns which emerge among the essays include comparisons between ancient and modern athletes (Romano, Brunet, Simpson), the nature of victory (Romano, Stocking, Simpson) Pindaric and other rhetorics of victory (Stocking, Lee, Pressly, Keen, D'Angour), and the varying social contexts of 'Olympic' ideals (Spivey, Volonaki, Simpson, Challis). There is also a timely interest in the English dimension of the revived Games (Lee, Pressly, Challis). Chapter 1, 'Pythagoras and the Origins of Olympic Ideology', investigates the prehistory of the concept that comes to be called 'Olympism', seeking the roots of what became a tradition, and in the process challenging received history. Chapter 2, 'True Heroes and Dishonorable Victors at Olympia', pursues the theme of the contradictory use of Olympic values. To its examination of the complexi-

16

ties of 'victory', both ancient and modern, Chapter 3, 'To Give Over One's Heart: Pindar, Bataille and the Poetics of Victory', responds by suggesting instead that the Pindaric ode is rooted in an experience of victory that can be shared across history. Chapter 4, 'Epideictic Oratory at the Olympic Games', considers the ideological investments of public oratory at the Games, including one occasion where Olympic 'harmony' was interrupted by orchestrated violence. Chapter 5, 'Living in the Shadow of the Past: Greek Athletes During the Roman Empire', discusses how later athletes approached Olympic tradition, and thus provides a bridge to the second part of the collection.

The next two chapters investigate certain eighteenth-century attitudes that preceded international discussion of a revival. Chapter 6, 'Gilbert West and the English Contribution to the Revival of the Olympic Games', reveals West's hitherto neglected role in the reinvention of the Games, while Chapter 7, 'James Barry's "Crowning the Victors at Olympia": Transmitting the Values of the Classical Olympic Games into the Modern Era' reinterprets James Barry's impressive mural to suggest a covert but ambitious political allegory. The nineteenth-century Crystal Palace Olympics are considered in the context of Victorian fears about physical and mental degeneration in Chapter 8, 'The Race for a Healthy Body: The Ancient Greek Physical Ideal in Victorian London', which also discusses the work of Charles Kingsley and his extension of the Greek athletic ideal to women as well as men. In Chapter 9, the role of the Olympic movement in overcoming mid-twentieth-century wartime tensions is investigated by analysis of Olympic architecture in 'Nervi's Palazzo and Palazzetto dello Sport: Striking a Delicate Balance between Past and Present in 1960 Rome'. The 2004 Olympics are represented by the two final chapters. Chapter 10, 'Trailing the Olympic Epic: Black Modernity and the Athenian Arena, 2004', examines the representation of the conjunction between ancient Greece and modern Africa in publicity for the 2004 Games. Chapter 11, 'Pindar at the Olympics: The Limits of Revivalism', is a consideration of the place of the modern Pindaric Ode by the scholar who was invited to compose it for the Athenian Games. Apparently a similar Ode will grace London 2012, but what will its significance be?

Notes

1. *London 2012: Wrestling*. Accessed 2010.
http://www.london2012.com/games/olympic-sports/wrestling.php.

2. Schaus and Wenn 2007 considers ancient and modern Games, but not the classical tradition that allegedly binds them.

3. The most recent is Golden 2008. The invention of tradition that characterises the Olympics has been well discussed; see e.g. Biddiss 1999, Toohey and Veal 2007.

4. Of the many sources, some are hagiographic (Rioux 2000), some polemical (Soldatow 1980: 33-46). Toohey and Veal 2007: 35-8 perhaps achieves a balance. On Coubertin himself, MacAloon 1987 remains authoritative.

5. References are to *Olympism: Selected Writings*, published in 2000, but I give the date of the first publication in parentheses.

6. The International Olympic Committee was established by Coubertin, and remained largely identical with him until his death. An unelected body with de facto international powers, it oversees each session of the Games, chooses the host city, and obtains almost unimaginable revenue from the events. It is accountable to no other body, and its workings regularly come under intense critical scrutiny (Shaw 2008). Although the IOC has overcome some of its earlier challenges, such as its relation to apartheid South Africa or to political divisions in Germany and Korea, it continues to struggle with doping incidents, and has recently been severely criticised for condoning environmental damage. Its decision to award the 2008 Games to China was highly controversial (Broudehoux 2007). In this Introduction the IOC and 'official' views on the Olympics are synonymous.

7. See also Gold and Gold 2007: 61.

8. Curtius lectured on Olympia in Berlin 1852, and led the German expedition to Olympia 1875-81.

9. See especially Young 1996a, Hill 1992: 11-15.

10. See Turner 1981: 450 on connections between the nineteenth-century rediscovery of Greece and the transformations of modernity.

11. (1894) 2000: 532, (1906) 2000: 254-5, (1929) 2000: 564. Versions of this balance can be read in the discourse of the London 2012 Olympics, e.g. Coe 2007.

12. See e.g. (1918) 2000: 277; (1919) 2000: 172; (1920) 2000: 674; and (1919a) 2000: 739-40.

13. Coubertin quoted no sources, but probably referred to passages such as the fragments of Euripides' satyr play *Autolykos,* which are very critical of athletes' morals.

14. See e.g. Toohey and Veal 2007: 7-8, Dyreson 2007: 336-9.

15. See Young 1996a: 166, Kanin 1981: 32.

16. Although for different reasons, the IOC has also always generated new and improved versions of its central enterprise, as with the Winter Olympics, the Olympic Academy, the Olympic Museum, the Olympic Studies Centre, and the new (for 2010) Youth Olympics.

17. See *Value System*, 2004. 'Greek culture has provided humanity with enduring and imperishable values, all of which revolve around the notion that everything has to be in moderation.' The 'globally comprehensible, Greek values' are said to include democracy, humanitarianism, universality, and harmony, as well as 'the Olympic ideal'. Accessed 2010. http://www.cultural-olympiad.gr/.

18. See *London 2012: Get Involved*, 2009. Accessed 2010. http://www.london2012.com/get-involved/cultural-olympiad/index.php.

19. My discussion of the medals is indebted to Van Alfen 2004.

20. See *Athens 2004 Collection*, 2004. Accessed 2010. http://www.olympic.org/en/content/Olympic-Games/All-Past-Olympic-Games/Summer/Athens-2004/Athens-2004-Collection/?Tab=1.

21. See Van Alfen 2004: 23 on the particularly egregious winner's medal for Antwerp 1920.

22. The book of this title by Eliza Butler appeared in 1935.

23. *Antigone* had been performed in 1896 and *Oedipus Tyrannus* in 1906 (Jenkins 2008: 12).

24. The film is much discussed; see e.g. Downing 1992 and Mackenzie 2003.

25. See e.g. Maraniss 2008: 81-2, 144.

26. Jesse Owens won his events in 1936, and Abebe Bikila of Ethiopia won the

marathon (bare-footed) in 1960. Cassius Clay also gave an outstanding performance at Rome and, in a characteristic gesture, wrote the commemorative poem
'How Cassius took Rome'. See Maraniss 2008: 352.

27. See e.g. Moragas Spà and Rivenburgh 1996: 320-1.

28. Hamilakis 2007: 286 registers an analogous disappointment with the new
Acropolis museum. He also offers an account of the other controversies that dogged
the Athens Olympics.

29. See the contemporary comment by Coonan 2008.

30. See the report in the *Daily Telegraph* for 25 August 2008, subtitled 'Western
countries will never match the success of the Beijing Olympics 2008 opening and
closing ceremonies because trade unions would never allow it, according to the
man responsible for both spectaculars'.

31. See e.g. the IOC press release on the Vancouver 2010 relay:
http://www.olympic.org/en/.

32. *Olympic Movement promotes peace worldwide*, 2009. Accessed 2009.
http://www.olympic.org/en/content/Olympism-in-Action/Peace-through-sport/Ol
ympic_Movement_promotes_peace_worldwide.

33. See Barney, Wenn and Martyn 2002: 278, and Swift 1996.

34. Munich 1972 admitted as much (Pro Sport München 1972 vol. 1 part 1: 73).

35. See MacAloon 1996 on its significant differences from the Opening
Ceremonies.

Pythagoras and the Origins of Olympic Ideology

Nigel Spivey

'To put it bluntly, about no one else have greater and more extraordinary things been believed.' This judgement of the reputation of the sixth-century BCE philosopher and 'guru' Pythagoras, made in late antiquity, has hardly lost its force.[1] Only, perhaps, has the extent of belief waned: summarising the ancient biography of Pythagoras as 'a mass of incredible fiction' would probably gain assent from most scholars of Presocratic philosophy.[2] So it is with several misgivings that I propose to add a further element to the Pythagorean legend, by constructing around his name an answer to the following question: *What were the ancient Olympics originally about?*[3]

Clarification of that question comes shortly. In Pythagorean spirit, however, this essay is eccentrically organised: not as a fluent hypothesis, but as a ten-fold set of separate meditations. This is not for the sake of being enigmatic – simply done in acceptance of the enquiry as highly speculative, and defiant of sequential argument. I cannot resolve the problem of an elusive subject, whether it is the person of Pythagoras or the protohistory of the Olympic Games. But this attempted approach may at least define more sharply the limits of our historical understanding about how competitive sport was formalised in ancient Greece. It is all too easy to accept the traditional date of the first Olympiad, 776 BCE, as marking the birth of an institution that endured for over one millennium, and was then 'revived' in 1896. The truth is that whatever can be termed 'the Olympic movement' in antiquity did not exist in 776 BCE: it is a phenomenon that should be located over two hundred years later.

I. Odysseus on Scheria

It is one of the most satisfying minor episodes in Homer's *Odyssey* when the hero, shipwrecked on the island of Scheria, home to the Phaeacians, shows his mettle at an athletics contest. As Homer's readers/audience, we have shared with Odysseus the near-death experience of clinging to a raft for three weeks before being plunged into open sea for two days and nights. Crawling ashore, he sleeps among a bed of leaves before making his alarming appearance at the river where the Princess Nausicaa and her maidens are washing clothes. It will be Nausicaa's father, Alcinous, king of the Phaeacians, who receives Odysseus with courteous hospitality, promising him safe passage home. But the hero has scarcely recovered by the next day when, after feasting and recitations, his hosts propose a display of their prowess at boxing, wrestling, jumping and running. Odysseus is among the numerous spectators of this display when some of the young Phaeacian noblemen challenge him to join the sports. *'Nothing makes a man so famous for life as what he can do with his hands and feet'*, says the king's son Laodamas (*Od.* 8.147-8). Odysseus, still exhausted, declines; whereupon one of the lads, Euryalus, pours scorn on him. Despising the visitor as a mere trader, mindful only of his cargo and 'greedy profits' – not deemed sources of fame, evidently – Euryalus derides him with aristocratic arrogance: *'One can see you are no sportsman.'* (There is perhaps anti-Semitic sentiment here, if the imputation is, as some commentators suppose, that Odysseus is perceived as if he were a Phoenician merchant).

In a moment worthy of Hollywood, Odysseus rises to the taunt. Without warming up, or so much as removing his cloak, he seizes a discus that is considerably larger than any of those so far used by the Phaeacian youths. He sends it spinning – and the crowd has to scatter as it flies beyond the markers of all other contestants.

The point is made. Odysseus cannot resist inviting all-comers to try him at the combat sports, archery, or even running (though here he admits he is not in his best shape) – but wisely King Alcinous intervenes, and steers the occasion back to music, stories and dancing. Soon enough the insolent Euryalus will make amends with a gift to Odysseus, and all ends happily. Beyond its narrative importance, however, the episode is instructive to students of the ancient Olympics.

It is not the only place in Homeric epic where the recreation of athletics is featured. Most conspicuously, of course, there are the Funeral Games organised by Achilles in honour of the dead Patroklos, occupying a substantial part of *Iliad* 23, but there are other allusions: for example, vignettes of Penelope's Suitors at ease 'on the levelled ground' (*dapedon*), throwing the javelin and discus (*Od.* 4.626-7). Yet the minor 'showdown' on Scheria serves to epitomise what we might term the ancestral tradition of sport in the Classical world. The Homeric hero is by definition good at games – and, if he reaches old age, like Nestor, fond of boasting about his former all-round athletic prowess (*Il.* 23.257-61). Tests of strength, speed and handling of weapons have an obvious carry-over to the codified encounters of largely individual prowess on the battlefield. Among the Phaeacians this heroic attribute devolves into the etiquette of palatial society. Odysseus, though battered and ostensibly destitute, has been received as one of royal rank. The invitation to compete with members of the local court is not made with the intention of humiliating the visitor.

1. Pythagoras and the Origins of Olympic Ideology

Odysseus might well have felt slighted had he not been asked. The breach of manners occurs only when Euryalus, in effect, refuses to believe that Odysseus is part of the peer group – marked by the antithesis made between someone belonging to the class of busy 'traders' (*prêktêres*) rather than being 'one who competes for prizes' (*athlêtêr*) – in other words, a leisured aristocrat.

The incident serves to foreshadow the ultimate homecoming of Odysseus on Ithaca, when it will be essential that he sustains the mistaken identity of beggar before revealing himself as king. But let us consider what Homer does *not* mention with regard to athletics. The poet is aware that special areas need to be designated for sporting contests, *ad hoc* as they must be for the heroes camped outside Troy. The Phaeacians have a 'track' (*dromos*) marked out for running (8.121) – but this too seems an improvised area. There is no allusion to athletic nudity; and Homer's picture of civilised life does not include any place remotely describable as a gymnasium. The young Phaeacian aristocrats may be proud of their fitness for athletic contests, but they appear to have no dedicated training facilities. Furthermore, while it may be apparent from the episode on Scheria that athletics is an essentially Greek habit, or more specifically an aristocratic Greek habit, and a prime source of 'renown' (*kleos*), Homer shows no sensibility of inter-Greek sporting festivals, whether at Olympia or elsewhere. If the existing compositions of Homer relate, as most Homeric scholars believe, to the period of *c.* 750-700 BCE, we may surmise that in the second half of the eighth century the gymnasium was not yet conceived as an institution; and that 'the Olympic Games' were not yet a significant part of Greek culture.

Agreed, the dates of an Ionian bard designated as 'Homer' are not definitive; and some commentators might want to claim that an eighth-century Homer was evoking the heroic past, and therefore perhaps conscious of formal games and gymnasia as anachronisms in his epic. But suppose that Homer does not allude to institutional athletics because institutional athletics had still be invented – that he could not sing of running in a stadium because he did not know what a stadium was? Then we are bound to draw at least two historical conclusions. Firstly, that the traditional absolute date for the first Olympiad does not mark the 'launch' or 'inaugural event' of an institution: that is, whatever was happening at Olympia in the eighth century, it bore little resemblance to the 'Olympic Games' as conducted *c.* 500 BCE, the close of the so-called Archaic period. Secondly – and more importantly to our present enquiry – the ideology of athletics in 'the world of Odysseus' must be set aside from the ideology of athletic competition at Olympia (and the other formal locations of games recognisably prestigious by the fifth century, including Athens, Delphi, Nemea, and Isthmia). This is not to dissociate athletics from the profile of heroism in Classical Greece – not at all, as we shall see – but simply to narrow our search for the origins of an Olympic ideology. Ancient 'Olympism' is not rooted in the so-called 'Dark Age' of Greece; still less in the Prehellenic palace culture of the Minoans and Mycenaeans.[4]

II. The formation of athletic space

Any deduction from archaeological evidence is subject to change in the light of future discoveries. In particular, ongoing excavations at Olympia should eventually clarify how the stadium we now see at the site – a structure of the fourth century BCE – relates to a presumed *Ur-Stadium*; and we can hope that the remains of some Greek city or colony will one day be shown to include a gymnasium datable to a period prior to the Late Classical or Hellenistic. As it stands, however, the material record confirms that athletics lacked formal facilities not only in the eighth century, but also throughout the seventh century too. The first visual testimony of a dedicated area for sporting contest comes *c.* 570 BCE, on a fragment of an Athenian black-figure bowl painted by Sophilos, 'illustrating' the Funeral Games of Patroklos – though this may show a makeshift grandstand for spectators rather than a proper hippodrome. The historical tradition suggests that civic gymnasia at Athens were in existence during the time of Solon, and then monumentalised during the tyranny of the Peisistratids.[5]

The representation of athletes on painted pottery is a largely Athenian phenomenon, and therefore limited in its general implications. But the precise chronology of Athenian vases is a bonus, and allows us to claim that the subject of civic athletics enters the iconographic repertoire only *c.* 550 BCE – that is, on vases primarily intended for use at the symposium, with scenes generally taken as reflective of the 'lifestyles' of symposiasts. We can distinguish these vases from the oil-containing amphorae produced as prizes for the contestants at the *agônes* (contests) of the quadrennial Greater Panathenaia festival, instituted in 566 BCE; and distinguish the imagery from 'mythologised' scenes of athletics – Herakles wrestling with one of his foes, say, or evocations of *Iliad* 23 (the Funeral Games of Patroklos, again, are specifically represented on the François Vase of *c.* 570 BCE). What we find among the output of, for example, the Amasis Painter, are the more generic depictions of young Athenian men practising and competing in the various disciplines of organised athletics, often in the presence of senior figures who must be either trainers or referees. Wrestling, boxing, sprinting, jumping with weights – the figures represented in such activities on the vases are usually naked, and sometimes named: it is reasonable to suppose that symposiasts using the vessels saw themselves generically reflected there. The imagery suggests a 'lifestyle' of regular attendance at the gymnasium, and a social code whereby military service on behalf of the *polis* both obliged male citizens to practise athletics and qualified them to do so.[6]

This ties in obviously with the date assigned to the foundation of the Panathenaic Games; and in turn the Panathenaic Games may be seen as institutionally catalysed by the establishment of the Pythian, Isthmian and Nemean 'Crown Games' *c.* 580 BCE. At Olympia, the first monumental building to be raised was the limestone temple of Hera, *c.* 600 BCE; but the Panhellenic identity of the sanctuary is not signalled until *c.* 570, when representatives from the colony of Gela in Sicily establish a Treasury on a terrace below the Hill of Kronos (archaeologically this seems to be the earliest of the Treasuries at Olympia, even if Pausanias [6.19.1] reports that the Sikyonians set the precedent).[7]

So it seems that during the first half of the sixth century the facilities for athletic training and the opportunities for athletic competition began to take shape. What we now need to discover are signs that will lead us to some of the ideological motives for the effort involved in both training and competition. *'Just do it'*, a modern slogan exhorts. But why bother?

III. A plethora of athletes

Imagine the following Olympic scenario: in the final of one of the most spectacular events, the 100 metres sprint, no fewer than the first seven athletes all come from the same place. There have been occasions of national dominance of the victory podium in the modern Olympics – but nothing quite so remarkable as the occasion at ancient Olympia when athletes from the colony of Croton achieved just this in the *stade*-race – a distance the length of the stadium, just under 200 metres. *'The last of the Crotoniates is first among all other Greeks'*, the saying was coined. Alas, our historical source – Strabo's *Geography* (262) – does not relate when exactly this 'clean sweep' of sprinting honours occurred. Circumstantial evidence, however, would suggest the sixth or early fifth century BCE: a period in which Croton enjoyed particular success at the Olympic festival.[8]

Strabo knew as much. And, having alluded to the plethora of prize-winning athletes from Croton, he goes on to specify that the colony, situated on the sole of the 'stiletto boot' of southern Italy, was known also for its Pythagorean philosophers; furthermore, that the most celebrated athlete from Croton, the wrestler Milo (or Milon), was a 'disciple' (*homilêtês*) of Pythagoras himself.

Strabo, writing at the turn of the millennium, as Augustus was formalising the administration of 'the Roman Empire', was perhaps only relating what might be described as the salient historical facts about Croton – a city which, though colonised by the Romans in 194 BCE, had fallen into decline. Its civic apogee lay distinctly in the second half of the sixth century, marked not only by Olympic success and the presence of Pythagoras, but also the establishment of a medical school. Strabo contents himself with the report that Croton was a healthy place to live; various other sources, however, speak of the pre-Hippocratic physicians trained at Croton, in particular Democedes and Alcmaeon. Admittedly Democedes, known primarily through the narrative of Herodotus (3.125;

129-37), seems mostly to have practised abroad – at first on Samos, and then, after capture by the Persians, in the service of King Darius; eventually returning to Croton, where he married a daughter of Milo. But Herodotus is aware that Crotoniate doctors generally enjoyed high esteem in the late sixth century. From other sources, meanwhile, we understand that the reputation of Alcmaeon was largely based upon the development of a therapeutic physiology of 'humours'.[9] To what extent Alcmaeon himself should be classified among *hoi Pythagorikoi* (the 'Pythagoreans') is debatable, but a doctrine conspicuously attributed to him (Aët. 5.30.1), asserting the 'due proportion' of humours as the foundation of good health, shows strong intellectual consonance with Pythagorean ideals of equilibrium and *symmetria* in music, mathematics, and cosmology. It becomes tempting to suppose that this period of glory for Croton was not a matter of coincidence.

IV. 'Pythagoras planned it'?

Diogenes Laertius (8.47) reports that there was a young Samian boxer by the name of Pythagoras who distinguished himself at the 48th Olympiad (588 BCE) by fighting 'cleverly' (*entechnos*). It seems that even in antiquity some historians (notably Eratosthenes, who compiled the first list of Olympic victors) took this athlete to be the philosopher in his youth – but Diogenes appears unconvinced, and it remains difficult to reconcile with a more credible chronological tradition that has Pythagoras the philosopher leave Samos during the tyranny of Polykrates, c. 532 BCE, and transfer to Croton, where he would establish a 'Pythagorean Order' or 'Community', before being forced – by political upheavals – to retire to Metapontum.

This tradition – attributed to the Sicilian-based historian Timaeus, writing in the late fourth century BCE – implies a biographical *floruit* of Pythagoras over two decades at Croton. No definite date is given for his death, but if it is guessed as a little before 500 BCE, we see that the lifespan of Pythagoras would have to be implausibly elastic if he were also once an Olympic boxing champion in 588. (This does not inhibit a number of ancient authors from attributing great longevity to the philosopher). But amid the farrago of information bequeathed to us about Pythagoras there is a distinct aspect of the philosopher as a figure with expertise in athletics. Porphyry and Iamblichos, the principal 'Neo-Pythagoreans' of late antiquity, do not relate the tale of Olympic glory for the young Pythagoras.[10] But several sources report that Pythagoras, while still resident on Samos, supervised the training of an athlete who went on to gain victory. Porphyry (op. cit. 15) specifies the boy's name as Eurymenes, and says that the success of Pythagoras here consisted in dietary advice. Previously, the staple foods of athletes were cheese and dried figs. Pythagoras put Eurymenes on a regime of meat; presumably (Porphyry does not elaborate) this high-protein strategy resulted in gains of muscle and bulk. The ensuing success is supposed to have taken place at the 62nd

1. Pythagoras and the Origins of Olympic Ideology

Olympiad of 532 BCE – which some commentators cannot resist suggesting as the occasion when Pythagoras met young Milo, destined to become Croton's multiple prize-winner at the Olympics and other Crown Games.[11]

Iamblichos wants to separate this Pythagoras *paidotribês* (trainer) from the philosopher (*VP* 25); but he too is at pains to show us that the founding-father of 'the Pythagorean life' considered athletic ability a necessary element in the recruitment and training of disciples. As Iamblichos describes it, the intellectual apprenticeship of Pythagoras was mostly served abroad – first in Ionia (with Thales at Miletus and Bias at Priene), then in the Levant, Egypt and eventually Babylon. On his return to Samos, the philosopher yields to the demands of his fellow-countrymen that he share his 'alien wisdom'; but on his own terms. It is at the local gymnasium that Pythagoras picks out a 'gifted and well-coordinated' athlete to become an experimental pupil (*VP* 21). The young man will receive instruction in arithmetic and geometry; and, as he learns, be rewarded with a cash allowance, so as to keep up his athletic training. Eventually this arrangement reverses, when Pythagoras tests the acolyte's devotion to study by pretending he, the boy's mentor, can no longer afford the three obols of reward.

Iamblichos says it was this Samian pupil, confusingly also named Pythagoras, who went on to become an authority on athletic massage and diet. Yet while recounting how Pythagoras senior transferred his system of *paideia* (education or training) from Samos to Croton, Iamblichos holds to the thread of concern for physical comportment that runs throughout the diverse areas of Pythagorean teaching. The philosopher, on his arrival at Croton, made for the gymnasium (*VP* 37), where young men 'flocked around him' to hear a homily on respect for the elderly and the value of self-control. The success of this discourse leads to Pythagoras being invited to address other sections of Croton's population, including women, and children. When it comes to establishing a community, however, the gymnasium is evidently the breeding-ground for full-time followers of Pythagoras; and even then, the young men who wish to become Pythagoreans are put through a scrutiny (*dokimasia*) of aptitude tests (*VP* 71). Critical among these are assessments of their physical aspect (*eidos*), gait (*poreia*), and 'mobility' (*kinêsis*).

These are not factors taken into official consideration by university admissions interviewers today. Why should they have mattered then?

V. On being born again

Of the various elements of Pythagorean doctrine one stands out as a 'core' principle: the faith in metempsychosis, or transmigration of the soul. Notoriously summarised in the anecdote about the philosopher intervening to stop a man beating a dog because he heard in the dog's yelps the voice of a departed friend, it was evidently a faith that Pythagoras based in personal experience – according to the testimony of Heraclides of Pontus (Diog.Laert. 8.4). 'Pythagoras knew his own previous lives, and began his training of others by awakening their memory of an earlier existence', reports Iamblichos (*VP* 63) – identifying in particular the philosopher's previous reincarnation as Euphorbos, a minor hero of the Trojan War. Homer's plangent simile for the death of Euphorbos at the hands of Menelaus (*Il.* 17.45ff.) was, we are told, a favourite recitative piece of Pythagoras; and the shield of the hero, displayed at the Argive Heraion, was allegedly recognised as a personal possession of the philosopher's *proteros bios* or 'earlier life' (cf. Hor. *Carm.* 1.28; Paus. 2.17.3, etc.).

Why Euphorbos? Heraclides appears to have supplied a complex 'family tree' of previous lives for Pythagoras, but again we are left with a matter of guesswork. Homer has little to say about Euphorbos: still, that little may be precious enough. When brought down by Menelaus, it is the beauty of Euphorbos that is remarkable. And we have been primed for that by the single previous mention of the hero (*Il.* 16.808-9) – as an outstanding athlete.

The grace and physical presence of Pythagoras himself are repeatedly stressed by his doxographers. But vanity cannot be the motive for this psychic affiliation with Euphorbos. Pythagoras taught his followers to aspire to a state of divine immortality. They must strive to be godlike: in other words, they must try to be heroes, or 'halfway-gods' (*hemitheoi*). A noble aim: yet where should the effort be made? Within the collective discipline of the hoplite phalanx, individual distinction on the battlefield was not so readily available as it would have been for Homer's champions. The obvious alternative was to show excellence, *arête*, in the realm of competitive athletics.

VI. Games for heroes, heroes of games

The concept of the *epitaphios agôn*, the contest staged as a funerary rite due to a hero, is not only Homeric: Pindar invokes it to furnish an aetiological explanation for the games at Isthmia, as a particular form of sacrificial 'honour' (*geras*) manifest at other sites of heroic veneration – Thebes, Argos, Sparta, Aegina and Megara.[12] Games were one mode of making the veneration of a localised hero 'apparent from afar' (*têlephantos*) – attracting pilgrims from beyond the locality with the spectacle of a commemorative event. The Olympics were no exception, fundamentally: for it was next to the ancient burial-place (*sêma*) of Pelops that Herakles founded the Games (*Ol.* 10.24), and it is the *kleos* (renown) of Pelops that irradiates far from the race-tracks of Olympia (*Ol.* 1.94).

Naturally – in Pindar's vision – what happens here is a sort of paradigmatic refrain. The commemoration of an original hero offers opportunities for fresh displays of heroism. Pindar's well-known trope, whereby victory in the realm of athletics is radically or genealogically connected to some prototypical (and often bloody) triumph from the mythical past, is more than a poetic strategy. It is inextricably bound up with the agonistic ideal of heroic *mimêsis*, according to which the proud wrestler could aspire to be a second Herakles, or the champion pankratiast imaginatively re-enact the deeds of Theseus. Within the so-called 'economy of *kudos*', hero-cult provided traditional resources and motives for glorious emulation. Pindar and the other epinikian poets promote the ideal by stressing its benefits: not only blessings upon the individual athlete, but lasting honour also to his family and homeland.[13]

This is a phenomenon historically known beyond Pindar, with a series of celebrated cases: Euthymos of Locri, Theagenes of Thasos, et al.[14] And within the records of heroic status accorded to athletes, we find several instances of what might be called applied merit: that is, occasions when the victorious athlete makes a notable appearance in the theatre of war. Among such instances are a trio from the golden age of Croton's athletic success. One of them is Philippos, an exiled Crotoniate who joined the Spartan Dorieus in his doomed colonising quest to Sicily *c.* 510 BCE.[15] Philippos, as Herodotus reports (5.47), met his end in a battle against combined Phoenician-Sikel forces representing Segesta: but his fame as an Olympic victor (in 520 or 516, it is assumed) was preserved. Because Philippos was acknowledged as not only a prize-winning athlete but also 'the most beautiful of the Hellenes of his day', the Segestans went so far as to establish a *hêrôon* (hero-shrine) at his burial-site, and henceforth honoured the spirit of Philippos with sacrifices.

To be revered both as a great athlete and on account of outstanding *kallisteia* (beauty) may be a 'first' for Herodotus, but it can hardly surprise us. We do not know whether Philippos was a Pythagorean: nevertheless, this story advertises him as a typical representative of Croton during the city's 'Pythagorean' epoch. Historically it resonates in a subsequent passage of Herodotus regarding an individual Crotoniate who volunteers his services in the wider theatre of military action: this involves the well-known pentathlete Phayllos, three-times victor at Delphi, and accredited with 'record-breaking' achievements in both long-jump and discus. In 480, Phayllos contributed and captained his own ship on behalf of the Greeks at Salamis (Hdt. 8.47; cf. Paus. 10.9.2). Herodotus, by mentioning that Phayllos was from Croton and *tris Pythionikês*, need hardly say more: Phayllos is therefore of heroic potential.

Yet neither Philippos nor Phayllos can eclipse the formidable figure of Milo, whose talismanic deployment on the battlefield is famously evoked by Diodorus Siculus (12.9.5-6). The circumstances were as follows. Croton harboured a number of exiles from Sybaris, after that city came under the tyranny of Telys. Sybaris put pressure upon Croton to yield up these exiles. Some at Croton favoured *entente* with the Sybarites (among them, incidentally, the athlete Philippos); however, as Diodorus relates, it was Pythagoras who urged resistance. This developed into a military show-down, *c.* 510. Despite their reputation for effeminacy, the Sybarites were able to field a huge force, outnumbering the Crotoniates by three to one. But the Crotoniates resorted to an extraordinary advantage. Their multiple Olympic wrestling victor and staunch Pythagorean Milo took command of their army, and presented himself dressed up like Herakles, with lionskin and club, and wearing his six Olympic crowns. Whether Milo himself routed the enemy, or generated panic among them by his appearance, is not specified: Diodorus simply assures us that Milo's presence was perceived as the cause (*aitia*) of victory. The ensuing rout led to the complete destruction of Sybaris.

The episode invites incredulity. Of what use was a wooden club against a hoplite phalanx; and what manner of head-protection offered by a stack of brittle olive wreaths? But before we dismiss the tale as pure fiction, it is worth remembering that a conspicuous disregard for personal safety, on the part of a commander, had its own strategic logic – as Alexander the Great would several times demonstrate; and worth remembering, too, the attestations of heroic epiphany in the midst of battle, as variously reported and depicted in antiquity. Marathon in 490 is a well-known example: combatants claimed to have seen Theseus in action there (Plut. *Thes.* 35); while fifth-century paintings of the battle on view in the Stoa Poikile in Athens showed not only Theseus, but also Athena and Herakles, and two further heroes, fighting on the Greek side (Paus. 1.15.4). The morale-boosting effect of such phantom experiences was understood by Herodotus (describing the defence of Delphi against the Persians: 8.38-9), and the Crotoniates were on at least one occasion victims of this effect, according to reports of their battle with the Locrians at the River Sagra, *c.* 540 BCE: here not only the Lesser (Locrian) Ajax joined the outnumbered Locrian ranks, but also the Dioskouroi, despatched as divine allies from Sparta (Conon, *Narr.* 18, Strab. 261, etc.).

That prize-winning athletes made formidable warriors was an expectation eventually destroyed by the rise of professional armies; and not all Olympic victors were accorded heroic status (though epitaphs indicate that an *Olympionikês* would never omit this distinction from his tombstone).[16] Nevertheless it remains true to say that, as an *ideal*, the athletic games, rooted in hero-worship, generated new heroes. The Pythagorean doctrine of the soul's cycle at once shaped and responded to this ideal. In other words, it is utterly plausible that when Milo appeared on an all-Greek battlefield in the late sixth century, dressed in Heraklean mode, and wearing his Olympic crowns, it *was* taken as a supernatural event – no less than an epiphany of Herakles.

VII. The athlete's grave at Taranto

The deceased colonist remains anonymous. But to define his status as an athletic hero, from the remains of his inhumation, is irresistible. The skeleton has been analysed as that of a well-muscled middle-aged man,

Fig. 1.1. Detail of a Panathenaic amphora from 'the athlete's grave' at Taranto, *c.* 475 BCE. Taranto, National Archaeological Museum inv. 115474.

about 1.70 metres tall; it was placed inside a stone sarcophagus that in turn was lowered into a rectangular rock-cut tomb. Within the sarcophagus, the corpse was laid on a wooden couch, with just one accompanying object, a small alabaster oil-flask (*alabastron*) – a characteristic attribute of the gymnasium-regular. It seems that his prize possessions were kept on display outside: so, on the corners of the tomb, four Athenian vases. Their form and decoration are unmistakable: these made a quartet of Panathenaic prize amphorae, datable on stylistic grounds to between 500-460 BCE. The Kleophrades Painter is suggested as one possible specific source for the three vases that survive more or less intact.[17]

The imagery on these three surviving pieces may be telling (Figs 1.1-1.3). As usual with Panathenaic amphorae, each features an image of Athena Promachos on one side and a scene of athletic endeavour on the other. One shows figures preparing for the discus and long jump, with an *aulos*-player present – a reference, presumably, to the pentathlon; another shows chariot-racing; and the third, a pair of hefty boxers. If the logic of prize-giving at the Panathenaic festival was that vases (filled of course with oil, and in considerable quantity) were decorated according to the nature of the event in which victory had been achieved, we would have to conclude that the subject of burial here was a remarkable all-rounder, not only talented in the various disciplines of the pentathlon, and a prize

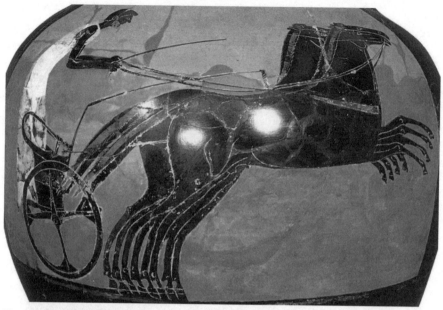

Fig. 1.2. Detail of second Panathenaic amphora from 'the athete's grave' (inv. 115475).

Fig. 1.3. Detail of third Panathenaic amphora from 'the athlete's grave' (inv. 115473).

boxer, but also wealthy enough to maintain – and enter for competition, possibly with himself as driver – a chariot and team of horses.

So much is speculation, assuming in the first place that the Tarentine owner of Panathenaic vases was indeed a successful competitor at the Panathenaic festival – or, to be more precise, at the quadrennial Greater Panathenaic festival, when contests were thrown open to Greeks beyond Athens. (Panathenaic prize amphorae have also been found in Etruscan tombs – where they are taken to be collectible *objets d'art*, not personal trophies.) The style of deposition, however, combined with the osteological analysis of the human remains, does suggest the veneration of a 'big man' – who in his abbreviated lifetime had accrued various athletic honours. It is conceivable that Olympic victories were among them: several Tarentine names, including the distinguished pentathlete and coach Ikkos (cf. Pl. *Leg.* 839e-840a), are known from the Olympic lists of the first half of the fifth century.

Was this athlete – whose tomb made a posthumous journey, as an archaeological exhibit, to the Beijing Olympics of 2008 – a Pythagorean? Perhaps: if not, it is at any rate credible that he realised the heroic value of his athletic success as sanctioned by Pythagoras. Surveying further funerary evidence from South Italy, meanwhile, the Pythagorean pre-mium put on 'the beautiful and good among men' (*hoi kaloi kagathoi tôn andrôn: VP* 42) comes to mind with the burial assemblages from Locri, where in the early twentieth century Paolo Orsi explored some 1700 tombs of the so-called Lucifero necropolis. Panathenaics are not unknown here, too: but more striking, in graves of the late sixth century onwards, is the custom of depositing typical 'gender' attributes. For women, objects typi-fying the hearth and home; for men, objects that evoke a less domesticated 'lifestyle'. Some weapons and hunting accoutrements are among them: predominant, however, are the key symbols of gymnasium-attendance: the strigil and the oil-flask.[18]

VIII. 'They supposed the elements of numbers to be the elements of all things'

Aristotle's comments on the mathematical principles developed by the Pythagoreans (*Met.* 985b23ff.) have been linked with the medical practice of Alcmaeon at Croton: as already noted, Alcmaeon proposed an 'equal distribution' (*isonomia*) of bodily parts as the basis for good health. But another potential link has also been suggested – with the aesthetics of Classical Greek sculpture. It is well-known that the custom of commemo-rating athletic victors with statues began in the late sixth century BCE, with an image of Milo one of the early recorded figures on display at Olympia; and that, during the fifth century, a number of sculptors special-ised in epinikian commissions. Among their names – including Myron, Hageladas and Naukydes – is one Pythagoras, from Rhegion, who had (so

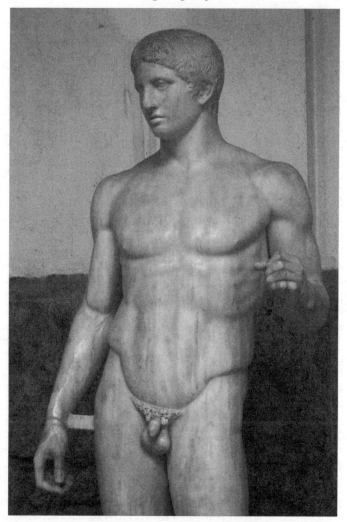

Fig. 1.4. 'The Doryphoros': Roman marble statue after an original bronze by Polykleitos, *c.* 450 BCE. Naples, Archaeological Museum.

far as we know) no connection with his philosophical namesake. But to the best-known of these sculptors, Polykleitos of Argos, a Pythagorean aspect has been speculatively assigned. It is to do with the reputation of the so-called 'Canon' developed by Polykleitos as a method of representing the human body. As reported by diverse ancient sources, the sculptor devised a strict and painstaking system of proportional measurements that would generate aesthetically pleasing images. He worked in bronze, and there is no surviving statue that can be definitely pronounced as a Polykleitan original: nonetheless, there are sufficient 'copies' to yield a clear idea of the

Fig. 1.5. Detail of the Parthenon Frieze, *c.* 440 BCE. London, British Museum.

formulaic style that Polykleitos achieved. Even when fragmentary, the 'foursquare', chiastic aspect of a figure done in the manner of Polykleitos is striking (Fig. 1.4). The type, developed by Polykleitos for recurrent commissions (at Olympia and elsewhere) to commemorate athletic victors, passed into the mid-fifth century repertoire, equally serviceable for representing warriors and heroes: it stands out clearly, for example (and literally), on the Parthenon Frieze (Fig. 1.5).

The Pythagoreans invoked an enigmatic 'foursome' (*tetraktys*) in their explanation of *harmonia*, whether it came from the oracle at Delphi, or in the songs of the Sirens. Pythagorean doctors would apply a fourfold

Nigel Spivey

principle in their doctrine of the bodily 'humours', the balance of which was critical to health. Beyond this quadruple 'ethos', however, was Polykleitos implementing a more complex procedure of proportions and ratio? As John Raven pointed out, while we cannot prove a direct connection between Pythagorean number-theory and such citations of the Polykleitan Canon as survive, 'coincidence' seems an inadequate explanation. There is enough in the allusions to Pythagorean mathematics by Aristotle, Sextus Empiricus and others to warrant the conjecture that Pythagoras, who may be claimed as a 'fashioner' (*tektôn*) of prize-winning athletes (cf. Pind. *Nem.* 5. 48-9), indirectly offered a theoretical method to Polykleitos, the sculptor *par excellence* of memorials to prize-winning athletes.[19]

IX. Pythagoras at large

Aristotle (*Fr.* 191; cf. Ael. *VH* 2. 26) is named as the source for several remarkable stories about Pythagoras. One attests his capacity for being in two places at once – the power of bilocation, later accredited to certain Christian saints; another tells how 'many people' heard Pythagoras being hailed by a river; and finally there is a vignette of Pythagoras at the Olympic festival, where allegedly the philosopher got up among the spectators *en theatrô* (in the stadium, presumably), and showed that one of his thighs was of gold.

We do not have Aristotle's rational comments on such phenomena. But we understand from Plato (*Rep.* 600a-b) that Pythagoras had the charisma to inspire a 'way of life' (*odos tou biou*) among his followers; and from various sources it is clear that 'Pythagoreanism' was a discipline that could be practised collectively. 'Associations' (*hetaireiai*) of Pythagoreans evidently spread beyond Croton: schools were established at Catania, Locri and Rhegion, and certain legislators were historically defined as Pythagorean – most famously Plato's acquaintance, Archytas of Taranto, the 'mathematician king'.[20] As Pythagoras himself had shown at Croton, 'the Pythagorean life', whatever its religious peculiarities, was neither opposed to nor distinct from participation in the life of the *polis*. Clarity, alas, does not extend far: the history of the Pythagorean 'diaspora' among the Achaean colonies of Magna Graecia is complex and obscure, with stories of a schism in the movement compounding doubts over its political coherence.[21] For our purposes, however, it is worth singling out the phrase used by Iamblichos to describe the oligarchic constitution created by a group of Pythagoreans at Rhegion (*VP* 130). This was a *gymnasiarchikê politeia*: which, if understood in relation to remarks by Aristotle (*Pol.* 1297a) regarding the obligatory nexus, in some constitutions, of 'bearing arms' (*hopla kektêsthai*) and 'exercising naked' (*gymnazesthai*), implies that the ruling elite of Rhegion was defined by athletic prowess – or at least enjoyed exclusive access to athletic training and contests.

36

It seems probable, though never proven, that the Pythagorean emphasis upon athletics (not to mention *mousikê*) as a part of the education of young citizens eventually informed Plato's approval of a 'traditional' curriculum (*Rep.* 376a). Centuries later, the delineation by Iamblichos (*VP* 96-100) of *gymnastikê technê* (gymnastic skill) within the daily regime of the Pythagoreans at Croton finds a visual evocation in the stucco decorations of the subterranean Neo-Pythagorean 'Basilica' by Rome's Porta Maggiore. Romanised as it may be, Pythagorean *paideia* here encompasses both gymnastic manoeuvres and weapons-training.[22] Chronologically we may have come a long way from 'the world of Odysseus'; ideologically, however, little has changed.

X. Before Panhellenism

By the principle of ring composition, and in hope of a conclusive answer, we return to our starting question: *What were the ancient Olympics originally about?* Here is a response that attempts to incorporate the diverse strands of this essay into a synthesis.

Some kind of rustic festival was undoubtedly celebrated at Olympia during the eighth century BCE: in that sense, the year 776 may continue to serve as a date for the 'First Olympiad'. But, as archaeology indicates, this gathering was a predominantly local affair, scarcely registering in the minds of Greeks beyond the Peloponnese. It did not concern Homer – whose heroes, nonetheless, were keen athletes.

The Olympic Games developed into a prestigious occasion because Greek cities around the Mediterranean sent representatives to participate. The greater the participation, the more the sanctuary flourished – becoming, like Delphi, a monumental focus of pilgrimage in the otherwise 'out of the way' region of Arcadia. (In fact Olympia, like Delphi, was relatively easy of access to Greeks in the West). The success of the site in attracting Greeks from beyond the mainland in turn fostered a concept, albeit fragile and fractious, of Panhellenic unity: such a concept appears to have been articulated during the fifth century BCE, during and after the Persian wars.[23]

Olympia was home to an oracle. But that was not why athletes came from beyond the Peloponnese to compete there. They came because Olympia offered a more or less neutral location for contest; for establishing who was 'best of the Achaeans' in the post-Homeric Greek world. (One could, in this sense, describe Olympia as a regular and 'civilian' rehearsal of the Trojan War.) The reason that this mattered to them was that victory at Olympia (and, indeed, at the other Crown Games and the Greater Panathenaia) marked a distinct social and political status – in addition to any economic reward. In short, it offered the possibility of heroisation: a sort of immortality.

Who blessed this ideology with philosophical conviction? We cannot point to any individual in antiquity to compare with Pierre de Coubertin as prime mover of the revived Olympics – even if some of the sentiments lodged in the Baron's voluminous testimonies sound oddly akin to ancient motives (*'une école de noblesse'*, etc.). And, as stated at the outset of this argument, it must be perverse to attribute any sort of historical purpose to the person of Pythagoras, from whom we have no more secure report than the often indistinct snatches of his 'sayings' or *akousmata* ('things heard'). Yet, indistinct and anecdotal as it may be, the evidence about Pythagoras adds up to yield something like a fundamental charter for ancient athletics. Porphyry (op. cit. 15) says that Pythagoras came to advise against winning at the Games, as a precaution against envy – but everything else we hear about his teachings, in their content and their conduct, suggests that Pythagoras was first among the Greeks to articulate the moral and medical justification of sport. Homer had made it an essential part of heroic identity. Pythagoras brought aspirations of heroic virtue into the archaic *polis*. In other words, he raised the stakes of any athletic contest; and one effect of this – we may conclude, in our own idiom – was to put Olympia on the map.

Notes

1. Porphyry, *Life of Pythagoras* 28.
2. Burnet 1920: 87. The sentiment is echoed in subsequent studies, e.g. Philip 1966: 3.
3. This essay derives from a paper given at a colloquium at Leeds in January 2005. Since then I have seen Teja and Mariano 2004, and Christesen 2007b – both of which concord a good deal with the argument presented here. (Crowther 2007 runs complementary rather than counter to this case.)
4. *Contra* Renfrew 1988.
5. See Delorme 1960: 37ff.
6. See Kyle 1987: 54-5; Delorme 1960: 471ff.; and Mann 1998: 7-21.
7. Scott 2010 gives a more nuanced survey of the evidence at Olympia (146ff.) – and offers useful caveats regarding use of the term 'Panhellenic' (256ff.).
8. The 51st Olympiad (576 BCE) is conjectured by Moretti (1957: 69), proposing an emendation of Strabo's text; however, given the remarkable record of *stade*-victories by Crotoniate athletes between 508 and 480 (seven titles from eight consecutive Olympiads), a later date may be more plausible: *cf.* Dunbabin 1948: 369.
9. See Longrigg 1993: 47-81.
10. Iamblichos is well served by modern scholarship: Clark 1989; Dillon and Hershbell, 1991; von Albrecht et al. 2002; and Romano 2006.
11. See Moretti 1957: 74. Whether Milo was competing at Olympia for his first victory (as a boy) or second victory (as a young man) is uncertain. Delatte 1922: 175, is dismissive of Pythagoras as an athlete or trainer – though various ancient sources (e.g. Lucian, *Gallus* 8) repeat the trope.
12. Pindar *Isthm.* Fr. 6.5 (1); 5.26-35; 8.74. Further discussion in Gebhard and Dickie 1998.
13. See Kurke 1993: 131-63; and note Nagy 1990: 199-214.

14. Fontenrose 1968 remains a fundamental collection of *exempla*, along with Bohringer 1979. The fortune of Euthymos is examined in detail by Currie 2002.

15. On Philippos, see Giangiulio 1989: 200-4.

16. On athletes' inscriptions, see Brunet in this volume.

17. Thus De Juliis and Loiacono 1988: 139-51, following the optimistic interpretation of Lo Porto 1967 (esp. 'Tomb C', 69-84). See also La Regina ed. 2003: 234-41, and Bentz 1998, nos. 5.028/029/030. The attribution of the vases to the Kleophrades Painter or his 'workshop' remains debatable: thus Matheson 1989: 111-12.

18. See Cerchiai 1982.

19. Thus Raven 1951: see also remarks by Pollitt 1995: 22-3.

20. Cf. Huffman 2005.

21. See von Fritz 1940.

22. See Carcopino 1926: 117ff. and Teja 1994.

23. On the rhetoric of Panhellenism at the Olympics, see Volonaki in this volume.

2

True Heroes and Dishonourable Victors at Olympia

David Gilman Romano

In 2008 the XXIX Modern Olympic Games were celebrated in Beijing, China, where 11,028 athletes from 204 nations competed in 28 sports and 302 individual events.[1] In addition, there were 5,500 officials and some 21,600 journalists who were in attendance. By most accounts it was a very successful Olympics and according to Nielsen Media Research, more than two out of three people all around the world watched a portion of the Games, a total of 4.7 billion people; 1.3 billion Chinese watched it alone![2] By comparison, 3.9 billion people worldwide had watched the Athens Olympic Games of 2004 and 3.6 billion people the Sydney Games in 2000.[3]

Eighty-seven different countries or National Organizing Committees were represented in the medal standings, the largest number in the history of the Games. There were 37 different venues for the competitions including the Equestrian facility in Hong Kong. According to an article in the *Los Angeles Times*, the total price tag for the sixteen-day event totalled $43 billion, almost three times what the Athens Olympic Games cost at $15 billion.[4] The Olympic stadium in Beijing, the 'Birds Nest', alone cost $500 million.

These are indicators of success, but how else might we measure it? In this essay I shall examine several versions of success and victory, noting its complexities both now and in the distant past. Beijing certainly scored highly as a media event. I spent a lot of time watching the Beijing Olympic Games on television, both from Athens during the first few days of the Games and from Philadelphia later on. I personally preferred the European coverage to that of NBC, as there was less beach volleyball and a greater variety of events covered. I watched ping pong, as well as swimming, gymnastics, wrestling, weight lifting, baseball and many others, but my personal favourite events were probably the women's and the men's marathon races. These were both interesting contests but there was the additional element of being able to see many aspects of the city of Beijing through the wonderful air photography that was used to follow the races. Although there was some rain during the events of the Games, the pollution in Beijing did not seem to create the difficulties that had been feared in the months and years preceding the Games.

2. True Heroes and Dishonourable Victors at Olympia

The Beijing Olympiad was themed 'One World, One Dream' a global sporting event, but it was also, like many other Olympics before it, billed as an attempt to promote unity, friendship and peace. Yet there were many concerns about the Chinese political repression at home and around the world. Certainly some of these issues were brought to the attention of the world during the Olympic torch relay and some others during the Games. The torch relay, which covered 85,100 miles (not including travel in China but including miles by air travel), was interrupted a number of times by political demonstrations and some portions of the relay were cancelled. In the weeks and months preceding the Games there was talk from many nations of the idea of boycotting the Games or some portion of the Games, perhaps the Opening Ceremony, although this did not take place.[5]

There were 132 Olympic records set during the Games, 43 world records and 302 gold medal winners.[6] The overall medal count by nation produced some debate itself, at least in the US – the question of whether it is the number of gold medals or the number of total medals that is most important in the medal standings. With respect to gold medals, China finished first with 51, the United States second with 36, Russia third with 28 and Great Britain fourth with 19.

There were many memorable athletes. For the United States Michael Phelps was far and away the most conspicuous of these, at least on NBC. With a total of eight gold medals in swimming, Phelps eclipsed the record seven gold medals at a single Olympics by Mark Spitz from the Munich Games in 1972. Phelps now has a total of 16 medals, 14 of them gold and two bronze, from Olympic competition, including the eight that he won in Athens in 2004. Previously the greatest number of Olympic medals won by a male was held by the Soviet gymnast Nikolai Andrianov who won 15 medals between 1972 and 1980. For a female the record is held by Larysa Latynina, another Soviet gymnast, who holds the overall record with 18 medals: nine gold, five silver and four bronze.

The total number of medals won by an athlete is one of a variety of ways of comparing the greatest of Modern Olympic athletes. Most would say, I think, that it is difficult to compare athletes living and competing in different centuries for a number of reasons having to do with coaching, competition, equipment, training, facilities, and diet. And in the modern era another element has entered into the mix – performance-enhancing drugs.

There have been several attempts in recent years to rank the most famous Modern Olympic athletes, and the *Times* of London has published two of these. David Powell in the *Times* on 8 January 2008 published his list of the Top 50 Track and Field athletes at the Modern Olympic Games.[7] Without clear criteria, this list is based on the journalist's strong instinctive input, according to his own admission. Powell does say that he ruled out all athletes with proven or strong circumstantial links to doping as well as athletes who did not actually win events in the Olympic Games. Powell cites Carl Lewis as his no. 1 Olympic athlete, Paavo Nurmi no. 2 and Jackie Joyner Kersee as no. 3. The first British athlete on the list is the middle distance runner Sebastian Coe who is no. 24, and Jesse Owens, the great US sprinter from 1936, is no. 12.

On 30 July 2008 Calvin Shulman published the 'Top 100 Olympic Athletes' which is a listing of the greatest track and field athletes according to this journalist who devised a system of points as criteria.[8] All top-eight finishers in track and field events are awarded points according to a scale. Competitors in relays and team events are given half the points. Schulman's list includes athletes who competed in now discontinued events at the end of the nineteenth and beginning of the twentieth centuries. He also includes the records of the athletes who competed in the unofficial 1906 Interim Athens Olympic Games.

According to this listing, Raymond Ewry is the greatest Modern Olympic athlete of all time. He won ten gold medals in track and field over eight years but in events that were discontinued years ago, the standing high jump, standing long jump and standing triple jump. Two of his medals were from the interim Games of 1906. Paavo Nurmi is in second place, with nine gold medals and three silver. Nurmi dominated middle distance and distance running from the 1500 metres to the 20 kilometres during the 1920s. He was declared a 'professional' before the 1932 Olympic Games and not allowed to compete. Carl Lewis is in third place in this ranking, having won nine gold medals and a silver medal during his career. He won four gold medals in Los Angeles in 1984 in the 100 m, 200 m, long jump and in the 4 x 100 metres relay.

In both of these listings, Carl Lewis features prominently, first in Powell's list and third in Schulman's. This is notable since in 2003 Lewis admitted to failing three drug tests during the 1988 Olympic Trials that should have prevented him from competing in the 1988 Seoul Olympic Games a few months later.[9] Lewis claimed that he had inadvertently taken the banned substances as a part of an herbal remedy. Sebastian Coe and Jesse Owens are tied at no. 38 in the listing.

Both of these modern rankings were completed before the 2008 Beijing Olympic Games began, so neither includes the results of the latest Olympic Games, and certainly now there would be some new names to add to these lists from the track and field events.

One new name would be Usain Bolt of Jamaica, the winner of the 100 metres and 200 metres and a member of the victorious 4 x 100 metres relay team, the first man since Carl Lewis to win all three events at a single Olympic Games. Bolt set world records in the 100 metres in 9.69 seconds, the 200 in 19.30 seconds, as well as in a leg of the 4 x 100 metres relay, the first time that this has been accomplished in the Olympic Games. By all appearances Bolt is a true phenomenon and he might easily now appear on a list of the greatest Olympic athletes. But these days the proof of athletic achievement takes time and is more complicated. Due to the possibility of drug-enhanced performances, it is not always completely clear at the moment of victory who has won fairly, and who has had illegal assistance. The *New York Times'* sports headline during the Beijing Olympic Games on Friday 22 August 2008 read 'As Records Fall, Suspicions of Doping Linger'.[10] There is recent history that is hard to forget.

Marion Jones, for instance, won three gold medals and two bronze at the Sydney Olympic Games in 2000. She won the 100 metres and the 200 metres by vast margins and was celebrated as the first female athlete to win five medals in track and field at the Olympic Games. She was praised as a true modern heroine and as a result appeared on the cover of *Sports Illustrated* as well as on the cover of *Vogue Magazine*.[11]

After a long investigation, in October 2007 Jones gave back her five Olympic medals and agreed to forfeit all other race results going back to 1 September 2000.[12] 'Her track and field times from the 2000 Games onward were wiped from the record books – as if she never existed.'[13] In a further move in April 2008, the International Olympic Committee voted to strip Jones's teammates in the 4 x 100 metres and 4 x 400 metres relay races from the Sydney Olympics because of Jones's drug use, although this decision was overturned by the Court of Arbitration of Sport in 2010.[14]

Katerina Thanou of Greece, who ran second to Jones in the Sydney Olympic 200 m, was involved in an incident preceding the Athens Olympic Games in 2004 in which she and her training partner Kostis Kenteris (the Olympic 100 metres victor in Sydney) failed to appear for a drug test (their third missed test) and were involved in what has been described by the IOC as a staged traffic accident. Before the Beijing Olympic Games, Thanou was barred from Olympic competition by the International Olympic Committee.[15]

On 8 January 2008 Marion Jones was sentenced to six months in prison and ordered to serve 800 hours of community service after she pleaded guilty in October to lying to federal agents about her use of performance-enhancing drugs and her connection to a cheque fraud case.[16] Jones entered federal prison in Fort Worth, Texas on 7 March 2008 to serve a six-month term, and it must have been from there that she watched (if permitted) part of the Beijing Olympic Games on television.[17] On 19 August she was moved to a half-way house in San Antonio until her release on Friday 5 September 2008.[18] In April 2009 Jones told an audience at the University of Pennsylvania that her six months of prison time was 'start of a new beginning' for her.[19] In March 2010 she joined the Tulsa Shock of the WNBA.[20]

In Beijing, 4,770 doping tests were undertaken, including 3,801 urine and 969 blood tests.[21] Forty athletes were caught for drug-related reasons before the Games, six during the Games and at least one after the Games. Test samples are now kept frozen for eight years in order to repeat tests on athletes done earlier as new techniques develop to identify and meas-

Fig. 2.1. Herakles wrestling the Nemean Lion. Attic red-figure stamnos by the Kleophrades Painter, *c.* 490 BCE, in the collection of the Mediterranean Section of the University of Pennsylvania Museum of Archaeology and Anthropology, L-64-185.

ure drug substances.[22] So what all of this means is that to be sure that our victors have won honourably, we now may need to wait up to eight years! Our Olympic champions are very literally on ice in the meantime.

Both in antiquity and in modern times victorious athletes have sometimes been characterised as 'heroes'. Literature and myth provide us with a number of ancient athletic victors, some of whom could be called 'true heroes'; among the most prominent are Herakles, Pelops, Atalanta and Odysseus. None of these figures competed in the historical ancient Olympic Games, of course, but each was represented as outstanding for his or her strength, speed, guile and prowess as an athlete. What was 'heroic' about their feats and their victories? How did they assume heroic stature? Many would agree with Gunnel Ekroth that 'to qualify as a hero in ancient Greece, one had to be extreme, in every sense of the term, in life or death; virtue was not necessarily a qualification'.[23] In each of the following examples the mythological hero uses his or her prowess as an athlete to exemplify their superhuman status.

Herakles, considered the greatest of Greek heroes, and renowned for attaining the status of a god, was in myth forced to complete twelve labours in order to free himself from the slavery of King Eurystheus. The Pythia at Delphi had promised him immortality as a reward.[24] Herakles was also known as one of the mythological founders of the Olympic Games, and whether this was the Herakles reputed to be son of Zeus and Alkmene, or one of the Daktyloi, his name is associated with early Olympia.[25] He is depicted, during his first labour, wrestling the Nemean Lion on a stamnos by the Kleophrades Painter in the University of Pennsylvania Museum of Archaeology and Anthropology (Fig. 2.1), which may be understood as symbolic of the athletic prowess necessary to complete the rest of the series. According to Pindar (*Olympian* 10) it was Herakles who measured out a sacred area at Olympia, fenced the altis, gave a name to the Hill of Kronos and who then offered sacrifice and founded the four yearly Olympic Games. Herakles' fifth labour occurred in the area of Olympia, cleaning the stables of King Augeus, which he accomplished by means of rerouting the Alpheios river. At Olympia the twelve sculpted metopes of the Temple of Zeus, found in the front and back porches of the building, were devoted to the labours of Herakles.

Pelops was another hero who also was credited with the founding of the Olympic Games. According to Pindar (*Olympian* 1), Pelops came to the region of Elis as a suitor vying for the hand of Hippodameia, the daughter of the rich King Oinomaos. The king had challenged each of the thirteen previous suitors to a chariot race, defeated them all and had them murdered. Pindar gives Pelops a golden chariot and horses to defeat Oinomaos[26] but according to Apollodoros, Hippodameia, who had fallen in love with Pelops, persuaded Myrtilus, the charioteer of Oinomaos' chariot, not to insert the axle pins into the wheel hubs, thereby causing Oinomaos' chariot to fall apart during the race and ultimately ensuring the death of the king.[27] The moment before the race is depicted in the east pediment of the Temple of Zeus at Olympia, where all the principal members of the story are present.

Atalanta was one of the most famous heroines of Greek mythology.[28] A native of Arcadia, she was exposed at birth, nursed by a bear and brought up in the woods by hunters. As a virgin she spent her time hunting with Artemis, killing centaurs who tried to rape her, and she took part in the hunt of the Calydonian Boar. At the games held in honour of Pelias she defeated Peleus in wrestling and later, when her father wished to give her in marriage, she promised to marry the man who would defeat her in a footrace. After several suitors were defeated and put to death, Hippomenes was victorious in the contest, by means of dropping golden apples on the track surface which Atalanta stopped to pick up. Although Atalanta is not necessarily related to Olympia, there could be a possible connection through the festival and games in honour of Hera for unmarried girls, organised by a committee of sixteen Elean women. Some resemblance has on occasion been seen between the costume that the girls wear in the races for Hera, as described by Pausanias, and as found in the several bronze miniature depictions of female athletes, and in depictions of Amazons. This conclusion has, however, been shown to be without foundation; the girls' garment is more likely to be modelled on a man's lightweight, short chiton, named the *exomis*.[29] The Atalanta myth is known early, from Hesiod, *c.* 700 BCE. and the Athenian dramatists Aeschylus, Euripides and Sophocles all wrote plays about Atalanta; she is known as beautiful, strong and brave.[30] The Hera games at Olympia may have a relationship with Spartan education and may be related to initiatory practice, and it is certainly a possibility that there could have been a mythological connection (now lost) of Atalanta with Olympia.

Odysseus is one of the most prominent of the Greek heroes from the *Iliad* and the subject of the *Odyssey*. In the *Iliad* he shows martial prowess, courage and resourcefulness as well as wisdom and diplomacy, whereas in the *Odyssey* he is better known for his attributes of guile and deception. In the 23rd Book of the *Iliad* he participates in two of the eight contests of the Funeral Games of Patroklos, the wrestling contest and the footrace. Odysseus ties with Ajax in the wrestling event and wins the footrace over Ajax and Antilochus. In order to win the footrace Odysseus asks for the help of Athena, who is willing to assist, causing Ajax to slip on ox and cow dung during the race. The prizes for the wrestling event are divided between the victors, a great tripod with the worth of twelve oxen and a woman with the worth of four oxen. The prize for the footrace is a mixing bowl of silver, which we are invited to think of as substantial, since the second prize was a great ox and the third prize half a talent of gold.

In *Odyssey* 8.105-255 we see Odysseus again as a competitor, when after years of wandering he arrives on the shores of Phaeacia. After he is entertained at dinner with songs from the Trojan war, his host Alcinous introduces athletic contests as a kind of after-dinner entertainment. There were five events: the footrace, wrestling, the long jump, the discus and boxing. Following the boxing contest the winner of the event, Laodamos, challenges Odysseus to try his hand at some contest, 'if he knows any'. He adds that Odysseus has the look of an athlete and that 'there is no greater fame for a man than that which he wins with his feet or by the skill of his hands'. Odysseus is not immediately interested, but when Euryalus, the winner of the wrestling event, goads him further and says to Odysseus that he is no good at athletics and only a sailor, and ends with the words, 'You are no athlete!' Odysseus of course reacts to this and picks up a discus heavier and bigger than the ones that were used in the discus competition by the Phaeacians. Odysseus throws and surpasses the marks of the others. It is Athena, disguised as a Phaeacian, who marks the throw and tells the crowd that no Phaeacian will come close to this mark. Odysseus adds that he will take on any man (except his host Alcinoos) and in any event except the footrace, for he has spent too much time on ships lately and his knees are bad! There are no material prizes for these after-dinner games, and the only reward appears to be one's honour.[31]

What about the historical record of ancient Olympic athletes?[32] What we know about ancient Olympic victors comes to us as a result of a victor list that was put together beginning in the fifth century BCE by Hippias of Elis. Hippias was a sophist from Elis who compiled his list in *c.* 400 BC. During the fourth century the list was revised by Aristotle and Eratosthenes, and in the third century BCE it was used as a kind of chronological system by Timaeus of Sicily. Later in antiquity the catalogue was revised by Eusebius, Phlegon of Tralles and Julius Africanus.[33]

The ancient Olympic Games, held every four years, continued over twelve centuries, and altogether the victor list consists of over 1,029 ancient Olympic victories and information about over 794 ancient victors. The first recorded victor was Koroibos of Elis who won the stadion race in 776 BCE. The last victor about whom we have information was Zopyrus, a boxer from Athens in 385 CE.[34] Between these two dates there were 291 Olympic festivals. In addition there were probably two additional ones after 385 CE for which we have no information, a total of 293 festivals.

According to my own estimate, the total number of possible victories at Olympia for the entire history of the festival, all 293 Olympic Games, should be approximately 4,760. This estimate would take into consideration the changing number of events during the history of the festival. Our known 1,029 victories constitute less than 22% of that number and should serve as a caution for our research. If the same relationship between victors and victories should prevail throughout the history of the festival, which it may not, one would expect to have a total of 3,672 ancient victors, of which we know of approximately 794, leaving a startling 2,878 Olympic victors for which we have no information at all. So any discussion of ancient Olympic victors is sadly incomplete and may be very misleading.[35]

Who are the greatest of the historical ancient Olympic victors? One indicator of Olympic success is the total number of recorded Olympic victories. I mention here the six who, according to the Olympic Register, won the most victories.[36]

Leonidas of Rhodes won a total of twelve victories in the *stadion, diaulos,* and *hoplitodromos* at four successive festivals; 164, 160, 156, 152 BCE.

Herodoros of Megara won ten victories in the contest for heralds in ten successive festivals; 328, 324, 320, 316, 312, 308, 304, 300, 296, 292 BCE. This was an event introduced in 396 BCE.

Hermogenes of Xanthos probably won a total of eight victories in the *stadion, diaulos* and *hoplitodromos* in three successive festivals; 81, 85, 89 CE.

Astylos of Kroton/Syracuse won a total of seven victories in the *stadion,* *diaulos,* and *hoplitodromos* at three successive festivals; 488, 484, 480 BCE.

Hipposthenes of Sparta won a total of six victories in boys' and then men's wrestling, in six festivals; 632, 624, 620, 616, 612, 608 BCE.

Milo of Kroton won the boys' wrestling and the wrestling event in six consecutive festivals from 536-516 BCE.

Another indicator that might be useful to determine the best ancient Olympic athlete of all time would be to consider the finest one-day athletic Olympic achievement, although it is difficult to compare these for various reasons. We often have incomplete or non-existent information about the competition in each of the events, and the effects of lottery selection of opponents and of byes in certain field events, the weather, or other factors may have influenced the outcomes. We do know that all of the track and field events were held on a single day during the ancient Olympic Games.[37] There are seven Olympic athletes who won three times, as 'triastes' in a single day. The triastes victors are the following:

Phanas of Pellene won three victories in the *stadion, diaulos, hoplitodromos* in 512 BCE.

Astylos of Kroton/Syracuse won three victories in the *stadion, diaulos, hoplitodromos* in 480 BCE.

Nikokle of Akrion won three victories in the *stadion, diaulos, hoplitodromos,* 100 BCE.

Leonidas of Rhodes won twelve victories in the *stadion, diaulos, hoplitodromos,* 164, 160, 156, 152 BCE.

Hekatomnos of Miletus won three victories in the *stadion, diaulos, hoplitodromos,* 72 BCE.

Polites of Keramos won three victories in the *stadion, diaulos, dolichos,* 69 CE.

Hermogenes of Xanthos won three victories in the *stadion, diaulos, hoplitodromos,* 81, 89 CE.

The *stadion* at Olympia was a footrace of 192 metres and the *diaulos* a footrace of 394 metres. The *hoplitodromos* was a footrace run in armour of 394 metres. The only athlete who definitely accomplished this feat on more than one occasion was **Leonidas of Rhodes** who achieved triastes status at four consecutive festivals. Was Leonidas the greatest ancient Olympic athlete of all time? Arguably he could be, based on his total number of victories and his series of Olympic appearances.[38] It is also possible that a boxer or wrestler or pankration athlete could be the greatest Olympic athlete as opposed to a runner. For instance, Milo of Kroton won six times in the wrestling event at Olympia between 536-516 BCE. 'Most victories' is not necessarily the best indicator of the greatest Olympic athlete of all time.

2. True Heroes and Dishonourable Victors at Olympia

It is known that there were some irregularities in the ancient Olympic Games and in fact there are a number of cases of cheating reported to us through ancient authors. As far as I am aware, there were no incidents involving drug-enhanced performance, although there were a number of occasions when athletes at Olympia were involved in scandals. As an example, Pausanias tells us of the case of Kallippos of Athens, who was a competitor in the pentathlon in the Olympic Games of 332 BCE.[39] Kallippos was caught trying to bribe those who were going to compete against him, and as a result both he and his antagonists were fined. We do not know the amounts, or the names of the antagonists. As a result the Athenians commissioned the famous orator Hypereides to persuade the Eleans to drop the fine. When the Eleans refused, the Athenians would not pay the fine and announced that they would not send athletes to the Olympic Games, essentially staging a boycott. The Athenians subsequently appealed to the Oracle at Delphi who declared that no oracle would be delivered to the Athenians until the Athenians paid the fine. Eventually the Athenians did pay the fine to the Eleans, and it was used to erect six bronze statues of Zeus along the path to the stadium. These are some of the statues that the Eleans called the Zanes, and each told the story of an athlete who had broken the rules of the contests. Of course most of the statues at Olympia were set up to commemorate victors in the ancient Olympic Games as well as to commemorate political and military events. The Zanes were purposely located where they were since they would have been the last statues that the athletes would see before entering the stadium, and would serve as a warning to would-be cheaters.

We don't know for certain the timetable for this incident, so we don't know when the infraction was discovered, whether it was at the time of the pentathlon event or before or later. Kallippos is included in Moretti's list of Olympic Victors although Pausanias does not clearly name him as a victor. Victor Matthews has recently questioned how Kallippos could possibly be an Olympic victor, having so obviously cheated to win.[40] But maybe we have a better idea now, based on the events of the past eight years of the modern Olympic Games, of what the organisers at Olympia could have been coping with in 332 BCE?

If the pentathlon event had already been already contested and Kallippos crowned the victor before the infraction was discovered, involving not only Kallippos but also his antagonists in the same match, what was the solution for the Elean officials? Was the solution to disqualify all the athletes, thus leaving an event with no victor? It may have been to heavily fine the city-state of the athlete, Athens, and the city-states of the other athletes in the match, and to use the fines to erect the six bronze statues in the altis at Olympia. Since possibly all the athletes in the match were implicated in the scandal, and since Kallippos may already have won the event, the organisers could have made an example of this scandal as a public humiliation for generations to come. So the fine may have in some

49

David Gilman Romano

Fig. 2.2. Al Oerter competing in the 1956 Olympic Games in Melbourne, Australia. Photo: Associated Press.

ways literally paid for the dishonourable victory and the story of the incident to make future athletes aware of the risks of dishonesty. We know that fines were used in other cases of dishonesty at the ancient Olympic Games as well.[41]

Perhaps this kind of financial penalty would provide a better resolution to the current and ongoing drug scandals of modern times, severely fining the countries of the athletes who are implicated and making an example of the athletes to other would-be offenders. After all Marion Jones did actually win the 100 metres and the 200 metres in Sydney (even though with the assistance of drug enhancements). Although it is now known that she did not win fairly, at this moment, ten years later, we do not have an official victor of either race.

There are many true track and field heroes in the history of the modern Olympic Games, and these are of course not mythological heroes but mortals. I would like to pay tribute to an especially outstanding example, Al Oerter of the United States, who died in 2007. Al Oerter, the four-time Olympic discus champion who won gold medals in 1956, 1960, 1964 and 1968, and who competed at international level through his forties, has few equals in the modern day (Fig. 2.2). He has been called the 'greatest competitor ever to compete in the discus'[42] and this is true of the modern age as well as from antiquity. 'Oerter's sweep of Olympic victories was all the more remarkable because in each case he broke the Olympic record, beat the world record holder, overcame an injury and was not the favorite to win.'[43] His track and field equal in the modern day could only be Carl Lewis, who won the Olympic long jump four times from 1984 to 1996,

50

although Lewis has been implicated in drug-enhanced performance issues. Al Oerter ranks no. 15 on David Powell's top 50 Olympic athletes list and no. 22 on Calvin Shulman's top 100 Olympic athletes list.

Oerter compares well with the best of the athletes from the ancient Olympic Games, as there were only a handful of ancient athletes who won four or more consecutive victories in one event. There are only three who are known from antiquity to have equalled or surpassed this feat. In antiquity, the discus was not an individual event, rather it was one event of the five-event pentathlon, and as far as we know, there never was an athlete who won four consecutive pentathlon victories at Olympia.

Another famous United States athlete, Jim Thorpe, who ranks no. 29 on David Powell's top 50 Olympic athletes, is worthy of mention. Thorpe won both the pentathlon and the decathlon in the 1912 Olympic Games in Stockholm, setting world records in both events. In 1913 he was stripped of his medals for having played semi-professional baseball for $25 a week before competing in the Olympic Games, and thus violating the existing amateurism regulation. Despite this, in 1950 he was named the outstanding US athlete of the first half of the twentieth century. Only later in 1982 (Thorpe died in 1953) were his Olympic medals restored by the International Olympic Committee. Thorpe, who was Native American and who attended the Carlisle Indian School in Carlisle, Pennsylvania, was one of America's most versatile athletes, playing professional football and baseball.[44]

So, given the complexities of victory in ancient as well as modern Olympics, what light can the athletic identity of mythological heroes shed? Certainly the athletic dimension of 'heroism' is a very old concept; the stories of Herakles, Pelops, Atalanta and Odysseus bear this out. What are the most salient characteristics of these early heroes? They are resourceful and clever as well as being strong and fast, using the contest and struggle as a kind of definition of who they are. But these heroes had vices as well as virtues and some not so attractive sides to their characters. For instance Herakles was said to have murdered his wife Megara and his children in a fit of madness sent by Hera, Pelops was responsible for killing Oinomaos, or having him killed, in order to avoid his own death and marry Hippodameia, and Odysseus killed Penelope's suitors on his return to the palace in Ithaca. Even Atalanta was said to have killed centaurs in her youth. Each of these mythological 'heroes' was also able to have a malevolent and less attractive side, and overall this did not seem to diminish their importance.[45] Perhaps we should not be surprised that some of our modern athletic heroes also have a less attractive side. Honesty and integrity do not necessarily come along with great athletic talent even though it may be taught in competitive situations by coaches. In the modern day athletes are often trying to gain victory by any means possible even if this should include slightly or more than slightly dishonest means. The assumption seems to be that the 'the other guy' is going to take any possible advantage, so why shouldn't you?

How do the mythological athletic heroes relate to the ancient historical victors at Olympia? They were obviously known to the athletes and the visitors who came there. As we have seen, Herakles and Pelops were an integral part of the architectural sculpture of the Temple of Zeus, Pelops in the east pediment and Herakles in the metopes. Herakles had made dedications to Pelops (Pausanias 5.13.2) as well as to Zeus (5.14.2). The stories of Odysseus and Atalanta were myths known from the oral tradition and at Olympia, in the games in honour of Hera in which young female virgins ran every four years, Atalanta may have had a prominent role. From these games we only know the name of one victor, Chloris, daughter of Amphion of Thebes.[46]

We can't possibly know how the individual historical athletes from antiquity may have been influenced by the stories of the 'true heroes'. We are led to believe that the historical athletes trained and competed to honour Zeus at Olympia. The victor was the athlete who was chosen by Zeus; the best representation of this concept may be the miniature bronze figurine found at Olympia depicting a Greek athlete standing at the start of a footrace, with the inscription on his right thigh, ' ΤΟ ΔΙϜΟΣ ΕΙΜΙ', 'I belong to Zeus' (Fig. 2.3). This must have been a dedication of a victorious runner at Olympia around 490 BCE who believed that he had been selected by Zeus as the winner of the race. Could it be the dedication of Astylos of Kroton who won both the stadion race as well as the diaulos race in the Olympic Games of 488 BCE and who features prominently in the lists of the greatest Olympic athletes of all time (above)?

What can we say about the relationship of ancient heroes and modern? Were the ancient victors any more or less honourable than their modern counterparts? We certainly don't have the reliable statistics from antiquity that would enable us to talk about the incidence of cheating in the ancient Olympic Games for comparative purposes. Nor do we have these statistics for the modern age. But it would seem to be a common characteristic of both ancient and modern athletes that there are specific competitors who were, and still are, willing to try to win at any cost. It would clearly appear that the winning is the most important thing (and of course in ancient times winning was the only thing as there were typically no second and third places) and it would outweigh the resulting public disgrace if an athlete were caught cheating.

It is one thing in the modern day for an athlete to try to cheat the judges and the International Olympic Committee, but did the ancient athletes really think that they were going to fool Zeus? Weren't ancient athletes supposed to be training and competing to please the god?[47] Wasn't athletics a part of a religious festival with dedications, sacrifices, processions, as well as other cultic ceremonies? Hadn't the ancient athletes taken an oath before the Olympic Games began in which they swore in front of Zeus Horkios, Zeus the Oath Giver, to do no wrong?[48] Was Kallippos thinking of Zeus when he bribed his competitors in 332 BCE – or was he thinking more

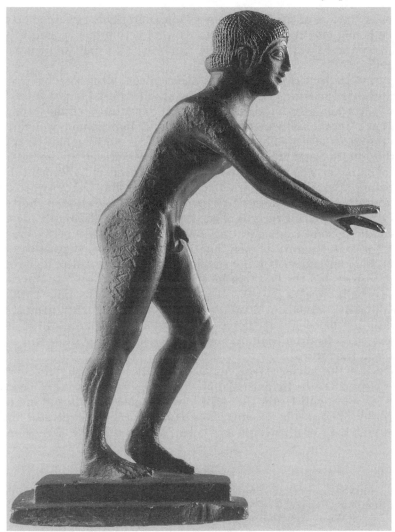

Fig. 2.3. Bronze miniature of a runner at the start of a race, *c.* 490 BCE.
Olympia Archaeological Museum, Hellenic Ministry of Culture and Tourism,
7th Ephorate of Prehistoric and Classical Antiquities and Archaeological

about Herakles or Pelops or perhaps Odysseus? Was it more the model of
the strong, clever if sometimes unscrupulous mythological hero that was
in his mind? It is hard to tell for sure but it is likely that Kallippos may
have been thinking about the lucrative awards that he would receive as
an Athenian citizen when he returned home as Olympic victor. It is known
that in several city-states lucrative prizes were awaiting Olympic or
Panhellenic victors.[49] Whereas the victorious athletes received a wreath of

leaves at the site of the Games, they were often richly rewarded on their return home. It is clear that city-states were very proud of their athletic victors and were willing to pay them handsomely as they would a victorious general.

Even with lingering suspicions about illegal drug use by Olympic athletes in the modern era, it seems that spectators and fans want to have their sports 'heroes', almost regardless of the way in which they won. One might ask 'does it really matter if the Olympic champion has won fairly or with the assistance of enhancement drugs?' This question may be applied to other professional athletes in the modern period who are under suspicion of using, or who have been found to have used, enhancement drugs, for instance Barry Bonds, Mark McGuire and possibly Lance Armstrong.[50] Are these individuals 'heroes'? Or perhaps simply celebrated sports figures known for setting records of one type or another, even with questions raised and in some cases cheating. Are we in the modern period creating myths of contemporary heroes that are in some ways suggestive of the myths from antiquity? Is it not so important how the athlete has won his or her victory, but the fact that he or she did win victory?[51] In the case of Carl Lewis it appears that the judges and officials were quite content to look the other way about drug test results, in an era when drug testing was less developed. Marion Jones on the other hand was caught in an era of more rigorous drug examination of Olympic athletes. How will things change in the future?

Who are the modern 'true heroes?' Are there modern 'true heroes'? Eight years after the Beijing Olympics in 2016, after retesting of blood and urine samples, will Usain Bolt still have his gold medals and his world records? Will he still be recognised as a phenomenon, a superstar athlete and a 'true hero' or discovered as a cheat? Would it matter if he were?

Notes

1. '2008 Summer Olympics,' *Wikipedia*, http://en.wikipedia.org/wiki/2008_Summer_Olympics

2. Nielsen Wire 2008. Additional data from Nielsen Media Research, 5 September 2008.

3. Sports Marketing Surveys, International Olympic Committee, 13 October 2004 as reported on the Beijing Olympic Games Official Website, 8-24 August 2008.

4. Demick 2008.

5. Booth et al. 2008, Lichfield 2008.

6. '2008 Summer Olympics,' *Wikipedia*, http://en.wikipedia.org/wiki/2008_Summer_Olympics

7. Powell 2008.

8. Shulman 2008.

9. MacKay 2003. Lewis admitted to testing positive for banned substances but claimed that he was only one of 'hundreds of people getting off'. The U.S. Olympic

Committee had originally denied claims that 114 positive tests between 1988-2000 were covered up.

10. Longman 2008: D2.

11. *Sports Illustrated*, 2 October 2000; *Vogue*, January 2001.

12. O'Keefe 2007.

13. Maggie Jones 2010: 32.

14. *ESPN Track and Field* 2008; Hersh 2010.

15. Zinser 2009.

16. Schmidt and Zinser 2007.

17. UPI.COM 'Marion Jones begins federal prison term', 7 March 2008.

18. Frank Shorter, who was the Chairman of the US Anti-Doping Agency, which he helped to found in 2000, has called Marion Jones 'a convincing liar'. Shorter has been outspoken in support of drug-free sports and independent drug testing (Epstein 2008). Shorter himself, who won the Olympic Marathon race in Munich in 1972 and won a silver medal in the same race in the 1976 Olympics in Montreal, alleges that Waldemar Cierpinski, the East German who won the Montreal Marathon, was guilty of using enhancement drugs, and has called this use of drugs as 'fraud perpetrated on sport' (Longman 1998).

19. Fitzpatrick 2009.

20. Marion Jones has written a book about her experiences, *On the Right Track* (2010).

21. Official website of the Olympic Movement, 25 August 2008, http://www.olympic.org/en/content/Media/?MediaNewsTab=0&currentArticlesPageIPP=40&currentArticlesPage=20&articleNewsGroup=-1&articleId=53533

22. Macur 2008. In a related story, lab samples were found to be missing from the Beijing games approximately one year after the Olympics, as reported in the *Daily Mail* on 16 October 2008.

23. Ekroth 2009: 121.

24. Apollodorus II.5.

25. Diodorus Siculus 5.64.3; Strabo 8.3.30; Pausanias 5.7.6-10.

26. Pindar *Olympian* 1.

27. Apollodorus 3.12.6.

28. Apollodorus 3.9.2.

29. Pausanias 5.16.2-3; Scanlon 2002: 98-120; Serwint 1993: 415-16.

30. Scanlon: 175-95.

31. Odysseus does also win the 'reward' of becoming able at this point to tell his story. See also Spivey in this volume.

32. The Olympic Games in honour of Zeus were the most famous of the four Panhellenic festivals that also included games to Apollo at Delphi, Poseidon at Isthmia, and Zeus at Nemea.

33. See the new study by Christesen 2007a.

34. Sinn 2000: 134.

35. Romano 2004.

36. For a full listing of the literary references for each of the Olympic victors see Moretti 1957 and 1970.

37. Lee 2001.

38. There are of course other athletes who won victories in the ancient Olympic Games who are very famous but do not appear on such a list of 'most victories.' For instance Pausanias (6.11.2-9) gives us an account of Theagenes of Thasos who won at Olympia in the boxing match in 480 BCE and the pankration in 476 BCE. He also won three victories in boxing at Delphi, and nine Nemean and ten Isthmian

victories in boxing and pankration, and had a grand total of all athletic victories at 1400. He was heroized in antiquity, after his death, and there was a shrine set up to his memory in the agora at Thasos immediately adjacent to the Sanctuary of Zeus. Pausanias' story goes on that a local enemy of Theagenes would flog the statue in the agora and that one night the statue fell and killed the enemy. As a result the Thasians found the statue guilty of homicide and threw it into the sea. During a subsequent difficult period on Thasos the Delphic Oracle suggested that in order to appease the spirit of the dead athlete, the statue should be recovered. It was, and as a result Theagenes was made a god. See Daux 1968: 31-4. For further consideration of Theagenes as hero see Fontenrose 1968. Farnell 1921: 365 suggests that the heroising of the successful athlete was injurious and degrading to the religious sense of the cult and cites Theagenes as a prime example.

39. Pausanias 5.21.3.

40. Matthews 2007; see also Kyle 1987: 119-21 and 204.

41. Romano 2007: 107-9.

42. USATF Hall of Fame, http://www.usatf.org/halloffame/TF/show-Bio.asp?HOFIDs=124

43. Litsky 2007.

44. A new biography of Jim Thorpe has appeared: Buford 2010.

45. See Anderson 2009, who considers some of the ways in which Greek poets and artists approached ethics and how they confronted their heroes with moral challenges and how they provoked ethical inquiry in their audiences.

46. Pausanias 5.16.4.

47. Pausanias 5.21.16 mentions his surprise that an athlete would have so little respect for the god of Olympia that he would give or take a bribe in the contests.

48. Pausanias 5.24.9.

49. *IG* I^2 77 is an Athenian inscription from the mid-fifth century BCE in which it is stated that athletic and equestrian victors from Olympia, Delphi, Isthmia and Nemea will receive a free meal in the city Prytaneion every day for the rest of their lives.

50. Professional athletics introduces a whole different set of parameters with respect to steroids and the use of enhancement drugs. The release of the Mitchell Report in December 2007 drew attention to the fact that performance enhancing drug use had been pervasive in professional baseball in the United States for over a decade.

51. Barry Bonds, who holds the record for most home runs in a career, was invited to throw out the first ball of game 3 of the National League Championship Series between the Giants and the Phillies in October 2010. Bonds, who has been clearly linked to steroid use in his pursuit of his total of 762 home runs, was invited back 'because he is San Francisco's baseball hero'. His trial, scheduled for 2011, is supposed to determine whether he lied or told the truth about knowledge of taking steroids (Rhoden 2010).

To Give over One's Heart: Pindar, Bataille and the Poetics of Victory

Damian Stocking

But we ourselves are aware of the aspects of social life in which man is relegated to the level of things … It is this degradation that man has always tried to escape. In his strange myths, in his cruel rites, man is in search of a lost intimacy from the first. (Georges Bataille)

What is it that moved Pindar to compose the Victory Odes? Among critics of the last twenty years or so, the answer to this question has proved surprisingly uniform. Recoiling from the excessive formalism of the New Critical, Structuralist and Post-Structuralist studies bequeathed upon us by Bundy's efforts to understand epinician as a literary genre, and reasoning too that poetry, as just one among any number of social practices, cannot be understood apart from the larger material and ideological forces that constitute society as a whole, critics of the last two decades have sought to confer meaning upon Pindar's work by placing it within a relevant social context, by ascribing to it an important social function. With almost universal agreement, this function has been understood to be the maintenance and stabilisation of a certain socio-political order (more often than not, an 'aristocratic' one). Such, for instance, is the basis of Kevin Crotty's well-known argument for epinician as a ritual of cultural reintegration, one whereby the athlete might be restored from a condition of 'ambiguity' and 'liminality' (Crotty: 111-12) back into his community 'and the values of his community' (Segal 1998: 3); so too of course runs the argument of Leslie Kurke's highly influential *Traffic in Praise: Pindar and the Poetics of Social Economy.* Basing her interpretation of the odes on Marcel Mauss's description of pre-industrial society as a dynamic and 'total' economic system, one sustained solely through gift-exchange (Kurke 1991: 92, 94), Kurke argues for Pindaric ode as a site for the exchange of 'symbolic capital', an exchange aimed specifically at 'defusing the political tensions' that must inevitably come in the wake of an (aristocratic) athlete's victory in the Games (Kurke 1991: 182, 208). And though many of the most recent Pindaric studies have sought to distinguish their own work from these two seminal pieces by placing a greater emphasis upon the particular historical circumstances that would have shaped each individual ode, they do not differ in the least from their predecessors' general determination to understand the poems as performing the basic function of political stabilisation.[1]

Widely accepted as that assumption may be, there is, I think, a certain difficulty with such readings of the Victory Odes – namely, their relative neglect of a central feature of the poetry's own 'self-representation'. What I am thinking of here is the close association drawn everywhere between the odes themselves and that peculiar Greek 'institution' or social grouping that goes by the name of the *kômos*. As Gregory Nagy observes, though they were composed as choral lyrics, 'in the victory songs of Pindar (and of Bacchylides), it is in fact regularly the word *kômos* – and not *khoros* – that designates the joyous ensemble that celebrates the victory' (Nagy 1994: 22). What, then, is the *kômos*? On the one hand, the term designates the group of companions who celebrate a friend's victory by moving in procession, singing (more or less) ritualised cheers and songs with the victorious athlete as they go.[2] Pindar makes reference to such a *kômos* in the opening lines of *Olympian* 9, where the victor, Epharmostos, and his friends regale themselves by singing by the so-called *kallinikos* song of Archilochus (the tradition was to repeat the refrain *tênella kallinike* three times):

> The song of Archilochos
> sounding out at Olympia,
>   that three-ply exultant song of victory ...
> for Epharmostos, with his dear companions, as he went in *kômos* ...
> (*O*. 9.1-3, 5)[3]

Now throughout the Victory Odes, Pindar is at pains to relate his own carefully prepared, formal songs in honour of the victor to these informal, ebullient *kômoi*. Sometimes, it seems, he would have us imagine his epinicians being sung as part of a *kômos*: 'Stand beside Arkesilas, O Muse, so that you might lift a breeze of hymns for him, as he celebrates in *kômos*' (*stamen ... Moisa ... ophra kômazonti sun Arkesilâi ... auxêis ouron humnôn, P*. 4.2-3).[4] The epinicians will in fact often simply refer to themselves as 'at-the-*kômos*' songs, either *en-kômion* (*O*. 13.29, *P*. 10.53, *N*. 1.7), or *epi-kômion* (*P*. 10.6, *N*. 6.32, *N*. 8.50). More controversially, though perhaps much more interestingly, there are those cases in which Pindar seems to want us to think of epinician as being itself a kind of metaphorical *kômos* – as when, for instance, the poet begs the Muse to be present at the singing of an ode in Aegina, where 'young men, fashioners of honey-voiced *kômoi*, yearn for your voice' (*meligaruôn tektones kômôn ... sethen opa maiomenoi, N*. 3.4-5); or again, when he identifies himself, the singer of epinician, as the 'steward' or 'the head' of the *kômoi* (*tamias ... kômôn, I*. 6.58).[5] Whether we understand the relation to be metaphoric or metonymic, however, it is clear enough that Pindar would have us import the whole performance context of the *kômos* into his victory songs. As Hayden

Pelliccia so insightfully puts it, the ode 'is designed to create its own party, chorus or *kômos*, wherever it is performed, whoever performs it, whoever hears it' (Pelliccia 2009: 254).

On the other hand, though, *kômos* may also be taken to signify certain social practices organised around drinking, indeed, around a ritualised drinking to excess (cf. Aloni 2009: 175). In such cases, *kômos* refers once again to a gathering of companions who are moving outside in procession – only this time with much more riotous results. Understood in this particular sense, *kômos* refers to the custom among Greek males of drinking themselves into such a pitch of excited inebriation that they would finally burst out onto the street, whence they would proceed, singing and revelling by torchlight, to the homes of friends and neighbours (or perhaps simply to the dwelling 'of some attractive person' (Bowie 1997: 2)). There they would request that the disturbed occupant either allow them in, or join them outside. Actually opening one's doors so as to 'receive the *kômos*', was, one takes it, a somewhat bold undertaking, given the general condition the komasts were likely to be in when they arrived. As the fourth-century comedian, Eubulus, has Dionysus himself explain, the first three rounds of drinks at a symposium, which belong to Health, Love, and Sleep respectively, should suffice for 'right thinking' men. The fourth, however, as Dionysus puts it, is 'no longer within our possession' – *ouketi hêmeteros esti*; the fifth belongs to shouting – *esti boês*; and the sixth round, that in fact is what belongs to *kômos* (fr. 94b, Hunter 1983: 66).[6]

Now what is interesting to note concerning these two senses of *kômos* in relation to Pindar's Victory Odes is just the way the poet himself refuses to delimit or divide them (as his translators are sometimes wont to do).[7] No less than the victory processional is the *kômos* as 'drunken rout' implied in that 'party' brought into existence by the odes whenever and wherever they are sung.[8] In *Isthmian* 8, for example, Pindar opens with the excited exclamation, 'In honour of Kleandros, go to his father's shining door, and awaken the *kômos*!' (*Kleandrôi ... patros aglaon ... para prothumon iôn anegeiretô kômon, I.* 8.1-4). Clearer still are implications of the opening and closing strophes of *Nemean* 9: 'Let us go in *kômos* ... to Aetna ... O Muses ...' calls out the singer, (*kômasomen ... Moisai ... es Aitna*), 'where the doors, flung open wide, have been overwhelmed, vanquished, by *xenoi*: guest-friends/strangers!' (*entha anapeptamenai xeinôn nenikantai thurai*: (*N.* 9.2-3). Eruption, irruption, and even a little destruction: all the more 'disruptive' aspects of *kômos* are in evidence here, all likewise taking their origin from the excited intoxication of wine and song:

> But the voice becomes bold near the wine bowl.
> Let someone mix him in–the sweet spokesman of *kômos*!
> In silver bowls let someone serve him forth – the violent
> Child of the vine! (*N.* 9.49-52)

The relation Pindar wished to draw between his epinician songs and *kômos* has not gone unnoticed by critics, of course; but, for the most part, they have been content to use the connection to try to settle historical questions of performance.[9] These are not unimportant questions, to be sure, but it does seem to me that a whole series of more difficult, and in some sense, more fundamental, questions remains to be asked. In particular, how does the inebriated *kômos*, that 'ritual drunken riot ... performed in public with the intention of demonstrating the power and lawlessness of the group' (Murray 1990: 150; cited in Nagy 1994: 25), relate to the ebullient victory procession that goes by the same name? Even more difficult, what is the meaning of this drunken ritual? Why would such a strange practice exist at all? And of course, of most pertinence to a study of Pindar, why is the poet so intent on relating his Victory Odes to these customs?

Clearly, the centrality of *kômos* in Pindar makes such questions crucially important for any adequate evaluation of his poetry. One can see, however, why the majority of contemporary critics – even so formidable a critic as Kurke, whose work marshals together in brilliant fashion nearly every other major conceptual term enunciated in the odes – would somehow allow these more difficult questions concerning *kômos* to pass. Critical perspectives that aim, in accordance with classical sociological notions inherited from Mauss and others, to make a deep-seated anxiety for the restored equilibrium of the group the sole motivating force in social life, may well find unthinkable any practice as riotous as the *kômos*, a practice which is after all little else than the ritualisation of an experience of unrestrained and 'lawless' self-abandon.

But I suspect, in this last formulation, we in fact have the answer to at least the first question I posed above, namely, that concerning the relation between the drunken *kômos* and the reception of the victor. For *the experience of victory is itself an experience of exuberant, unruly, uncontainable self-abandon.* We can verify the truth of this easily enough within contemporary times by 'looking no further' (to quote Pindar's *Olympian* 1) than our own responses to a tennis victory, to a favourable football final, or indeed (as Pindar himself suggests), to our experience of the Olympic Games, whose *raison d'être*, so it seems to me (the platitudes of Pierre de Coubertin to the contrary notwithstanding) is nothing other than that wild exuberance we feel in the moment of our favoured athlete's victory. The possibility of such an experience, I submit, is primarily why we ourselves watch the Games. And if we needed to verify that this is an experience we share in common with the spectators of ancient times, we have, among many other tales, the story of Kallipateira. As we learn from Pausanias' *Description of Greece* (5.6.7-8), Kallipateira's son, Peisirodos, was competing in the games at Olympia, but as a woman, Kallipateira was denied entrance into the stadium. The penalty for any woman discovered attending the Games was to be cast down from atop Mount Typaeum; but

Kallipateira, undeterred, disguised herself as a trainer, just so that she might watch her son compete. Peisidorus, as it turns out, was victorious – and Kallipateira, we are told, apparently *unable to restrain herself*, 'leapt over, beyond' (*hyper-pêdôsa* [*hyperpêdaô*, 'to overleap,' but also, 'to escape, transgress, surpass']) the *eruma*, the 'enclosure' in which the trainers were kept (but *eruma* also denotes, significantly, 'defensive wall, safeguard'). In casting aside her self-protections, so to speak, in abandoning herself to the moment of victory, Kallipateira was 'exposed' (*egumnêsthê*); happily, in light of her family's illustrious Olympic history, she was allowed to live.

This experience of the Games, of victory, thus coincides with those of the *kômos*. It is my contention that this experience is central to the purposes and aims of epinician as well. In other words, I think we can best account for the principal structures and content of Pindaric Victory Ode by understanding them as the effort to recreate, within the confines of civic life, this 'common' (i.e. common to us *and* the ancients) experience of uncontainable self-abandon that comes of watching athletic victory. As far as I know, such a strategy for interpreting Pindar has never really been adopted before. Indeed, it is curious to note, given contemporary criticism's keen interest in relating Pindaric poetry to every imaginable social context, that the one context nobody ever seems interested in is, as a matter of fact, the experience of athletic victory itself. Criticism has attempted to generate meaning out of the odes by recourse to everything but the Games. Still, this critical 'blind spot' afflicts more than just Classicists. In our determination to 'think the modern Olympics' in terms of *their* ideological, historical and economic import, *their* function in the maintenance of a given social order, we tend to think of them too strictly in terms of their larger, social effects – leaving the actual experience of victory (which is, again, our reason for attending the Games) untouched, and so to speak, utterly 'unthought'.[10]

The attitude with which we approach the modern Games is thus, by and large, the same approach we take to Pindar himself, whose basic response to victory, it would seem (on the reading of contemporary critics, at any rate), was to view it as, at best, a cause for anxiety over a threatened socio-political order, or, more suspiciously, to see it as a serviceable opportunity to create that order through rhetorical manipulation. The possibility of him valuing the exuberance of the Games themselves does not enter into the discussion.

Such thinking, I suspect (though this is to anticipate somewhat), comes from a deep-rooted assumption about what constitutes (and what is of real value) in 'social existence', and how poetry is related to that. Poetry, it is often pointed out, is a social thing; but since – and this is the key assumption – 'society' is nothing other than the maintenance of a certain kind of order and equilibrium, poetry too must perforce serve that order. But the very existence of the *kômos*, its prominence within Pindaric Ode, and many other features of epinician as well, can best be understood, as I hope to show, from the perspective of another possibility – namely, that sociality, genuine community, is not incompatible with a certain *disequilibrium*, and may in fact depend upon it. In that case, poetry (and the Olympics, and poetry *about* the Olympics) might serve an important social function precisely to the extent that it disorders us, casts us into states of instability. Against the poetics of 'social economy' and its objective orderings, I propose to read Pindar against a poetics of victory, and its subjective 'disorderings'. But to make this reading possible, to answer successfully questions about the existence of the *kômos*, the communal importance of victory, and Pindar's interest in both, would require a different logic than the 'logic of equilibrium' with which classical sociological thought has made us familiar; it requires a different political economy than the political economy of anxiety that underwrites all our present analyses.[11] We would require a logic of disequilibrium, and a political economy, so to speak, of exuberance – just such a logic and political economy, in fact, as we find in the works of Georges Bataille.

Over the course of several decades, through a series of works which would profoundly influence the thought of Lacan, Foucault, Derrida, Baudrillard and many others, Bataille sought to formulate the principles of what turned out to be (somewhat to his own chagrin) a new 'political economy' (1991: 9). In Bataille's view, all political economies up to his own time had been interpreted on the basis of 'conservative' principles: the point of all social behaviours, what they lead to and seek, is restored equilibrium within a system. The universal object of any economy, so it seemed, was to accumulate and preserve, and to accumulate precisely so as to preserve. Against this seemingly incontestable view, Bataille proposed a different principle (one he formulated, in fact, originally, as a critique of Mauss):[12] the real object of any economy, its true *telos*, was not to save, but to spend. Only in expenditure, a 'non-productive expenditure' 1985b: 118) that contributed nothing to further growth and development, would socio-economic systems (and the human beings that constitute them) come to actual fulfilment.

This was not to deny, of course, that a great part of human social existence is given over to producing goods, and saving them too. Bataille merely wished to point out, a little archly one suspects, that 'human activity is not entirely reducible to processes of production and conservation' (1985b: 118); ultimately, such processes exist, he insists, for the sake of a final, sumptuous expenditure, a non-productive consumption of our energies and goods.

Bataille understood, of course, that such a notion would encounter a certain amount of resistance: 'Minds accustomed to seeing the development of productive forces as the ideal end of activity refuse to recognise that energy, which constitutes wealth, must ultimately be spent lavishly (without return), and that a series of profitable operations has absolutely no other effect than the squandering of profits' – for to hold such a position is to go up squarely against the 'judgments that form the basis of a rational economy' (1991: 22). But such 'rationality,' Bataille insists, takes only a 'restricted view' of things. From a larger, *general* perspective, what people anxiously hide from themselves is the fact that they are only fulfilled when they throw all their savings away. It is true that we are taught to think of ourselves as 'productive' members of society, but 'in the final analysis it is clear that the worker works in order to obtain the violent pleasures of *coitus* (in other words, he accumulates in order to spend)' – and not the other way round 1985c: 99). Pouring out one's capital (physical, material, cultural) is the culmination of all political economies – such is the working principle of Bataille's 'General Economy', the economy, that is, taken in its widest view (1991: 39-40).

But why, one wonders, should this be the case? Why is it that persons are fulfilled strictly in the extravagance of a wasteful *'dépense'*? The answer to this question takes us to the heart of Bataille's most revolutionary insights – insights concerning the nature of community, personhood, and the relation between them. As inheritors of a tradition of Cartesian subjectivity, of Lockean theories of government by social contract, and of Adam Smith's notion of an economy motivated by the maximisation of utility, we are accustomed to thinking of ourselves as self-subsistent, autonomous, fully individuated creatures, creatures whose actions and social connections lie within their own disposing. Bataille, in common with Heidegger, and the whole tradition of postmodern thought that they themselves inspired, would strenuously contest this assumption. They would treat as ludicrous the idea that a person ever 'appears' fully formed on the scene of the world, ready to refuse or entertain connections with (similarly fully formed) beings, just as he or she wills; rather, no person exists without 'always already' being in relation to others: 'Nowhere do there exist "isolated beings" ...' (1976: 553). Our actions, our thoughts, desires, words do not issue from some secret interior place within us – even when completely 'alone', everything we do and think and feel results from, is 'contingent upon', a felt relation to another. Our being is in fact nothing other than a 'being in relation' (1985a: 174), or to use Bataille's usual formulation, a being-in-communication: *'Existence* is communication!' (1988: 98).

What this implies, of course, is that as human beings we depend, existentially, upon the 'difference' of the other – 'relation' and 'communication' presume such difference (for where there is only sameness, no relation is possible). The irony, however, is that as human beings we typically try to take control of the differences of others, in just such a way as to appropriate them into sameness with ourselves. For insofar as my being is contingent upon the other (and hers upon others, and so on, *ad infinitum*), my existence has no guaranteed stability, no guarantee of continuance into the future. I therefore become anxious. I attempt to assimilate the other, to absorb her into my own self and projects; I give her intelligible, calculable dimensions, physically and intellectually reduce her to a measure that is commensurate with myself: I render her an 'object' to my 'subject', a mere *thing* in the '*order of things*' (cf. 1991: 56-7). By my appropriative, 'homogeneous representations' I render the other, and the whole world of others, 'fit only for the fabrication, rational consumption, and conservation of products' (1985c: 97), a calculable world in which I may maintain my own stable, calculable identity.

But as I say, there is an irony here. To the extent that I am successful at reducing the world of others into total homogeneity with myself, I may well allay my anxiety for my continuance – yet in eradicating the differences of others, I also forsake that 'being in relation' which was my essential ground, from out of which I so richly existed in the first place. 'No one can make a *thing* (of another),' says Bataille, 'without at the same time estranging himself from his own intimate being, without giving himself the limits of a *thing*' (1991: 56). And therein, I believe, lies Bataille's answer to the mysterious satisfactions of extravagant, unrestrained expenditure. For by such expenditure, I relinquish my appropriative designs upon the world, and allow it become once again a source of communicative being: 'The animal or plant man uses as if they had value only for him needs restoration to the truth of the intimate world – so he may receive a sacred communication from it' (1991: 57-8). In my uncalculating *self-abandon*, I open myself up and expose myself (*egumnêsthê*) to the possibility of a genuine being in relation with others: 'And if I thus consume immoderately, I reveal to my fellow beings that which I am *intimately*: Consumption is the way in which *separate* beings communicate. Everything shows through, everything is open, between those who consume intensely' (1991: 58-9).

Here then we have a basis upon which to understand the value (to Pindar, to ourselves) of that exuberance which is so characteristic of the Olympic Games, both ancient and modern. In the moment of victory, we forsake all defensive, anxious calculation; we make an instant consumption of all that we have – expending all available energy in upward leaps and screams, dispossessing ourselves of hats and clothes, and significantly, embracing even strangers. For the result, the 'social function', if you will, of Olympic victory, is nothing less than a genuine communing with others – others, who (for once) are not calculable objects fit by my appropriative imagination within a projected order of things, but other beings I am content to leave indeterminate in themselves, and with whom I therefore enjoy a non-productive, pointless, and lavish intimacy. At the moment of victory, 'Everything in me gives itself to others' (1988: 130). The Games convert what was a mere 'society' – a mere regulation of people into an alienating system of production and conservation – into a place of communication; a 'community'.[13]

It is this experience of athletic victory, I submit, which *kômos* (that *other* form of 'intense consumption') ritualises – and it is likewise this experience which gives life and meaning to the Pindaric ode. But before seeing how that is so, an additional question remains to be answered concerning the 'existential dynamics', the 'phenomenology', if you will, of victory; namely, how does something like athletic victory cause us to forsake our usual, calculative dispositions? One answer to this question, entirely consistent with Bataille's formulations, would be to see the athlete as a sacrificial offering. In sacrifice, Bataille tells us, a given social group (the Aztecs are his favoured example) takes a portion of its otherwise productive wealth, and 'wastes' it, uselessly and 'sumptuously'; this free expenditure thus creates a sacral intimacy amongst those who sacrifice (cf. 1991: 55ff.). And as it turns out, classical scholar David Sansone (an indirect follower of Bataille in this, though apparently an unwitting one[14]) has made the case that Olympic athletes were indeed treated as sacrificial offerings: their 'ritual separation' from their home cities before the games, the decking out of athletes in fillets in the manner of sacrificial beasts, the procession to the double flute which accompanied sacrificial and athletic processions, and (finally) the resemblance of the cleaning 'strigil' to a religious instrument for sacral laceration – all this would seem to suggest that athletes were viewed by the Greeks in terms of sacrifice.

Without wanting to dispute Sansone's claim in all its particulars (for I think he is right to point out the basically sacral character of the Games), I would suggest there is something rather more subtle (and certainly more informative for the analysis of Pindar) occurring in the event of an athlete's victory than a simple matter of religious sacrifice. (For one thing, there is no reason, on Sansone's evidence, why winning would matter at all – and clearly it did; the losers featured in Pindaric odes hardly have a 'sacral' character! Cf. *Pythian* 8.81-7). I propose that instead of a simple case of sacrifice, the experience of victory is actually a case of what Bataille would have called a 'heterological' experience. As we have already seen, human beings proceed through life, for the most part, by appropriating what is foreign to them, 'homogenising it' into conformity with their own selves, with their own bodies, ideologies, projects, and so forth. The foreign material item is digested into food, the foreign sense datum is rendered into a serviceable concept (1985c: 95). Occasionally, though, we encounter something foreign that we cannot assimilate, either physically or psychically, something Bataille calls *le tout autre* (after Otto's famous *das ganz Anderes*; ffrench 2007: 33). We might of course just avoid such a thing, so as to continue on our appropriating, homogenising way. But what if, instead, we take the foreign body, with its 'irreducibly heterogeneous elements' (1985c: 95) into ourselves – not through a process of objectification, but in a manner similar to what Lacan identified as 'subjectification' (ffrench 2007: 37)? What if we risked absorbing this 'total Other,' and, instead of objectifying it (for by definition it defies objectification into a rational order of things), we identified with it and 'became' the Other we contemplated? We would, says Bataille, as a result, suffer a kind of 'expulsive or projective "charge"' (1970: 58) within our psyches, one that would totally destabilise us as subjects – for we would become incalculable to ourselves. But this, I believe, is what occurs in athletics all the time. Athletic victory is practical heterology.

In the first place, we should recognise that we look to athletes to be nothing less than potential 'total Others'. Their training, their natural capabilities make them (potentially) capable of things beyond what we can calculate or know from within our own experience. And then again, crucially, in any athletic competition, we require the athlete to submit herself to the vagaries and contingencies of risk: in setting up a bar to jump over, a target to hit, a time or opponent to beat, the athlete forswears all secure self-possession, and submits herself to the incalculability of chance. This alone is enough to detach the athlete from the 'order of things' for us, and we in fact demand such detachment (to cheat in athletic competition is felt to be intolerable – no less to the ancients than ourselves – precisely because it degrades the athletic 'event' to an expected, scientifically calculable result; insofar as cheating just re-enacts our usual calculating, objectifying ways, it robs the athletic event of the ability to let us escape from those ways).[15]

So as the athlete approaches the starting line, we do not know what to expect – and insofar as we have identified ourselves with her, 'subjectified' her, so to speak, we too forsake the certainty of our own self-possession. We expose ourselves, brutally, to the anguish of time, the anxiety of future expectation. Pindar's *Olympian* 12 enacts this anguished anxiety for us with exquisite skill: beginning with an invocation, significantly, to 'Chance – our Saviour!' (*sôteira Tucha*, O. 12.2), it subjects us, through 'stylistic enactment' (Silk 2007: 180), to the torturing, tortuous vagaries of these expectations: 'the hopes of men, often up, then down again, deceptive, vainly blown on the wind, cleaving (the waves), rolling (in the waves)', where, in the original Greek, the definite article 'the' (*h'ai*) and its noun, 'hopes' (*elpides*) are the first and last words in the phrase, so that 'the phraseology is drawn out like perilous hope' (Silk 2007: 180):

> ... *h'ai ge men andrôn*
> *poll' anô, ta d' au katô*
> *pseudê metamônia tamnoisai kulindont' elpides* (O. 12.5-6a)

Uncertain abilities and risk alike therefore detach us from the stabilising order of things. But of course, not just the risking matters here; for what happens when we watch someone forsake self-possession, calculable certainty ... and then fail? Our appropriative gestures, our objectifying calculations, seem sadly justified, and we are condemned (once again) to the alienation, the destroying isolation they bring. But with victory, everything changes. What calculations are possible, after all, when success is the result of risk? In the victory of the athlete, calculation is overthrown, *for we no longer know what is impossible.*[16] The athlete, whose training and natural abilities had already detached her from the order of things for us, confirms her place outside it. And through a heterological movement of subjectification, she takes us with her.[17]

In victory, therefore, our calculative reduction of the world into the order of things is (temporarily) undone. Luxuriating in the possible, we relinquish anxiety, so that, in the moment of victory, the future ceases to be of concern; indeed, phenomenologically, the future ceases to exist at all. Released from temporal anguish – an anguish to which we had voluntarily subjected ourselves, *just for the chance to be released from it* – we let others be from our need to reduce them to objects; in complete self-abandon, we open ourselves up to being with others in that rarest of things, the present. 'If I am no longer concerned about what will be, but about "what is," what reason do I have to keep anything in reserve? I can at once, in disorder, make an instantaneous consumption of all I possess' (1991: 58). ('But *now*,' concludes *Olympian* 12, having drawn us out painfully upon the uncertainties of time, and addressing itself to a victor who had been in exile, 'at Olympia you are crowned!' (*nun d' Olumpiâi stephanôsamenos, O.* 12.17).[18] The result of that self-abandoning consumption, of course, will be nothing less than a rediscovery of that '*lost intimacy*' we had been in search of, '*from the first*' (1991: 57). Just such an intimacy, in fact, as one enjoys, among one's companions, in a *kômos*.

We experience the moment of victory, then, as a 'heterological' moment. By means of our identification with that Incalculable Other who is the Olympic victor, we are released from our own objectifying tendencies into the General Economy of abandon, into a non-objectifying intimacy with others, and the world. It is just that experience of intimacy, so I submit, which is now, and has always been, the real gift of the Games.

This is, sadly enough, a point which seems to be somewhat lost upon the majority of those who have undertaken to 'think the Olympics', whether critically or admiringly, and is lost upon them for the simple reason that (as Bataille notes in his introduction to 'The Notion of Expenditure', 1985b), 'on the whole, any general judgment of social activity implies the principle that all individual effort, to be valid, must be reducible to the fundamental necessities of production and conservation' (1985b: 117). To 'think the Olympics' has been, for the most part, to think them from within the perspective of the restricted economy, from within the perspective, that is to say, of a future-oriented, objectifying anxiety ('a flat, untenable conception of existence', Bataille hastens to add, to which personal experience 'each time gives the lie' (1985b: 117)). It is no doubt for this reason that intellectual evaluation of the modern Games almost inevitably revolves around the 'ideals' of its *fin-de-siècle* founding, whether it be to praise the holding of those ideals or to deconstruct the mythologising misappropriation by which they were formed, whether to subject the ideals themselves to ethical critique, or simply to lament the failure of the

Games to realise them; for it is precisely through such 'ideals' that societies are ordered, and it is for the most part only with a view to their utility
as a procedure for social ordering that the Olympics have (so far) garnered
any kind of intellectual attention whatsoever.[19] What I would like to
suggest, however, is that in an important sense, discussion of the 'ideals'
that underpin the Games, whether for or against, fails to capture what
matters most about them, even as it fails to notice what most essentially
unites our own experience with that of the ancients. Without a doubt ideal
(or what amounts to the same thing, 'ideological') values were, in ancient
and modern times alike, a crucial element in the establishment and
execution of the Olympics (it was, for instance, probably quite important
for de Coubertin to believe that in re-establishing the ancient festival he
might help develop the 'effeminate' bodies of his 'excessively intellectual'
fellow Frenchmen, and thus prevent further humiliation at the hands of
healthier countries such as Prussia; it was no doubt an incitement to
participation in the Games for not a few ancient Greek aristocrats to
believe that a victory in Olympia would demonstrate the superiority of
their *phusis*, and thus their right to rule in the polis).[20] Yet, as Bataille
himself rather laconically observes, 'moral ends ... are distinct from any
excesses they occasion. States of glory and moments of sacredness (which
reveal incommensurability) surpass results intentionally sought' (1998:
xx). It is not fundamentally the enactment of so many socially advantageous (or politically suspect) ideals or values that ties us to the Games; it
is not their advertised utility for moral improvement, commercial development, or the furtherance of any political agenda that continues to draw us
to them, as it drew the Greeks, for centuries on end. What truly binds us
to the Games – and what, by extension, most fundamentally connects us
to the ancients who first invented them – is the constantly rediscovered
'utility' of this invention for suspending us in anguish and abandoning us
to ecstasy, for opening us up to an experience of exuberant intimacy daily
denied to us by the usual objectifying procedures of everyday, civil life.

Yet if this point is by and large lost to us, it certainly was not lost upon
Pindar, whose odes are written (so I would argue) for the explicit purpose
of bearing – as a messenger might bear – the intimacy of the heterological
moment of victory back into society, back into the 'order of things'. But
that, perhaps is just the function of 'the Ode' as such; it is at any rate what
seems to inform the odes of the English Romantics. Shelley calls out to *le
tout autre* that is the West Wind, 'Be thou me, impetuous one!' precisely in
an attempt to restore a lost intimacy with a world now chained down 'by
a heavy weight of hours'; Keats, listening in intimate darkness to a
nightingale, bears the experience back into a world where 'men sit, and
hear each other groan'. Pindar too, as we shall see, must attempt to bear
the intimacy of victory back to a similarly hostile world, an objectifying
world of mockery, self-content, and bitter resentment. It has been said
that Pindar's 'social function' is to fold the athlete back into his commu-

68

nity; I would propose instead that Pindar's social function is to fold the community, the athlete, and us as well, back into the moment of the athlete's victory and its intimacy.

This would explain, I think, Pindar's insistent invocation throughout the odes of a term more important even than *kômos*, namely, *charis*. *Charis* has, of course, been a mainstay of those who wish to make political stability the *raison d'être* of Pindaric epinician, for the simple reason that *charis* (in certain contexts) implies or relates to the act of giving gifts. Any passage in which it occurs, therefore, is interpreted as evidence of the poet's interest in (Maussian) gift-exchange, and thus too his intention to use the poetry in the service of total social stability. The flaw in such readings, however, (the most serious one, at any rate) is their tendency to treat *charis* as a 'bond' between distinct, atomically self-contained entities (cf. Kurke 1991: 120); but that, it seems to me, is to miss the whole significance of the word. For what *charis* designates primarily (both in the singular, and in its pluralised, mythic personification as the *Charites*) is 'grace,' 'charm,' 'beauty' – in other words, *that quality in persons and things that causes the dissolution of the autonomous subject in its experience of them.* 'But I,' Pindar tells us in a fragment, 'melt like the wax of holy bees, stung by the heat of the sun' (*all' ego kêros h'ôs dachtheis h'elâi / h'iran melissan takomai*) just at the moment when he looks upon the '*charis* of the son of Hagesilas' (*charis h'uion h'Agesila*, fr. 123.10-11). As beauty, *charis* ruins our self-sufficiency, our 'autonomy'. In fact, even in its relation to so-called 'gift exchange' *charis* still betokens this same dissolution of the subject. As Benveniste points out in *Indo-European Language and Society*, *charis*, like the Latin *gratia*, is fundamentally 'ambivalent,' designating either the favour one shows another (graciousness, generosity), or the feelings (gratitude) with which one receives the act of generosity (Benveniste 1973: 159). This makes sense, of course, for insofar as *charis* signals 'gratuitousness', a giving and receiving that is outside the systematic economies of an order of things, it must perforce confuse the categories that inhere in that order: the active, the passive; the subject, the object. And as Bonnie MacLachlan notes, the ambivalence of *charis*, its ability to confuse the boundaries of subject and object, to join them both 'in a common experience' (MacLachlan 1993: 104), is something of which Pindar wishes to activate within his poetry: 'I will put my trust in *charis*', says the poet (*pepoitha ... charin*), 'eagerly loving the one who loves, leading the one who leads' (*P*. 10.66).

Of course, distinctions between 'beauty', 'generosity', and 'gratitude' are distinctions we ourselves place upon *charis*; to Pindar's audience, *charis* was *charis* – the situation it referred to was a complex one, no doubt, but unitary nonetheless. And the underlying 'unitary complex' to which *charis* refers, I would suggest, is precisely Bataille's opening of the heart toward the other in free expenditure, the other we have ceased to objectify and from whom we therefore receive our being-in-relation. From this perspec-

69

tive, we can see why it is precisely the *charis* of the Olympic Games that inspires Pindar to compose his odes: 'Given that the *charis* of Pisan (Games) has placed my mind under sweetest thoughts' (*ei ti toi Pisas ... charis / noon h'upo glukutatais ethêke phrontisin, O.* 1.18-19). Which is just to say, that the Games inspire the poet with simultaneous feelings of beauty, gratitude, and generosity – in other words, they effect in the subject a relinquishment of every appropriative attitude, a self-abandonment into communication, an opening of the heart.

And it is precisely this 'opening of the heart' that the poet must recreate in the world of the polis if he is to make it also a 'place of communication'. The way he achieves this end, as Pindar himself tells us, is by imparting upon the victor a subject-dissolving *charis*, that same *charis* he once possessed in his moment of glory at the Games. Through the enchantment of Pindar's poetic craft, 'upon you the dulcet-speaking lyre and the sweet pipe sprinkle *charis*' (*tin d' h'aduepês te lura / glukus t' aulos anapassei charis, O.* 10.93-4); as he goes in *kômos* he will 'let drip a pleasurable *charis*' upon the victor (*kômaxomai terpnan epistazôn charin, I.* 4.72b). (We might note, in passing, the insistently liquid, and *liquefying*, quality of Pindaric praise, a quality that undermines any notion of the poetry as merely attempting to 'bond' two self-sufficient 'parties' in a contract: praise involves us in the 'the outpourings of revel-songs' (*kômôn ... cheumasin, P.* 5.100); Pindar characterises himself as 'poured out' in poetic composition (*kechumai, I.* 1.4).)

The reason Pindar must work so hard to create this effect outside the Games, however, is just because the world 'back home' opposes it on every front, with *phthonos* and *koros*. What these terms designate (and they are as difficult for us to grasp, in their own way, as *charis*) is the precise inverse of Bataillean communication. Usually translated as 'envy', *phthonos* also seems to denote something like 'refusal' (as in *Odyssey* 11.149, say). Patricia Bulman explains the underlying unity of this particular concept by glossing *phthonos* as a 'malignant withholding that arises from unrestrained desire for what belongs to others' (Bulman 1992: 17). *Phthonos*, in other words, describes the disposition of one who refuses to 'be in communication' with the other, who will not relinquish his appropriative mindset: he 'begrudges' the heterological excellence of the victor (cf. for example *P.* 7.19-20: 'I am aggrieved at this, that *phthonos* is the response to fine deeds', *to d' achnumai, phthonon ameibomenon ta kala erga*). The *phthonos* man is like the 'blaming Archilochus' (*psogeron Archilochon*), who, instead of releasing himself into subject-dissolving praise, attempts to maintain his self-sufficiency by 'fattening himself on heavy-worded hatreds' (*barulogois echthesin piainomenon, P.* 2.54-5). The same holds true for the negative quality of *koros*, which paradoxically seems simultaneously to mean 'satiety' and 'greed' (Bulman 1992: 13; cf. *P.* 1.82 vs. *O.* 1.56). What unites these diametrically opposed senses of the word is an attitude set against all being-in-relation – an attitude that wants to view the subject as self-sufficient, and wishes to maintain that self-sufficiency by appropriating the other, by objectifying him or her. (Again, one thinks of Archilochus, whose *kakagoria*, 'words of censure' (*P.* 2.53) are only a means by which to objectify the other, to refuse the dissolving effect of their being upon us; one thinks too of the *ressentiment* of those intellectuals and comedians who try to undermine athletic achievement in our own time.)

Pindar's task, then, if he is to 'bring home' to us the 'communicating' experience of victory that is the gift of the Games, must, on the one hand, find poetic ways to recreate that sense of expenditure in us, here and now, in the moment of performance; and, on the other hand, must find ways to break us (and this 'us' includes the victorious athlete himself) out of the illusion of autonomous self-sufficiency that would foreclose the possibility of that experience. Or to put it another way, he must write a victory-inspired poetry that could transform a restricted economy of accumulation and conservation into a 'general economy' of release: 'Tire not of spending to excess (*mê kamne lian dapanais*), but let forth, like a helmsman, your sail to the wind!' (*P.* 1.91-3.).

There is of course no absolutely programmatic way to achieve this end; each situation in which the poet is called upon to make a mere 'society' into a genuine place of communication calls in turn for its own historically-specific response. Yet there were enough continuities between occasions to allow Pindar to develop some general techniques to achieve the ends we have articulated for him. The poet's famous use of the priamel, for instance, seem clearly designed to roll us into an expenditure of our energies:

> *êtoi Pisa men Dios, Olumpiada*
> *d'estasen Hêrakleês*
> *akropthina polemou.*
> *Therôna de tetraorias h'eneka nikaphorou*
> *gegônêteon, opi dikaion xenôn,*
> *ereism' Akragantos,*
> *euônumôn te paterôn aôton orthropolin. (O. 2.3-7)*

> Pisa belongs to Zeus; the Olympics
> were founded by Herakles,
> the prime fruits of war;
> But Theron, because of his four-horse chariot victory,
> Must be proclaimed! just in his respect for guests,
> Bulwark of Akragas,
> Highest and best upholder of his city of famous forefathers.

The verbal movement (so ably revealed by Race) from a stable (suppressed) copula, to a 'standing' (*estasen*) indicative, to an imperative that draws the listener into a discharge of activity; the movement from place, to festival, to person; the increasing specificity in time and place that is released, finally, in the here and now of the imperative, with an explosion

71

in the number of syllables in the climactic member of the priamel – all these things make the audience enact Bataillean expenditure; they are the expression, I submit, of a poetics of victory, a poetics of a General Economy.[21] The same might be said of the way the Victory Odes enrich the object of praise through long mythic digressions, digressions that circle back finally to the figure of the victor himself (as the mythic passage early in *Pythian* 4, 'ringed', as Nancy Felson points out, with a *chrêsen* at *P.* 4.6 and a *chrêsmos* at *P.* 4.60, that finally returns us back to the victor himself in the present moment of performance: *kai nun* (*P.* 4.63) (cf. Felson 1999: 18-19). Such passages, it seems to me, increase the incalculable otherness of the object of praise by presenting him as a node, a circuit through which the boundless energies of the past flower (*thallei, P.* 4.65) into the present – even as they contrive to have us 'subjectify' that 'object' through deictic manipulation, putting us in the position of heroes and athletes who are so strange to us, yet making us experience the world as though we were they: this, again, is nothing other than practical heterology.[22]

And on the darker side of Pindaric ode, we have all those poetic techniques marshalled against our assumption of a stable subjectivity, that is, of being a 'subject' that can know 'objects' within a given 'order of things'. The dense clusterings of metaphor that do not allow us to 'grasp' (the way a Homeric simile might) what is being said in any synoptic manner (cf. Steiner 1986: 8-18); condensed gnomic statements whose application to the story at hand is left obscure; a poetic technique in which 'each statement of theme is not completely clear in itself, but depends upon what follows and precedes it' (Lefkowitz 1976: 16), so that 'as to the whole, there is need of interpreters' (*es de to pan h'ermaneôn chatizei, O.* 2.85-6); the presentation of the poems by an 'I' who seems not to be in control of his own poem ('why do I vaunt against the occasion?' *ti kompeô para kairon; P.* 10.4) – all these techniques (and many, many more) ruin the possibility of 'holding ourselves' back, in self-satisfied distance, from the poem. We are forced to risk ourselves, as athletes do, in unknowing anguish, 'casting the javelin' of our understanding as the poet casts his of song (*akontizôn, N.* 9.55). For such anguished unknowing ('What is anyone? What is anyone not?' *ti de tis; ti de ou tis; P.* 8.94) is the condition of the joy of Pindaric ode, as it is of the Games from which they spring.

It has been the contention of this paper that the 'social function' of Pindaric Victory Ode, the function which provides the ground of its structures and characteristic themes, is not the stabilisation of political economies, but the destabilisation of our subjectivity in a moment of communicative self-expenditure, the release of self into that intimacy that is the 'Zeus-given-gift' (*diosdotos, P.* 8.96) of victory in the Games. From the point of view adumbrated here, that of Bataille's 'General Economy', the release into non-objectified communication with one another (in poetry, in the exuberance of witnessing athletic victory) is in fact the fulfilment of civic society, the *telos* of all its careful accumulation and preservation. The motive and meaning of our socio-political existence is thus not the achievement of order for its own sake, but – as Pindar sings on behalf of an exile hoping to return to the warm embrace of civic life – the possibility of 'giving over one's heart' (*thumon ekdosthai, P.* 4.295). This is the possibility the Games revealed to Pindar; it is, I believe, the very same possibility we see in them today.[23]

Notes

1. Cf. Kurke 1991: 103: 'If they wish to maintain the aristocratic system, they must follow the poet's example and choose praise.' For further of examples of critical literature offering (ultimately) political readings of the odes, see, e.g.: Pfeijffer 1999, Currie 2005, Nicholson 2005.

2. For a discussion of the processional *kômos* and its relation to epinician, cf. Thomas 2007: 144-6.

3. Greek texts of Pindar are from Race 1997a and 1997b; translations are my own.

4. For the argument that epinician was performed upon the arrival of the *kômos*, cf. Heath 1988: 189; for epinician as prelude to the *kômos*: cf. Mullen 1982: 24-7.

5. For 'metaphoric' vs metonymic views of the relation between *kômos* and epinician, cf. Morgan 1993: 9: 'Heath subsumes Pindar into the revel, whereas I would subsume the revel into Pindar.'

6. The situation degenerates even further, with every subsequent round of drinking, from causes for legal action, to physical nausea, and finally, with the tenth round, outright madness.

7. As Nagy archly notes, 'The spirit of merriment in a *kômos* is lost on most translators of Pindar' (1994: 25).

8. Clay goes so far as to suggest 'adding the epinician to the catalogue of Greek sympotic poetry' (1999: 34).

9. For a useful summary and bibliography of the question of whether Pindaric ode was performed by a solo singer or by a chorus, see Nagy 1994: 22, nn. 57-9.

10. Consider, for instance, the closing prefatory comments in *The Olympics at the Millennium: Power, Politics, and the Games*, in which the editors express the hope that they may offer their readers 'a more complex sense of why and how the Games matter to all of us–not only, *or even primarily, sports fans* – at the beginning of the new millennium' (Schaffer and Smith 2000: 16, emphasis added). In this essay, I adopt precisely the point of view of the 'sports fan', as (and this is the crux of my argument) it is from this position I believe Pindar composed the odes. As I shall attempt to demonstrate in the course of this paper, however little we hold in common with the particular ideologies supervening on the ancient Games, in our modern enactment of them we do in fact constantly recover what was most essential to them: a release from the alienation that belongs to civil existence as such. The original value of the Olympics was, and continues to be, a liberatory 'use value'. If the Olympics truly matter, it is not simply as (yet another) site of power/knowledge, but as a possible means of liberation and communal intimacy for the engaged spectator (a perspective necessarily lost, of course, upon the disengaged 'intellectual'). For further comment on the ideological function of the modern Games, see, inter alia: *Sport, Power, and Society: Institutions and Practices, A Reader* (2010); *Crafting Patriotism for Global Dominance: America at the*

Olympics (2009); *Sport, Revolution, and the Beijing Olympics* (2008); *Olympic Industry Resistance: Challenging Olympic Power and Propaganda* (2008).

11. Cf. Kurke, who reads Pindar as offering the patron advice on how to 'sav(e) himself from isolation and starvation' (Kurke 1991: 101); cf. also 1991: 92-4, in which Kurke explicitly bases her reading of Pindar on a view of community as driven entirely by 'scarcity'.

12. See Richman 1982: 8-39.

13. For Bataille as a thinker of community see Nancy 1981: 1-42.

14. Sansone's argument for sacrifice as an 'expenditure of energy' turns on a reference to R. Caillois: 'Play is an occasion of pure waste' (Sansone 1988: 63 n. 119). Caillois was the co-founder, with Bataille, of the College of Sociology. Sansone makes no reference to Bataille. Sansone oddly attempts (1988: 64) to assimilate Caillois' (and Bataille's) argument into an argument for the ultimate 'productivity' of expenditure. 'I am aware that by giving up part or all of my surplus I will ensure a surplus in the future.'

15. On penalties for cheating in the ancient Olympics, which could include whipping, fines, and the setting up of humiliating, admonitory statues, cf. Toohey and Veal 2007: 22, and also Romano in this volume.

16. How fast can Usain Bolt run? How many gold medals can a swimmer win in one Olympics? Our obsession with records stems directly from our need to establish, over and over again, the possibility of what was once thought impossible. On my argument, however, any athletic victory opens the horizon of the 'possible': cf. Scanlon 2002: 35. 'The abnormal, unusual, or fortuitous occurrence during a contest was best ascribed to the gods' participation'. For discussion of the ancient Greek obsession with records, yet another point at which ancient and modern experience coincide, see Young 2004: 31-3, 44-6; Brunet in this volume adds another dimension to the discussion.

17. Creating sufficient grounds for spectator identification is of central importance in all sport; the athlete must be, to borrow from Wallace Stevens, a 'song beyond us yet ourselves'. The creation of such grounds goes a long way, I suspect, in explaining the role of nationalism in the Olympics (we identify with the athlete as fellow countrywomen and countrymen), as well as the moral expectations placed upon athletes themselves (athletes who do not share the average ethical horizons of the spectator fail to provide sufficient points of identification for the spectators). With regard to the question of nationalism, it is interesting to observe how fluid our desire to identify with the athlete renders our criteria for nationality. Indeed, from this perspective, one might say it is less a case of the Olympics serving the cause of nationalist ideology, than nationalist ideology being made to serve the needs of the Olympics.

18. For Pindar's thematic concern for the present, cf. also *O.* 1.99, 'The good that comes each day is greatest for every mortal'; *P.* 3.62, etc. The gnomic exhortations to 'live for today' seem directed at the victor, who, perhaps more than anyone else at home, must be persuaded to forego his anxious, future-directed mindset if he is to commune in the present moment of joy; sadly, there was not sufficient room in the present article to discuss Pindar's poetics of victory from the patron's and/or athlete's point of view. I should like to point out, however, that the athlete's experience of victory need in no way coincide with the spectator's (as any athlete knows all too well). For athletes, 'sport' is all too often a Foucauldian discipline, an objectifying *technê*.

19. For a general endorsement of the Olympics as an means for the articulation of civilising ideals and values, cf. Guttman, 2002: 5: 'Pierre de Coubertin was

surely right about one thing: we need our ideals'; for a critical view of Olympic 'ideals' themselves, as well as the mythologising practices upon which they are based, cf. Toohey and Veal 2007: 21: 'The citing of amateurism as a practice in Greek athletics is another example of the use of a myth to perpetuate hegemonic twentieth century Olympic practices.'

20. Cf. Lucas (cited in Toohey and Veal 2007: 35): Coubertin believed that 'the nation had been humiliated by Prussia's ludicrously easy victory over an effeminate, non-sporting, excessively intellectual French population'. For an extensive analysis of the ideology of the ancient Greek aristocratic athlete, cf. Nicholson 2005.

21. See Race 1990: 9-40 for an excellent discussion of 'Climactic Elements in Pindar's Verse'.

22. Cf. Felson 1999: 5: Pindar uses deixis to make his audience 'travel across space and time'.

23. A note on tragedy: Insofar as the athlete/patron alone created, through his prowess and personal expenditure, the possibility for being-in-community (a possibility, however, realised only by the poet), power would have seemed, to many, intolerably concentrated in the hands of the aristocratic few. Thus, new forms of heterological experience were developed, in which the audience was led to identify not with the incalculably great and high, but with the revoltingly, unspeakably cursed and low. In this way, the citizenry was brought into being-in-relation, once again, by the unrestrained expenditure of 'giving their heart over' – not, however, to exuberant pleasure and joy, but to uncontrolled wails of misery. The Victory Ode was displaced, often within the context of ancient drama itself, by tragic songs of mourning; the aristocratic was displaced by a tragic hero whom none would 'own', and who therefore belonged to all.

Epideictic Oratory at the Olympic Games

Eleni Volonaki

This chapter addresses the ancient Olympics and considers the ideological investments of public oratory at Games ancient and modern. I will start with the rhetoric of the last two modern Games in 2004 and 2008 and subsequently explore the dual nature of epideictic oratory in ancient Games, based on the Olympic speeches that have survived from the first half of the fourth century BCE. As will be shown, the ideals of peace, concord and unity are common appeals for immense and wide audiences both in ancient and modern times. However, the epideictic oratory of the ancient Games played a prominent political role aiming to persuade audiences to action, while also offering skilful orators the opportunity for display. The ideology of public oratory used in the ancient festival may well have been received in the modern Games, but has been modified to address a global audience invested in certain moral and civic values alleged to increase social bonding.

Pierre de Coubertin is credited with the inspiration for and establishment of the modern Olympic Games; the renovation of the games took place in Athens in 1896. In 2004, the 28th Olympiad, the Olympic festival was hosted for the second time in Athens at their source. Jacques Rogge, the president of the International Olympic Committee, made a speech in the opening ceremony which thanked all the factors that contributed to the successful organisation of the Games, including the athletes. He repeatedly appealed to peace; he also called for tolerance and brotherhood. He finally underlined the importance of the Olympic Games as uniting people from different backgrounds: 'Athletes from the 202 countries show us that sports unite by overriding national, political, religious and language barriers.' Gianna Aggelopoulou Daskalaki, the president of the Organising Committee for Athens 2004, praised the athletes for their youth, excellence and competition in a spirit of peace, where divisions between nation and race should disappear.[1] As a whole, the rhetoric of Athens 2004 involved appeals for a spirit of peace, unity, and friendship in a fair contest.

The rhetoric of the Beijing Olympic Games 2008 was not dissimilar. The relevant website claims that ' "One World One Dream" is a profound manifestation of the core concepts of the Beijing Olympic Games 2008. It fully reflects the essence and universal values of the Olympic spirit – Unity, Friendship, Progress, Harmony, Participation and Dream. It expresses the common wishes of people all over the world, inspired by the Olympic ideals, to strive for a bright future of Mankind. The proclamation of the committee promoted the ideal of peace within the spirit of cooperation and mutual benefit.'[2]

The rhetoric of the Olympic Games both in antiquity and in modern times is characterised by the ideals of peace, unity and harmony. On these ideals are based the rhetorical appeals of speakers to their audiences. There is, however, a significant shift in modern times in the rhetoric deployed at the Olympic Games. Modern politicians and presidents of committees mainly address the athletes, encouraging them to continue their contests with the values of virtue, excellence and honesty. They praise them for their achievements and call for unity beyond any kind of social, political or religious differences. The ideal of peace is emphasised on a worldwide basis so that there will be no war or conflict but only a 'happy' future for all people; peace is promoted as a universal ideology in the face of reality. On the other hand, the unity is based on a non-discriminating social, political and religious basis; the political message is to override any kind of barriers that might interfere in people's lives.

The Olympic orations of antiquity emphasise a Panhellenic *homonoia* (concord), the unity of the Greeks against the barbarians. The appeal for unity is rhetorically used to encourage all the Greeks to make war rather than peace, but a war that will secure their freedom and will put an end to political conflicts. The speeches that have survived and were allegedly composed for the Olympic Games addressing either a reading or a listening audience have a complex political agenda, criticising Spartan influence upon the Greek states and nonetheless appealing for peace and unity among them.

The ancient Olympic Games and public display

The ancient Olympic Games were the oldest of the four Panhellenic or national athletic festivals,[3] and were held in honour of the god Zeus.[4] The traditional date of the foundation of the Olympic Games is 776 BCE, but it was in the last quarter of the eighth century that a wider participation in the Olympics began.[5] The Olympic festival was held every fourth year until 394 CE,[6] attracting citizens from all over the Greek world. In the early years of the festival, hundreds of people gathered from neighbouring towns and city-states of the Peloponnese, and later thousands of people used to come by land and sea from colonies as far away as Spain and Africa.[7] There was a tendency to view athletic success as a symbolic success in public life, and certain athletes went on to pursue political careers in their home towns.[8]

The Olympic Games offered an opportunity for the great assembly of all

77

Greek states to articulate a feeling of common identity, and apparently an opportunity for prominent orators to show off their skills. According to the programme of the festival, as reconstructed by modern scholars, orations by well-known philosophers and recitals by poets and historians were performed in the afternoon of the first day, which was among other things dedicated to various religious rites (e.g. sacrifices to Zeus) as well as to the athletes' oath-taking process.[9] Although the evidence of speeches composed for the Olympic Games is limited, it does reflect the persistence of public oratory as continuously playing a significant role in the festivals.

Three notable Greek orators used the occasion of the Olympic Games to plead for the cause of Panhellenic *homonoia* ('same-mindedness') or concord.

First was Gorgias,[10] the sophist from Leontini, in Sicily, who is said to have come to Olympia at the beginning of the fourth century (408 or 392 BCE). His full Olympic speech has not survived, but in the epitome he encourages the Greeks to be reconciled and fight against the barbarians. Philostratos briefly reports the following information (*Lives of the Sophists* 494) (all translations are my own):

> His *Olympian Oration* dealt with a theme of the highest importance to the state. For, seeing that Greece was divided against itself, he came forward as the advocate of reconciliation, and tried to turn their energies against the barbarians and to persuade them not to regard one another's cities as the prize to be won by their arms, but rather the land of the barbarians.[11]

Lysias, the Athenian democrat and metic from Sicily, allegedly delivered a speech in Olympia in 388 or 384, aiming to persuade all the Greeks present to remove Dionysios from his position as a tyrant in Syracuse and set Sicily free. A part of this speech has survived and is cited by Dionysios of Halikarnassos as an exemplary piece of Lysias' epideictic oratory. The speech appeals for the unification of all Greeks against the barbarians, namely the King of Persia and Dionysios, the tyrant in Syracuse. As with Gorgias' speech, here again the tone is both deliberative and persuasive.

Finally, another Athenian orator, Isokrates, composed a model Olympic speech, his *Panegyrikos* – a pamphlet which was not performed at the Olympic Games but was designed for a reading rather than a listening audience in the early fourth century (380 BCE).[12] In this oration Isokrates 'expresses a permanent Panhellenic ideal which transcends time, and affirms an Athenian leadership of Greece based on culture no less than on feats of arms'.[13] Isokrates makes use of a stock theme common in epideictic contexts, Greek *homonoia*, to call for a Panhellenic campaign against Persia. Isokrates exploits the context and themes of epideictic oratory for deliberative purposes.[14]

We will explore the role of epideictic oratory in the Olympic Games; first, as a demonstration of the rhetorical skills of the speakers, secondly, as enhancing their political status and voice, and finally, as influencing opinion in the audiences. Given the limited evidence from the fourth century BCE Olympic speeches, it is worthwhile to explore the rhetorical *topoi* (commonplaces) expected for display as well as the rhetorical purposes of the speakers. Lysias' speech, *Olympiakos* (33), is the only surviving speech (though only a fragmentary section) which could possibly have been delivered at the Olympic Games. It will therefore be taken as an example of epideictic oratory at the Games; our purpose is to examine the rhetorical means used not only to address the festival but also to persuade and give advice to a Panhellenic audience.

To understand the role of epideictic oratory at the Olympic Games as having an influence upon the Greeks, it is necessary to examine the characteristics of the genre. Aristotle (*Rhet. Alex.* 35, Loeb) distinguishes the types of oratory as follows:

> The concern of counsel/advice (*symboule*) is partly exhortation, partly dissuasion. For in every case people who offer private advice and people who speak in public on civic issues do one or the other of these. The concern of the lawsuit is partly accusation, partly defence. For inevitably people in dispute do either of these. The concern of display is partly praise and partly blame.

The term translated here as *display* is derived from the Greek noun *epideixis*, which means 'demonstration' or 'show'. As Carey (2007: 236) rightly points out, Aristotle's division has limitations and 'ignores the flexibility of and fluidity between literary forms in living traditions'. Epideictic oratory differs from forensic and deliberative oratory in having no immediate practical outcome; speakers in the courts and the Assembly need to persuade their audiences in order to reach decisions, which bring practical consequences.[15] Nevertheless, epideictic oratory aims to persuade as well. According to Isokrates (12.271), epideictic oratory should be taken seriously as contributing to rhetorical education; he also indicates that epideictic speeches can demonstrate methods of argumentation and consequently the rhetorical skills and ability of the orators (Isokr. 4.17).

There were two kinds of display: on the one hand, the funeral orations which played an important role in social definition since they constituted an integral part of the public funerals held each year at Athens for those who had died in battle and were delivered by prominent political figures, such as Perikles;[16] on the other hand, there were orations composed and normally delivered by distinguished orators at festivals, such as the Olympic Games or the Pythian festival at Delphi.[17] Isokrates alludes, if dismissively, to the practice of composing orations for festivals (5.13, Loeb):

> ... and, finally, that those who desire, not to chatter empty nonsense, but to further some practical purpose, and those who think they have hit upon some plan for the common good, must leave it to others to harangue at the public festivals, but must themselves win over someone to champion their cause from among men who are capable not only of speech but of action and who

occupy a high position in the world – if, that is to say, they are to command any attention.

As it appears, there was a lively interest in skilful and ambitious *rhetores* who could deliver speeches at festivals, since the audience, travelling and drawn from the whole of the Greek world, was available to listen to any speeches or other kinds of performance.[18] Isokrates 1.6 in fact discusses the size of this kind of audience while partly dismissing its political effectiveness:

> In addition this too is clear to everyone, that the festivals suit those in need of display (*epeidixis*) – for each can broadcast his own powers there to the largest audience – but those who want to achieve something practical should speak to the person who is to carry out the acts disclosed in the speech.

In the fifth and fourth centuries BCE the Olympic Games attracted a vast audience from all Greek cities and colonies. Isokrates refers to numerous crowds gathered at the city of Athens on the occasion of the state festivals (4.45), and we can conclude that numbers at the Olympics were comparable:

> And the crowds that visit our city are so numerous that any advantage accruing from our association has been secured by Athens. In addition to this, our city is the best place to find the most enduring friendships and the most varied society, and furthermore to see contests not only of speed and strength but also of reason and thought and all other activities – and for these the prizes are the greatest.

The fact that epideictic speeches had become a practice and a permanent feature of the Olympic Games from Gorgias' to Isokrates' time indicates that the audience was prepared to listen to prominent orators demonstrating their craftsmanship. Given that Greek society valued public speaking highly, the famous orators who used the occasion of the Olympic Games to speak publicly to these huge audiences must have gained in public standing and profit. The audience at the Games is likely to have included influential people from every city.

It appears that the competition among orators at the Games reached such a degree that their contemporaries could regard epideictic speeches as advertising.[19] In this context, orators differentiated their position from the tradition of the sophists; their intentions were not to praise but to advise their audience and tell them the truth. It was a common rhetorical strategy for public speakers at festivals to define their own limits within the tradition of the genre. For example, Lysias (33.3) presents himself as an honourable man and a worthy citizen (texts from Todd 2000):

> These were Herakles' instructions, but I have not come here to talk about trivialities or to fight about names. In my view these are the tasks of those

80

sophists who are wholly useless, and who are desperate for a livelihood, whereas the task of an honourable man and of a worthy citizen is to give advice about great matters ...

Isokrates also in his *Panegyrikos* (4.3-4) emphasises his own superiority to other sophists:

> I have come before you to give my counsels on the war against the barbarians and on concord among ourselves. I am, in truth, not unaware that many of those who have claimed to be sophists have rushed upon this theme, but I hope to rise so far superior to them that it will seem as if no word had ever been spoken by my rivals upon this subject.

The *display* was generally conceived as a highly competitive activity, as is clearly attested in the funeral oration ascribed to Lysias (2.1-2):

> If I thought it possible, you who are present at this burial, to make clear in speech the courage of the men who lie here, I would criticise those who gave instructions to speak in their honour at a few days' notice. But since for all mankind all time would not be enough to prepare a speech equal to their deeds, I think that the city gave the order at short notice out of concern for those who speak here, in the belief that in this way they would be most likely to be forgiven by their listeners. However, though my speech is about these men, my contest is not with their deeds but with those who have spoken in their honour previously.

The Olympic orations which are ascribed to Gorgias, Lysias and Isokrates make use of the stock theme '*homonoia*' (concord), which was not simply a suitable theme of epideictic oratory but was constantly used to enhance the ideal and concept of Panhellenic unity at Olympia.[20] The argument about Greek *homonoia* is stressed for deliberative ends, urging the audience to take action against the enemies, the barbarians. This practice of rhetoric confirms that there is flexibility between the genres of oratory.[21] The question, however, is how far the oratory of the panegyric speeches was genuinely deliberative. Gorgias seeks to persuade the Greeks to direct their aggressive inclinations towards the territory of the barbarians; however, this may not have been an argument for aggressive policy but simply a Gorgianic rhetorical ornament.[22] Lysias and Isokrates by contrast represent themselves as having a practical agenda.

Isokrates glorifies and praises the Olympic Games as an opportunity for strengthening the entity of Greece, and it is in this context that he calls for a Panhellenic campaign against Persia. The rhetorical *topoi* used in Isokrates' *Panegyrikos* could be taken as typical themes of epideictic oratory or at least of Olympic orations; among these topoi are the distinctive role of epideictic oratory and display (7-12, 43-5), the mythological and historical background of the city of Athens (23-34, 54-60), the superiority of Athens among the Greek cities (39-42, 47-50, 103-14), the achievements of the ancestors in the Persian Wars (61-73, 85-98), the criticism of the Lacedaemonians' policies (122-35) the need for an alliance of the Greeks against the King and the barbarians (138-40, 160-89), and the natural hatred against the barbarians because of their effeminacy and arrogance (149-59).

In the case of Lysias' Olympic speech, the deliberative goal becomes even more clear and urgent; Lysias not only calls the Greeks to unite against the Persian King and Dionysios I, the tyrant of Syracuse, but in particular he urges them to act out their hostility by removing Dionysios' representatives from the festival (Dion. Hal. *Lysias* 29). The encouragement of the audiences to make particular decisions of Panhellenic interest reflects the orators' tendency to foster their own political prestige.

Appeals and advice constitute a normal part of epideictic oratory. Lysias makes use of similar rhetorical *topoi* to those found in Isokrates' *Panegyrikos*, such as the appeal for the union of the Greeks against the barbarians and the criticism of the Lacedaemonians. Lysias criticises the Lacedaemonians for their humiliation of their subordinates and their support for Dionysios the Sicilian tyrant and the King of the Persians. Such a criticism would not fit the Panhellenic unity which is encouraged by orators at the festivals, even though it aims to appeal for Sparta's help in the future. Epideictic oratory may promote the ideals of Panhellenism, concord and unity but behind the ideal surface of the Games it shows, on the one hand, a tendency towards criticism of individual states, such as Sparta, and it encourages, on the other hand, the idea of a common war against the barbarians. The proposed violence interrupts the ideal of *homonoia* which is highlighted in the performance of epideictic oratory at the festival. There is a kind of ambiguity in the role of public oratory at the Games in that it promotes the tradition of articulating ideals but it can also interrupt the tradition by attempting to persuade the audience to take forceful political action.

Lysias' Olympic speech (33) – a speech for display?

We will now turn to an analysis of Lysias' Olympic speech, which offers valuable evidence of the role of epideictic oratory as advisory but also as encouraging the audience towards violence. An introduction to the speech by Dionysios of Halikarnassos has survived as a preface to Lysias 33, which briefly informs us about the historical context. Lysias warns the Greeks of the dangers that are great and surround them on every side, of Artaxerxes, the King of Persia and Dionysios, the tyrant of Sicily, who both possess ships and control the sea (§5). He explains that their powers have been substantially increased due to the civil conflicts among the Greeks and he advises now the Greeks to put aside their war and unite their forces for their own security (§6). He criticises the position of the Spartans, who neglect the destruction of Greece although they are worthily the leaders of the Greeks and have been the saviours of Greece in previous dangers; the speaker still expresses the hope that the Spartans will take precautions for the future (§7). Finally, Lysias emphasises that this is the best opportunity for all the Greeks to take action against the enemies (§8).

From 395 BCE Sparta was engaged in a war with a coalition of Boiotia, Corinth, Argos and Athens, fought in mainland Greece, the so-called Corinthian War. The cause of the Corinthian war was mainly the emerging power of Sparta over the Greek cities.[23] Sparta's intervention in support of Dionysios I retaining his position as a tyrant in Sicily aroused further hostility among the Greek states.[24] The Corinthian War ended with the victory of Sparta with Persian and Syracusan help (Xen. *Hell.* V.1.29) and resulted in the King's Peace of 387/6, the clauses of which meant the end of all alliances between Athens and Thebes and Corinth and Argos.

Two dates are possible for the performance of Lysias' *Olympiakos*. Diodoros of Sicily (XIV.109) places it in the Olympic Games of 388 BCE.[25] It is not unlikely, however, that the speech was delivered in the Olympic Games of 384, since the Corinthian War was still in progress in 388. In principle, there would not be a problem with the Olympic Games taking place in wartime;[26] on the contrary, appeals for *homonoia* and unification of all Greek cities against the enemies and the barbarians would have been far more effective during the Corinthian War. However, given that Athens made an alliance with the tyrant Dionysios in 386, it would be difficult to give a speech that urged the Greeks to take action against Dionysios after that date. On balance, taking the text into consideration, it seems reasonable to accept Diodoros' date of 388 BCE.

Dionysios of Halikarnassos (*Lysias* 29) quotes Lysias' Olympic speech as an example of his style in the genre of epideictic oratory,[27] whereas he does not mention the famous Funeral Speech (2) at all.[28] Diodoros of Sicily (XIV.109) also attributes the speech to Lysias and moreover considers that it was delivered by Lysias himself. However, the reception of the speech as genuine in ancient sources is no guarantee of authenticity. As recent studies have shown, Lysias' *Olympiakos* clearly diverges from the rest of the corpus Lysiacum.[29] Despite its peculiarities in language and style, the Olympic speech keeps the Lysianic line of forensic oratory (i.e. brevity, *charis* (grace) and sarcasm) and adjusts it to the needs of epideictic oratory, making use of the rhetoric of praise, respect, emotional appeal and exhortation to generate the audience's admiration and motivation.[30]

In antiquity, as we have seen, Lysias was thought to have performed the speech in Olympia. Modern scholars have disputed this view on the grounds that Lysias as a metic could not have delivered an Olympic speech, and argue that someone else, either Syracusan or Corinthian, could have delivered the speech.[31] There is no evidence, however, that only citizens could speak at the Olympic Games.[32] The Olympic Games were open to an audience of all Greek cities, and in such an occasion all philosophers, poets and orators could most probably participate. The festival might be particularly attractive to a man like Lysias, since it gave him a political voice. As an expatriate, he could neither influence Syracuse nor (as a metic) Athens.[33]

The rhetoric of the speech

In order to achieve an immediate result and have the envoys expelled, Lysias makes use of special rhetorical appeals to a Panhellenic audience. In the *prothesis* (§3, statement of the argument) Lysias differentiates his position from that of the sophists and expresses his intention to support the interests of the people rather than his own.[34] Lysias praises Herakles (in the proem, §§1-2),[35] who according to Pindar[36] had created Olympia and instituted the first games in honour of Zeus.[37] Furthermore, Herakles is said to have put an end to the tyrants and prevented their arrogance by establishing 'a contest of physical strength, a competition of wealth, and a display of wisdom' (§2). According to Lysias' description, the participants of the Games, at least when they were originally established, were expected to be excellent in physical and intellectual training as well as very wealthy. The respect for these aristocratic values reinforces their importance to the audience at the Games, who may have been an elite audience.

The praise of Herakles' achievements in the first Olympic Games is used to set an example for the present Games, uniting all Greeks together with friendship in order to stop the tyranny. Another example used to persuade the audience towards action is that offered by the ancestors (§6); the ancestors deprived the barbarians of their property, expelled the tyrants and established freedom for all. The theme that the ancestors set an example by offering freedom to all Greece is peculiar to epideictic oratory; in particular, the 'praise' section of the funeral orations included standard mythological and historical exploits, one of which was the praise of the ancestors and their accomplishments.[38] Most probably, Lysias refers to the Persian Wars and the victory by the Greeks over the barbarians – a common rhetorical topos used as a unique and exemplary action of bravery and freedom by the Greeks in epideictic oratory.[39]

Clearly connected with the example of the ancestors is the appeal to honour and shame. The Greeks should honour their ancestors and imitate their actions. They should also be ashamed for what has happened in the past and should be afraid of what is going to happen in the future (33.6). Lysias appeals to the common knowledge that shame brings dishonour to people whereas fear leads to action and liberation. In §9 the concept of 'shame' is rhetorically manipulated to make the Greeks responsible for having exacted no punishment for great and terrible crimes. In effect, Lysias' exhortation to remove Dionysios' envoys becomes a matter both of revenge and of duty.

Rhetorical *hyperbole* is widely used in the Olympic speech, when emphasising the dangers that are threatening Greece (§5), and the civil strife and mutual rivalry as the causes of the disasters in Greece (§§4, 9). The rhetorical exaggeration of the existing risks for the whole of Greece underlines the necessity to unite and secure safety. Lysias very cleverly shows respect toward the Spartans and he recognises them as leaders of the Greeks at the present, because of their innate merits and their knowledge of war, and as saviours of the Greeks in the past ('being leaders of the Greeks' ~ 'after having been the saviours of Greece in previous dangers'). Moreover, in §7 Lysias praises the Spartans' life style and customs to explain their freedom and independence. Finally, Lysias makes a special appeal to Sparta and bases his hopes for the future on the Spartans' precautions. There is a clear pro-Spartan tone on behalf of the Athenians, which is in line with the theme of *homonoia* that is emphatically stressed in epideictic orations. However, Lysias also criticises the indifference of the Spartans and charges them with passivity 'in tolerating the devastation of Greece' (33.7).

Lysias attempts to persuade the Greeks to take action against their enemies immediately (§§8, 9) and explains that there will be no better opportunity than the present one to stop the invaders attacking Greece.[40] The tone becomes deliberative when Lysias urges the audience to regard the disasters of those who had been so far ruined as their own concern and to prevent their enemies from any kind of disrespectful behaviour, while it is still possible. The emotional appeal aims to stimulate the audience's *pathos* (emotion) for revenge by emphasising that the motivation of the Great King and the tyrant of Sicily lies in greed and ambition.

The reference to the enemies' *hubris* (arrogance) and the rather intense phrasing, 'to restrain their enemies' arrogance', may involve an action that needs to be taken immediately and even though there is no other clear indication in the speech, we may interpret this phrase to mean that the orator urged the audience to remove an enemy. Such an assumption would be consistent with Dionysios of Halikarnassos' statement that the Greeks started their mission of hatred there and then by despoiling the royal tent (*Lysias* 29). Diodoros of Sicily, in his narrative of the incidents that occurred at the Games after Lysias had delivered his Olympic speech, reports: 'In the course of the contest chance brought it about that some of Dionysius' chariots left the course and others collided among themselves' (XIV.109.4). The ancient sources, though not necessarily reliable, seem to reflect a real event, which was probably widely known at the time, and in connection with the instruction, 'restrain their arrogance', as quoted in Lysias' Olympic oration (33.8), we can assume that the orator made a direct impact upon his audience. Lysias tried to impress his own political agenda and status on an immense audience.

In conclusion, epideictic speech is of ideological importance; its functions are more complex than Aristotle's description of it as involving what is honourable, in the form of either praise or blame (*Rhet.* 1406a-b).[41] According to Aristotle's categorising of the three 'species' of rhetoric – judicial, deliberative, epideictic – which remained fundamental in the history of classical rhetoric, a speech is called 'epideictic' if the audience is not being asked to take specific action; as Kennedy (1994: 4) points out, the concept of epideictic rhetoric needs to be broadened beyond this definition.[42]

The Olympic festival – though amenable to pure display – offered the possibility of influencing opinion in the Greek cities and getting beyond the limits of any one city. Furthermore, it gave an opportunity to skilful *rhetores* to impress their audience and advertise their own political opinions. Based on the evidence from *Olympic* speeches preserved to us, it appears that epideictic oratory revealed a dual nature; it presented the ideals of *homonoia, harmony* and unity among the Greeks but it could also interrupt the idealising tradition by criticising individual state policies and encouraging acts of violence. The rhetoric of the Olympic Games was based on the ambiguity of Panhellenic unity in the sense that the Greeks should all unite in order to get ready and prepare for a war against the enemies, the barbarians. The tradition of calling for a Panhellenic campaign against the enemies has the effect of exploiting the context and themes of epideictic oratory for deliberative ends. The festival was an occasion for pure display but also for actual action.

Notes

1. The evidence of the speeches has been taken from the Athens 2004 Olympic Games DVD.

2. The information has been taken from the official website of the Beijing 2008 Olympic Games: http://en.beijing2008.cn.

3. The other three were the Pythian Games at Delphi, held in honour of Apollo, the Isthmian Games, held at Corinth for Poseidon, and the Games at Nemea, which, like the Olympics, were in honour of Zeus; cf. Swaddling 1980: 12.

4. The mythical origin for Olympia's favour in the will of Zeus is recounted in Pindar, *Olympian* 3. The oracle is already in operation at the altar of Zeus, when Heracles establishes the athletic games at the site; cf. Spivey 2004: 174-5.

5. The question of the date of the institution of the Olympic Games must remain open; cf. Morgan 1990: 47-8, and Spivey in this volume.

6. On that date Theodosius I abolished the Olympic Games.

7. Swaddling 1980: 7.

8. For example, the history of the Diagorid dynasty of Rhodes; cf. Spivey 2004: 178. See also Stocking, Brunet and Pressly in this volume.

9. Cf. Glubok and Tamarin 1976: 15-27; Swaddling 1980: 37; Zaidman and Pantel 1999: 110ff.; Lee 2001: 30-47.

10. Gorgias is also credited with a speech delivered at the Pythian festival at Delphi; cf. Carey 2007a: 238.

11. Philostratos, *Moralia* 144c; cf. Spivey 2004: 190-1.

12. Epideictic oratory is considered to have developed in the fourth century BCE and have grown from the rise of book trade; speeches were composed for display

in the prospect of publication and tended to address a reading audience. Cf. Carey 2007a: 238-9.

13. Usher 1990: 21.

14. Carey 2007a: 248.

15. Carey (2007a: 237) explains that this kind of difference gives epideictic oratory an ambiguous status.

16. On the importance of the funeral oration to the political life of Athens, see the most extant and significant study by Loraux (2008; originally 1981).

17. Gorgias is credited with a speech delivered at the latter.

18. Carey 2007a: 238.

19. Cf. Isokr. 5.26.

20. For Greek *homonoia* used as a 'stock' theme of epideictic oratory, cf. Isokr. 4.3, Plutarch *Advice on Marriage* 144b; Carey 2007a: 248. As Spivey (2004: 192) suggests, one should speak of a rhetoric of Panhellenic unity at Olympia in the fifth and early fourth centuries BCE. Thus, the concept of uniting common interests was publicly demonstrated in Olympia; there was an altar to 'Unanimity' and, after the events of 364, there was an inscription 'From Eleans, for Concord' dedicated to a statue of Zeus. However, as Spivey (2004: 192) remarks, the *reality* of inter-Greek co-operation came about only by the domination of Greece first by Macedon, then Rome.

21. In Lysias' *Olympiakos* 3, the speaker's role appears to be deliberative, aiming to advise the Greeks how they can get rid of the barbarians and the tyrants, in the elevated style of epideictic oratory. We can also notice the combination of the elevated style of epideictic oratory with the practically important subject-matter of deliberative oratory in Isokrates' *Panegyrikos* 4; cf. Usher 1990: 150.

22. The speech has not survived and the evidence from Philostratus, *Lives of the Sophists* 493 cannot be conclusive.

23. Hornblower 1991: 190.

24. For the Spartan support of Dionysios I in Sicily and its consequences for Athens and Corinth, cf. Hornblower 1991: 187-9.

25. Diodoros' date may have derived from his tendency to place events in the wrong year by summarising earlier historians.

26. Todd (2000: 332) indicates that there may be two difficulties in our understanding of the speech, if the speech was actually delivered during the Corinthian war. The first difficulty involves §7, where the orator describes the Spartans as the leaders of Greece; it might be difficult to accept this description at a time when they were still fighting against other Greek cities. However, the description of the Spartans as the leaders of Greece (33.7) emphasises their virtues and life style, pointing to their superiority, and fits the pro-Spartan tone of the specific section. Furthermore, the present tense in the phrase 'tolerate the destruction of Greece' indicates that the war has not been over yet. The orator praises the Spartans at a time of conflict to call for their help in the future. The second difficulty involves §5, where the King of Persia is called the 'steward of money'; such a language might fit better a date after the Corinthian war, especially after 387/6 when the peace of Antalkidas was made on terms favourable to Persia and Sparta (cf. Medda 1995: 430-1). The emphasis placed upon the power of the King of Persia may be seen as an emotional evocation of fear and preparation for war.

27. Dionysios of Halikarnassos (*Lysias* 28) refers to Lysias as less forceful in his epideictic oratory though he should not be considered inferior to any of his predecessors or contemporaries for his efforts to be more lofty and impressive: 'In ceremonial oratory he is less forceful, as I have said. For he tries to be more lofty

and impressive, and indeed he should probably not be considered inferior to any of his predecessors or contemporaries; but he does not arouse his audience as powerfully as Isokrates and Demosthenes do theirs. I shall give an example of his ceremonial oratory.'

28. The fact that Dionysios of Halikarnassos quotes this speech as an example of Lysias' style in the genre of epideictic oratory and does not mention at all the most famous funeral speech (Lysias 2) may at first sight indicate that Lys. 33 is a genuine and Lys. 2 is not a genuine work of Lysias; cf. Todd 2000: 26-7, 331-2. However, given that Lysias was mostly popular for his forensic orations, it would seem particularly difficult to accept such an observation with reference to his skill as an epideictic orator, especially if we consider that Dionysios of Halikarnassos attributes only this specific epideictic oration (33) to Lysias. On the other hand, Dionysios' silence about Lysias 2 cannot be conclusive of the latter's authenticity; for the view that the Funeral Speech (2) is a genuine speech of Lysias, see Todd 2007: 157-64.

29. Usher and Najock 1982: 99-103.

30. Blass (1887: 434-36) indicates that Lysias does not use the epideictic characteristics found in Isokrates' *Panegyrikos* but, rather, adopts his own style of forensic speeches. One cannot exclude the possibility that the Olympic speech preserved in the Corpus Lysiacum was a rhetorical exercise imitating the Lysianic epideictic style; Lysias' work, however, focuses on forensic rather than epideictic speeches (only two epideictic speeches have survived in the corpus and have both been considered dubious), and one would expect students of rhetoric to imitate his forensic style.

31. Blass (1887: 431 n. 3) presents the scholars' views on this matter; Gröte argues that it was Lysias himself who delivered the speech, Schäfer assumes that an exile from Syracuse, called Themistogenes, could have delivered it, and Frohberger disputes that Lysias was in the position to deliver a public speech since he was not an Athenian citizen. There is also the possibility that the speech was composed for a Corinthian to deliver, since there is evidence that in the 340s Timoleon was sent out by Corinth to destroy Dionysios I, the tyrant. (Diod. Sic. XVI.83).

32. In the case of public funerals, one would have expected distinguished Athenian political figures to have delivered the speeches.

33. We cannot exclude the possibility that Lysias composed this speech for a reading audience. The publication of speeches involved a continuing contest to shape opinion and policy and consequently contributed to political rivalry and competition; cf. Carey 2005: 92-5. Thus, Lysias might have been interested in publishing such a speech for prestige and political influence.

34. This is a common rhetorical topos in all genres of oratory; for complaints about the triviality of other genres of oratory, as used in the epideictic speeches of Isokrates, cf. Todd 2000: 333, with n. 2.

35. The proem of the speech (§§1-2) is rather short and therefore the speech must not have been very long, or at least not as long as Isokrates' *Panegyrikos*, the proem of which is seven times longer (Usher 1990: 149) than the present one. According to Aristotle, the proem of epideictic speeches does not need to be relevant to the main subject of the speech but only whatever the speaker likes to say (Arist. *Rhet.* III.xiv.1) and should be either praise or blame (Arist. *Rhet.* III.xiv.2).

36. Pindar *O.* 3.19-22; cf. Lee 2001: 7, 11, 26.

37. It is considered more likely that athletic festivals like the Olympic Games

developed from the funeral games which were held in honour of local heroes; Pelops was the local hero of Olympia, and his grave and sanctuary were situated within the Altis. For this view, cf. Swaddling 1980: 9.

38. For the structure and the themes of funeral orations, cf. Loraux 2008; Hermann 2004.

39. For the *topos* of the Marathon battle in the funeral speeches, cf. Thuc. 2.34.1-7, Lys. 2.20-6, Plato *Menex.* 238c-246b2, Demosth. 60.9-10.

40. In forensic oratory the argument that the present trial offers a unique opportunity for the judges to take revenge and exact punishment upon the criminals constitutes a commonplace aiming to influence their verdict; cf. Lys. 12.90-1, 13.95, 40.6. Lysias draws on this rhetorical *topos* to focus the audience's attention on the importance of the matter and fight for their freedom.

41. For Aristotle's discussion (*Rhet.* 1367a32-4, 1367b21-8) of 'the language of praise (*logos epainos*) and its performative circumstances, cf. Haskins 2004: 61-4.

42. Kennedy 1994: 62.

Living in the Shadow of the Past: Greek Athletes during the Roman Empire

Stephen Brunet

When Samuel Kamau Wanjiru won the Marathon in the Beijing Olympics, he became the 24th man to win the event that, in spite of having no connection to the ancient games, has become emblematic of the Olympics. In the case of the women's Marathon, Constantina Tomescu became the seventh victor since this event was added to the Olympics in 1984. To take an event that would have been recognisable to the ancient Greeks, Usain Bolt joined 24 other runners who in the span of a little over a century could claim title to the men's 100 metres.

Compare their position with the situation faced by the pankratiast Demostratos Damas. The first of his two Olympic victories came about 173 CE and he may have been one of the most successful, if not the most successful athlete of the second century CE.[1] If one accepts the 776 BCE date for the founding of the Olympics, the games had been going on for nearly a millennium by Damas' time and the pankration – added in 648 BCE – for over eight centuries. This tradition meant that Damas stood 205th in a line of many exceptionally famous pankratiasts.[2] To cite three well-known champions: Arrhichion was a three time Olympic victor and his decision to die rather than lose was held up as a model of the fortitude athletes should demonstrate; Theogenes achieved the very rare feat of winning both the pankration and boxing at Olympia, although not at the same festival, and later was literally worshipped as a hero; finally, by winning both the wrestling and pankration in the same day Kapros of Elis became the first person since Herakles to win both events and one of only seven athletes in the history of the games to be designated 'successor of Herakles'.[3] Joining such illustrious company may have made Damas proud. Equally well, he may have found the experience of being essentially a junior member of such an illustrious club quite humbling.

The question to be considered here then is what did a successful athlete of the Roman period like Damas *think* about his life as an athlete, what did he *think* about the Olympics and its long history, what did he *think* about the seemingly disheartening situation of having to make his success stand out given the massive number of athletes who had won the Olympics during the prior eight or nine centuries. My contention here is that Damas and his fellow athletes were acutely aware of where they stood in the history of Greek athletics. This element of later athletic life is revealed in the claims athletes of the Roman Empire made about their triumphs as they sought to negotiate a position for themselves in the long tradition of prior athletic brilliance. Moreover, their desire to find a place in Olympic history explains many poorly understood features of later athletic inscriptions. Briefly, the complex structure of these documents and the very high level of detail were specifically designed to present their careers in ways that would ensure their not being overlooked.

Little thought has traditionally been given to the lives and concerns of later athletes because the history of ancient athletics has traditionally been built largely on literary evidence. Yet authors of the Roman period, like Pausanias, say very little about the athletes of their own time, preferring to look back to the great stars of the past. Our best evidence for the Roman period instead derives from the multitude of agonistic inscriptions set up throughout the Greek East in the first and second centuries CE. Due to the damage they often suffer, these documents sometimes present challenges in terms of restoration, which will not be discussed here unless necessary. On the other hand, they have one particular advantage over literary material for the purposes of this study. These career records tend to be set up by the athletes themselves, their families, their trainers, or the officials in charge of a particular festival. As a result, they reflect not the assumptions of an author removed from the realities of competition but what athletes or those closely connected to the world of athletics thought of their careers. We can actually perceive the athlete behind the inscription in an account of Damas' career set up after his death by his sons, themselves successful athletes. Certain anomalies in the list of Damas' honours have been traced to the record which Damas himself had produced during his lifetime but which his sons failed to adequately update after his death.[4] A similar situation obtains for an inscription honouring a runner from Rhodes. Most of the text is in Doric but the section in Attic summarising the runner's victories likely represents a text provided by the runner himself.[5] The point here is that by looking closely at what later athletes took pride in and even how they structured the documents detailing their successes, we can gain an insight into their concerns and their hope that they might make a name for themselves in the world of athletics.

Athletes' knowledge of the past

'Think' is probably not a word naturally associated with athletes of any period and even less with athletes of the Roman period. In the past our view of athletes like Damas has been very much coloured by the erroneous supposition that the Roman period marked a decline in the history of the ancient games as they were overrun by professionals. It would be hard then to envisage these hacks, concerned only as to where they might obtain their next prize, as being in any way concerned about who had won the Olympics a decade in the past, much less five or six centuries earlier.[6] The evidence, though, shows that the athletes of the Roman period were very much aware of the Olympics' long tradition and that this knowledge had a profound effect of their attitude to their careers. It would be too much to claim for them the wide-ranging interest of an author like Pausanias. For example, we have no indication that they knew or cared about whether the Eleans attacked the Altis in the midst of the festival held by the Arkadians (Xen. *HG* 7.4.26). On the other hand, when it came to factors most closely affecting their own position, they possessed an acute understanding of what their predecessors had accomplished dating as far back as the early days of the games. The proof comes out most strongly in the obsession athletes showed in noting the occasions when they had replicated great feats of the past or at times had exceeded those feats, in effect, being able to claim notable 'firsts'.

One of the longest and most complex series of such claims involves a group of wrestlers and pankratiasts who demonstrated their skill and determination not just by winning the Olympics but by doing so in a spectacular fashion. I have dealt with the epigraphic and chronological problems involved in these athletes' claims elsewhere and I want to focus here on the mindset that these claims imply.[7] Two of the three distinctions claimed by these athletes were open only to wrestlers and were directly related to technical features of their sport. Unlike the pankration or boxing where a victory depended on one's opponent giving up or being unable to continue, a wrestler won by being the first to throw his opponent three times. Therefore surviving all the rounds in a match without being thrown even once was a sign of a wrestler's superior skill, and wrestlers understandably took pride in any victory where they could be said to have won *aptôs* (*aptês*, *aptôtos*), 'not thrown'. Another way a wrestler could demonstrate his skill was to win without having been caught in a waistlock in any of his matches (*amesolabêtos*, 'not caught around the middle'). This hold, which was accomplished by grabbing someone around the waist from the front or back, gave a wrestler nearly complete control of his opponent, in particular allowing him to lift his opponent off the ground and throw him. For this reason, the Greeks considered it the most dangerous hold and in commemorating the death of one of their members, an association of athletes noted that this was the hold used by Death. The third distinction, *anephedros* (*anuphedros*), 'not having sat out a round', was shared by wrestlers and pankratiasts. Earning it was partially a matter of chance since it required an uneven number of competitors. In such case, wrestlers or pankratiasts drew lots to see who sat out a round. Moreover, in a feature of ancient sports that runs contrary to our sense of fair play, the Greeks never instituted a system to help out a competitor who never received a bye. It was entirely possible that at any point in the match he could face someone who had had the chance to rest. Winning under such conditions required extreme strength and endurance in two sports that already tested these qualities.

While we know of athletes who won other festivals *aptôs, amesolabêtos,* or *anephedros,* the Olympics dominate such claims. The table on pp. 94-5 includes all athletes who won or are likely to have won the Olympics with at least one of these distinctions. Also noted are other distinctions earned by these athletes or other significant features of their career. This information demonstrates that we are dealing with some of the superstars of ancient wrestling and the pankration. While many of these athletes are known from multiple sources, the list gives only the source for an athlete's having won *aptôs, amesolabêtos,* or *anephedros.* In the majority of cases, the information comes from an inscription, indicating the importance of these documents for our understanding of this aspect of ancient athletic history. All of these athletes were wrestlers unless it is noted that they won the pankration.

Taken individually, which is how they are normally encountered, these records are not particularly informative as to how these wrestlers and pankratiasts regarded their careers. When assembled as a chronological series, they essentially constitute a page out of the Olympic record book for a period stretching from the sixth century BCE to the end of the games. As such, they reveal a carefully modulated process in which the success of one wrestler or pankratiast was measured against what his predecessors had achieved. The initial mark was set by Milo, who had six Olympic wrestling victories to his credit and who was the subject of numerous stories. While an athlete might never hope to match Milo's overall fame, there was one concrete feature of Milo's career that a wrestler could use to determine where he stood in the field of Olympic victors. An epigram, which may date considerably after Milo's death but probably represents a traditional story, celebrates the fact he never fell to his knees. The implication is that he was never thrown and, in the terminology developed not long after Milo's time by wrestlers to mark their accomplishments, he would have been labelled in the record books as *aptôs.*[8]

To our knowledge, Xenokles was the first wrestler after Milo to claim that nobody was able to throw him in the Olympics. Nothing in the epigram celebrating his victory indicates that he had thought about whether other wrestlers had preceded him in the same fashion. He simply took pride in how thoroughly he beat his opponents. The next in the series, Hermesianax of Colophon, is a different case. He, of course, could not claim to be the first athlete to win the Olympics without getting thrown. Both Milo and Xenokles blocked him from making that claim. Taking stock of his situation though, he did find a way to mark out his place in the world of wrestling. The fact that Milo was from Croton and Xenokles from Arcadia, left him in the position to claim to be the first wrestler from Asia to win the Olympics without taking a fall. To put it in perspective, it was

Athlete (city)	First Olympic victory	Accomplishments	Source
Milo (Croton)	540 BCE	'He never fell to his knees', implying that he won *aptôs*	Epigram, possibly inscribed on a statue base and possibly dating to the Hellenistic period
Aristodamos (Elis)	388 BCE	'nobody seized him from the middle'	Eusebius' Olympic Victor list
Xenokles (Mainalos)	372 (?) BCE	*aptês*	Epigram inscribed at Olympia
Hermesianax (Colophon)	320 BCE	First from Asia to win *aptôs*	Epigram inscribed in his native city
Kleonikos (Miletos)	3rd c. BCE	*aptôtei* (adverb from *aptôs*)	Epigram inscribed in his native city, set up by his brother
Name and city unknown	224 (?) BCE	*aptôtos* Also seems to have achieved some first but the details are now lost	Epigram inscribed at Olympia
Hagesistratos (Lindos)	172 (?) BCE	*aptôs* First of Lindos to win the boy's wrestling at Olympia	Epigram inscribed in his native city along with a record of his father's victory at Nemea
Leon (Rhodes)	2nd/1st c. BCE	First of the Greeks in some respect *aptôs*, possibly in the Olympic Games	Career record inscribed at Olympia
Isidoros (Alexandria)	72 BCE	*aptôtos* in the *periodos*	Phlegon of Tralles
Heliodoros (Kos)	last quarter of 1st c. BCE or first quarter of the 1st c. CE	Survived five rounds First of all to win *anephedros* and *aptôs*	Record of Olympic victory, inscribed in his native city
Dionysides (Mylasa)	1st c. CE (before 93 CE)	First to win *aptôs*, *amesolabêtos*, *anephedros*	Inscribed on an altar to the emperor and Zeus Olympios, dedicated in his honour by a local association in his native city

much the same as being the first American-born golfer to win the British Open the first time out: not as great as being the first of all time to do so but something that not even Ben Hogan or Tom Watson could take away from Denny Shute.

One athlete's success, though, is often another athlete's loss, and that

Athlete (city)	First Olympic victory	Accomplishments	Source
Ti. Claudius Rufus (Smyrna)	Reign of Tiberius	Decree of the Eleans: *anephedros* (men's pankration) in all rounds, in the last round faced a man who had sat out a round, competed until nightfall and match declared a draw. Only one of all time to tie in the men's age-group. Decree of Smyrna: His fortitude is praised without providing details of the match. Bronze plaque: first to a tie in men's pankration.	3 inscriptions from Olympia: a decree by the Eleans, a decree by his native city, and a bronze plaque inscribed with the names of various athletes (the exact nature of the document is unclear except that it dates considerably later than the other two inscriptions)
P. Cornelius Ariston (Ephesos)	AD 49	*anephedros* (boy's pankration), amplified as 'not from the luck of the draw but without sitting out'	2 epigrams inscribed at Olympia, the author of which was himself a successful competitor, probably in poetry contests (he carried the title *Pleistonikes*, 'victor in very many contests').
Nikanor (Ephesos)	AD 89	*anephedros* (boy's pankration)	Record of Olympic victory, inscribed at Olympia by his brother
Antonius Asklepiades (Aizanoi)	AD 93	*aptôs, amesolabêtos, anephedros*	Dossier of his family's accomplishments, inscribed in his native city
Ioanes (Smyrna)	AD 384-392	*aptôtos* wrestler. No festival is specified. It might have been the Olympics or the term may have come to mean simply 'unequalled'.	Inscription in Greek and Latin set up at Rome

was certainly true for Kleonikos of Miletos, the next athlete on the list to win the Olympics without being thrown. Since Kleonikos was also from Asia Minor, Hermesianax' victory prevented him from claiming even a limited record, i.e. 'first' of Asia to win without taking a fall. It was still worthwhile for him and his brother, who set up his monument, to note and take pride in his particular success since it demonstrated his skill as a wrestler. In this he was followed by substantial number of other wrestlers and pankratiasts who continued to note the occasions when they had demonstrably dominated their competition at Olympia. It was not that they were not thinking about how a 'first' might put them in the record books. A glance at the list in fact shows how much of a premium they put on earning such distinctions. Two of the wrestlers, a third-century BCE wrestler whose name has been lost and Leon of Rhodes, took credit for some sort of 'first', the details of which have been lost because of damage to their inscriptions. Among the pankratiasts, Tiberius Rufus prided himself on being the only one ever to have earned a tie in the men's age category. The implication is that each of them looked back over the records set by their predecessors and while they found no way to glean a 'first' out of their *aptôs* or *anephedros* victories, they did find some else about their records that established a place for them in the history of their sport.

The process begun by Hermesianax does not stop there but continues into the Roman period. So about the time of Augustus, Heliodoros had a chance to claim a 'first' that put him one up on any previous athlete – he won the Olympics without ever being thrown and without sitting out a round. He recognised that individually these were not unique but together they represented a new standard of success. His record was quickly broken by Dionysides, who understood that he had dominated his opponents in a way that no wrestler had done in the prior eight centuries.

We have one final case of a wrestler being forced to take into account the tradition of his discipline. As Hermesianax had done to Kleonikos, Dionysides' success robbed another very successful athlete of the opportunity to take full advantage of his accomplishment. Asklepiades had shown the same dominance as Dionysides of his opponents when he won the Olympics not long after Dionysides. He recognised, though, that he could not claim to be the first to have done so or even the first from Asia since Dionysides was also from Asia Minor. The record his family set up thus records just his victory *aptôs*, *anephedros*, and *amesolabêtos*, something that placed him among the great wrestlers of all time but did not provide as much punch as Dionysides' record.

Additional examples of athletes who had their eye on the past history of the Olympics can be gleaned from David Young's attempt to prove that athletes did not become more specialised over time.[9] Instead of focusing on athletes who established a record for themselves with technical triumphs within their particular discipline, he examined athletes who had demonstrated their versatility by winning multiple events at the Olympics. Of particular interest to Young were runners since the sport by its nature tends to limit the ways in which an athlete can excel. Runners, sprinters in particular, remain at the top of their form for a relatively limited amount of time. Among winners of the modern Olympic 100 metres, for example, only Carl Lewis has been able to claim the title twice. In addition, long distance and short distance running requires different skill sets and training, making it exceedingly hard to do both well. In the case of the ancient Olympics, this meant that sprinters would specialise in one or more of the following: the *stade* (*c.* 200 metres), *diaulos* (*c.* 400 metres), or *hoplites* (a *diaulos* run in armour). Endurance runners concentrated on the *dolichos*, which has been estimated at 7.5 to 9 kilometres.

Among ancient runners with multiple Olympic victories, Young located six who set new records by pushing the limitations of their sport. The following chart makes clear the specific ways in which they outdid their predecessors, along with pertinent comments in ancient sources about their success.

Athlete (city)	Events and date (BCE unless noted)	Significant features
Pantakles (Athens)	*stade*: 696 *stade & diaulos* (?) 692	
Chionis (Sparta)	*stade*: 668 (according to Pausanias but wrongly, see below) *stade & diaulos*: 664 *stade & diaulos*: 660 *stade & diaulos*: 656	Pausanias: 'The *hoplites* had not yet been introduced' (on a stele at Olympia set up by the Spartans; see below)
Phanas (Pellene)	*stade, diaulos, hoplites*: 512	Eusebius: 'First to win a triple in these events'*
Astylos (Croton/Syracuse)	*stade & diaulos*: 488 *stade & diaulos*: 484 *stade & diaulos*: 480 Plus at least 1 *hoplites*	
Leonidas (Rhodes)	*stade, diaulos, hoplites*: 164 *stade, diaulos, hoplites*: 160 *stade, diaulos, hoplites*: 156 *stade, diaulos, hoplites*: 152	Eusebius: *triastês* (triple victor), a term used only of Leonidas Pausanias: 'the most famous runner ... he maintained his swiftness at its height for four Olympiads ...'
Polites (Keramos)	*stade, diaulos, dolichos*: 69 CE	Pausanias: 'You would also consider Polites a great marvel ... he exhibited every skill in running: he changed in the shortest time from the longest form of running and the one requiring the greatest endurance to the shortest and swiftest ...'

*On Phanas' record and the term *triastês*, see Harris 1968a.

We can guess from the comments in Pausanias and Eusebius' Olympic Victor list that Leonidas was the first runner to win three running events at four consecutive Olympics. Unlike the wrestlers discussed above, though, we lack a direct statement to this effect from Leonidas or any of the other runners. For this reason, I am less certain than Young that Astylos or Leonidas were aware of how much they had accomplished in comparison to their predecessors. Polites must be considered in an entirely different light. As Young realised, there is no way Polites could have accomplished the feat that draws so much praise from Pausanias (6.13.3-4) without a long term plan. Developing the ability to switch from the *dolichos* to the *stade*, something to which Pausanias specifically called attention, depended on his having invested a considerable amount of time in training for two very different types of events – sprinting and long distance racing. Unfortunately, while we now seem to have a record of Polites' career from his native city, it is so fragmentary that it is not helpful in this regard.[10] The most we can extract from it is the mention of a few victories at relatively minor festivals in the *stade* and *diaulos* along with possibly one victory in the *hoplites*. If we had a more complete record of his career, we might have seen a phase when he tried to gain experience in both the *stade* and the *dolichos* as preparation for the Olympics.

The chart reveals one aspect of Polites' career that Young did not note. Where is his victory in the *hoplites*? His skill in the *stade* and the *diaulos* suggests he had a good chance of winning this as well, as he seems to have done so at least one minor festival. It is not clear if he competed and lost, or he decided not to compete since even with a day's rest (the *hoplites* was the last contest) he felt he could not win. Either way, it suggests a willingness to forego a fairly certain victory for the chance of winning an event that the past history of the games indicated was out of his reach. The planning involved and his willingness to take risks indicates how far Polites would go to obtain a 'first' by doing something that no Greek had done before and, to our knowledge, nobody has done since, including in the modern Olympics.

Chionis' record can also teach us about the Greek attitude to athletic records. Pausanias understood that the monument he saw at Olympia could not have been dedicated by Chionis but had to be the work of the Spartan people. The one at Olympia (and he implies the same for the one at Sparta) carried the notation 'the *hoplites* had not yet been introduced' (6.13.2; 3.14.3). As Pausanias realised, there was no way that Chionis could have known that Eleans were going to add the *hoplites* to the Olympic program. Young (p. 189) supposed that the Spartans added this notation as a means of countering Astylos' record. Recently Christesen has gone even further in this direction.[11] He argues that Chionis' monuments were set up two centuries after his victory as part of a deliberate attempt by one of the Spartan royal families, the Agiads, to promote Chionis as a hero. Their plan was to use their close association with this early Spartan victor to strengthen their prestige in a time of political infighting. Enhancing the glamour of Chionis' victory would have been entirely to their benefit. So not only did they add the notation about the *hoplites* but they also made Chionis a founder of Cyrene and gave him one more victory than he actually earned. This would explain the conflict between the seven victories recorded by Pausanias (3.14.3, 4.23.4, 8.39.3), who was presumably misled by the monument at Olympia or the one at Sparta, and the six in Eusebius' Olympic Victor list. The Agiads then set Chionis' statue adjacent to that of Astylos with an augmented record designed to increase Chionis' prestige at Astylos' expense. The Agiads, in effect, sought to alter the tradition for their own purposes and, to the degree that they mislead Pausanias, they were successful. The underlying assumption behind their machinations was that athletic records mattered to the Greeks and that people did in fact look back in the history of the games to see if one athlete had outdone an earlier one.

The last case I want to look at is a runner from Miletos who is known from three inscriptions, a short record from Olympia and a longer decree set up at both Miletos and Didyma.[12] His name has been lost but we know he had a very successful career with victories in various combinations of the *stade, diaulos,* and *hoplites* at many major festivals including the Pythian, Nemean, and Isthmian games. Unlike Phanas or Astylos, he was not able to pull off a triple victory at Olympia but he did win the *diaulos* in 20 BCE. As one might expect for a sprinter, his career as a top level competitor appears to have been limited to five or six years. This judgment is based on the fact he won the Pythian games and the Eleutheria at Plataea twice as a man. Of interest here are the number and type of 'firsts' he claims, which are distributed throughout a long list of his victories but which can be summarised as follows.

First and Only: Eleutheria at Plataea, announced as 'Best of the Greeks' for winning the *hoplites* from the trophy [a special form of the *hoplites*] for a second time.

First of All: Nemean games, *stade, diaulos, hoplites* in succession in one year;[13] Aktian games, *stade, diaulos, hoplites* in one day; Games given by the guild of athletes, *stade, diaulos, hoplites.*

First of Asia: Eleutheria at Plataea, announced as 'Best of the Greeks' for winning the *hoplites* from the trophy [for his first victory in this contest].

First of Ionians: Pythian games, *stade* and *hoplites* twice; Nemean games, *stade, diaulos, hoplites* three times; Sebasta Romaia held by the Konion of Asia, *hoplites.*

First of Milesians: Isthmia, *hoplites*; Heraia in Argos, *stade.*

In discussing another runner's claim, which he also considered overblown, H.A. Harris commented: 'the lengths to which an athlete would go to find some category of priority for his achievements are amusingly illustrated by an inscription of a Milesian runner whose name is lost'.[14] Harris fails, however, to keep in mind that this Milesian was a top flight runner with the record to prove it. Not only did he win the Olympics but with his victories in the Pythian, Nemean, and Isthmian games he gained the much coveted title of *periodonikes* ('circuit victor'), the ancient equivalent of winning the grand slam. Moreover, his desire to list whatever 'firsts' to which he was entitled was legitimated by a long history of such claims, only some of which have been discussed above. Admittedly the number of his claims was greater than prior athletes but as will be made clear below, he had good reasons for doing so and this was not unusual for athletes of his particular time. So we are not dealing with a second-rate athlete who was trying to pump up his record in extraordinary ways but a very successful athlete making careful judgments about how to portray his prowess. Moreover, it is his precision and concern for getting it right, the very things Harris found amusing, that are most important here. He had made a thorough examination of the history of the games as it related to his career and for this reason he did not claim to be 'first of those from Asia' when 'first of the Ionians' is all to which he felt he was entitled. History mattered to this runner.

This is not the place to discuss whether the claims made by this runner or his fellow athletes were in fact justified, although I have found no evidence proving any of them to be false and Young makes the same observation for the material he studied.[15] What is germane here is how keenly aware these athletes were not just of who had won the Olympics centuries earlier but also what their own victories entailed in terms of the history of their sport. As a consequence of this knowledge, athletes of the Roman period, who had the luck or skill to be particularly successful, consistently tried to situate themselves in the long list of past champions, most often by making it very clear that they had equalled or, even better, exceeded the spectacular victories of their predecessors. In effect, they were thinking about the past because it determined how their present success would be seen in the future.

Strategies for recognition

The Greeks never conceived that it was necessary or useful to measure how fast a sprinter ran the *stade* or how far a pentathlete threw the javelin. This has led to some scepticism about whether they possessed a concept of athletic records.[16] The examples discussed above, however, indicate that they did believe it was of great importance to remember and to record when and how one athlete had matched or outdone the performance of an earlier one. This aspect of Greek athletic life has escaped much notice mainly because the occasions when an athlete could set a new record were much rarer than today. Over all, there were far fewer sports in which athletes even had a chance of setting a record and fewer ways in which they could earn a 'first'. So often centuries had to pass, as was the case for Heliodoros and his victory *aptôs* and *anephedros*, before one athlete could achieve something that no athlete had yet accomplished.

The lack of accurate measurements did have one profound but in some ways beneficial effect on the lives of ancient athletes with regard to records. With his 9.69 second time in the Beijing Olympics, Usain Bolt can have no doubts that he could have beaten any of the prior winners of the 100 metres, including the most famous Olympic sprinter of all time. While Jesse Owens may have set an at-the-time amazing record of 10.2, the end result of a match between him and any sprinter of the last decade would never be in doubt. In contrast, the records set by ancient athletes were not particularly helpful in proving that they were superior to previous Olympic victors. Leonidas' twelve victories, presumably a first in Olympic history, showed he was fast but not that he was faster than Polites, who also had a very significant 'first' to his credit.[17] What athletes increasingly needed then was an alternate approach to gaining the recognition they desired and the development of a new type of agonistic inscription represented a good solution. It gave them a way to portray all the highpoints of their career, including whatever 'firsts' they could glean, in a format that ensured that, while they might not be considered the greatest athlete of all time, they would be considered one of the greatest athletes.

This new type of athletic inscription, which became common throughout the Greek world in the first to third centuries CE, has not been properly appreciated, to say the least. For example, in his recent survey of Greek athletics, Stephen Miller dismisses these later inscriptions with the comment 'his many victories … are listed in excruciating detail'.[18] What Miller and others have not understood is that these inscriptions are not simple lists. When looked at closely, they turn out to be complex documents specifically designed to reveal the extent of an athlete's success. By way of illustration, I have translated the prose portion of a decree honouring Maron of Seleukeia in Cilicia, a wrestler who won the Olympics in the mid-second century CE.[19] Besides being well preserved and compact, it includes most of the typical features of such inscriptions. Also helpful is the fact that it was accompanied by a poetic account of his career which provides some insight into his attitude towards his victories. The terms in italics, which would have been easily understood by his contemporaries, are explained below.

The city of Seleukeia honors its own citizen, T. Aelius Aurelius Maron, also a citizen of Alexandria in Egypt, Athens, and many other cities, *Xystarch*, first of men to be *Periodonikes Teleios*, an *aleiptos* wrestler, crowned in the following sacred, eiselastic [allowing a triumphal entry into his native city] games (line 9):
Olympia, at Rome twice, Pythian games twice, Isthmian games three times, Nemea games three times, at Athens five times, the Aktian games, at Naples

twice, at Puteoli, the Haleia in Rhodes, Antiocheian games three times, at Ephesos twice, at Smyrna twice, Pergamon three times, Tarsus, The Shield at Argos, and forty-four cash prize games (line 18).

The decree follows the standard pattern of being divided into a heading (lines 1-9) and a body (lines 10-18), with the heading providing the elements of his career to which an athlete most wanted to call attention and with the body supporting and expanding on what one learns from the heading. The heading, representing more or less a *curriculum vitae*, is often the most damaged part of these inscriptions, a factor which does leave these inscriptions looking like simple lists. In the case of the Milesian runner, for example, we only have the body, which means we lack not only his name but details about his career that would have been helpful in contextualising and interpreting his claims. Here the athlete's name is preserved (although oddly without his patronymic), along with his original citizenship and the cities that made him a citizen. Where an athlete was born was an important fact because no matter how international sports became during the Roman Empire, winning a major festival brought an athlete considerable honour within his native city, just as it had centuries earlier. For Greeks of this period athletics remained a major element in the creation of a self-identity and athletic success was often used as a way for members of the elite to increase their status in their cities.[20] This is why the family of Asklepiades – the wrestler beaten out of a record by Dionysides – thought it very worthwhile to record his accomplishments in the family's dossier of political and religious successes. This is also why athletes continued to advertise cases where they were the first of their city to win a major contest, as did the Milesian runner discussed above.[21] Conversely, the importance cities themselves still attached to athletic success is made explicit in an inscription from Aphrodisias praising the pankratiast Menander for increasing his native city's reputation with his athletic honours, especially those he received from the emperor himself.[22]

The grants of citizenship in other cities functioned as a covert acknowledgement of his stature as an athlete since such honours were occasioned by his performance in that particular city's festivals. The Milesian runner, in fact, made a point of noting at the end of his victories that the Athenians had granted him citizenship, a statue, and a crown because of his manly virtue. Imperial appointments were also a vote of confidence in an athlete's ability since they tended to go to the leading athletes of the time. In Maron's case, we learn about his appointment as *Xystarch*, the official in charge of the operation of a particular city's festivals.[23] Damas' sons take care to reveal that he had obtained the much more select position of director of the imperial baths, which he, in turn, obtained for them from the emperor. The employment of athletes to oversee the athletic system represented one of the few advantages that athletes of the Roman period had over their predecessors. They clearly enjoyed the fact they had the option of continuing their careers in the world of athletics after retiring from actual competition. They might be honoured by their colleagues or the cities in which they served, as happened to Menander, who was praised by the athletic guild for his help managing a festival. In addition, they gained prestige by their association with the emperor. So Demetrios, the five-time Olympic victor whose claim Harris thought was overblown, gives pride of place to the fact the he was honoured by the emperor with *Xystarchies* for life.[24]

Next we get a series of athletic titles, which summarise the highpoints of an athlete's career in as concise a fashion as possible. First is *Periodonikes Teleios*, which when deciphered, means that he had won not just the Olympics and the three other games that made up the original *periodos*, 'circuit', but also the other games added to the *periodos* in the Roman period.[25] It was comparable to winning a grand slam in golf or tennis and it was this accomplishment which gave him his not insignificant 'first'.[26] Admittedly, this precise distinction was not an honour open to earlier athletes but the practice of advertising how one had dominated one's competition over a four year cycle had a long history. A further proof of his superiority is the notation that he was *aleiptos*, 'unbeatable', throughout his career. An indication of where this placed Maron in the history of athletics comes from M. Aurelius Asklepiades, one of the few pankratiasts of the Roman period whose record suggests he was even better than Damas. While he had only one Olympic victory to Damas' two or three, he remained unbeaten during his whole career and the remarkable nature of this feat becomes apparent when we contemplate the full list of his victories. It required Asklepiades winning virtually all the major games of the period, something that Damas never achieved.[27]

What this list did for Asklepiades is exactly what the body of the inscription was designed to do. It confirmed the impression of the athlete we gain from the heading and demonstrated that his success was not just a fluke. It forces us to realise that he competed against the best athletes of his day but they never (or virtually never) stood a chance. That these inscriptions at the most elemental level were designed to show an athlete's complete dominance is made clear in the last lines of the poem that accompanied the prose account of Maron's career. There he glories in having dispatched all his competitors: 'Maron of Seleukeia, you never yielded to your competitors in the stadium, as a boy, a young man, and a man.' He is not alone in expressing this sentiment. Aristomachos, a Magnesian pankratiast of roughly the same period, notes at the end of the poem that accompanied his list: 'why [did I win all the festivals listed]? I was unbeatable in all stadia'.[28]

Whereas the aim of the heading was conciseness, the body needed to be comprehensive if it was going to fulfil its purpose of testifying to the depth of an athlete's success and proving that he would have been a major contender in any period. In this regard, the comparative brevity of Maron's

103

list is unusual. In many other examples the body is two or three times as long as the heading. This length partially derives from the fact athletes often listed more festivals than we see here. These games were normally of somewhat lower calibre but their presence further emphasised that wherever these athletes went in the athletic world they were invincible. Sometimes an athlete felt that he had to make this point more explicitly. So Asklepiades stressed in the middle of his list that he had competed in Italy, Greece, and Asia, while the five-time victor Demetrios noted that, in addition to the claim discussed by Harris, he had won in every region of the world.

The even more striking absence is the failure to include those notations Harris found so amusing. The range of material that might be included goes far beyond any 'firsts' an athlete may have achieved, although these were an important element. Every detail that might point to an athlete's ability tended to be mentioned – winning two or three events in the same day, winning the same festival twice in a row, or winning the boy's age group and then winning the men's category at the same festival.[29] Such claims are not unfamiliar in connection with modern sports: 'Serena Williams won Wimbledon in straight sets' or 'Eli Manning pulled out the Superbowl in the last minute'. Today they seem particularly common in connection with sports where no objective standard exists for ranking players and there is a need for some other way to mark out the superior athlete in a crowded field. Basically these claims functioned in same way in the body of an inscription where the ultimate aim was to call attention to an athlete for having consistently dominated his competitors. Having a large number of victories helped to make this point but winning many festivals in a manifestly superior fashion made this point even better.

Finally, by an odd quirk of fate, it is the lack of objective records that allowed these inscriptions to do their job. If people knew that runners of the Roman period were faster or slower than six centuries earlier or that Milo was stronger or bigger than later wrestlers, there would be no question about who were the best athletes in the history of the games. With this issue up in the air, though, all the information packed into these inscriptions could accomplish two things. First, by providing a complete picture of an athlete's career, these documents made it abundantly clear that an athlete had been exceedingly successful over a long period of time – he was not a one-day phenomenon or a particularly precocious boy who otherwise did not amount to much. Second, this realisation made one think (and even today still makes one think) that you would not know where to place your bet if Damas met any of great pankratiasts of the past in the ring. Arrhichion or Damas? Kapros or Damas? Even a match between the two best pankratiasts of their century, Asklepiades and Damas, would be in doubt. In the end, you could never say that any Olympic victor was the greatest in his sport. You could, however, say of the particularly successful ones that they all were very great athletes and that they would have been greatly admired by the Greeks at any time in the history of the Olympics. Rhetorically then, these inscriptions are making a plea, with the fulsomeness of other contemporary orations, that these athletes deserved a place in the hall of fame for ancient athletics.

Conclusion

This does not pretend to be a complete study of later athletic inscriptions and many other factors undoubtedly played a role in their development. Certainly they were part of the general explosion of inscriptions in the Roman period which has been termed the 'epigraphic habit'.[30] Yet the adoption of this form of inscription throughout the Greek world by all sorts of athletes must be seen in the light of the challenges faced by athletes active during the Roman Empire. Standing in the shadow cast by the great champions of the past, they needed a way to represent themselves as being great athletes in their own right. These inscriptions became the dominant form of memorial because the complex format allowed ambitious athletes to amass a compelling picture of how successful they had been. Furthermore, how acutely they hoped that these inscriptions would establish a place for them in the long tradition of the Olympic games is apparent in the opening of the poem honouring Maron: 'Even if I am small to look at, you will say that no other is so great, once you have learned all the accomplishments due to my mastery of wrestling.'

Notes

1. Abbreviations follow Liddell, Scott and Jones, *Greek English Lexicon*, except *SEG* = *Supplementum Epigraphicum Graecum* (by vol. and entry no.). Modern Olympic records are based on the Olympic organisation database: www.olympic.org/en/content/All-Olympic-results-since-1896/ accessed 6 July 2010.
Moretti 1957 (*Olympionikai*) 878, 881, tentatively dates Damas' two (more is not impossible) Olympic victories to 173 and 177 CE. The evidence for Damas' career has been thoroughly reassessed by Strasser 2003. His work suggests that Damas retired between 176 and 180 CE and hence Moretti's dates are slightly too late. Damas or a member of his family is also depicted on a mosaic from southern Italy published after Strasser's article: Flesca 2004-05; D'Amore 2007 (*I.Reggio Calabria*) no. 35 with *SEG* 55 1056.
2. This count presumes that there was no pankration contest for men in 80 BCE when Sulla lured nearly all competitors to Rome to compete in his games but that they were held when Nero altered the schedule of games in Greece. On Sulla, see Matthews 1979; on Nero, see Kennell 1988.
3. Arrhichion's [or Arrhachion] decision is held up for praise by Pausanias (8.40.1-2) and especially Philostratos (*Im.* 2.6). For theories on the cause of his death, see Brophy 1978, Brophy and Brophy 1985, and Poliakoff 1986. On Theogenes' career, see Pouilloux 1994, Masson 1994, and Maróti 2004-05 (*non vidi*). Success in both the pankration and boxing was quite rare in comparison to the pankration and wrestling; see Strasser 2003: 278-81. On the designation 'successor

to Herakles', which seems to appear only in literary sources not inscriptions, see Kindscher 1845 and Forbes 1939.

4. See Strasser 2003: 267.

5. See Strasser 2004a: 142.

6. For a survey of changing views about the decline of Greek athletics and the role of professionalism, see Kyle 2007: 205-16.

7. For a full bibliography on the athletes and their claims, see Brunet 2010. To the examples cited there can be added an inscription from Phaselis in Lydia where an athlete won a local contest *aptôs* (completely restored) and *amesolabêtos*: Adak, Tüner Önen and Şahin 2005 no. 4. Christian Habicht has kindly pointed out to me that Leon has been securely identified as being from Rhodes, citing Kontorini 1989: 68-72. Hermesianax' father may have taken part in an embassy from Kolophon to Athens in connection with the Panathenaic games, see Catling and Kanavou 2007. Also of interest is an epitaph for Hermokrates, an athletic trainer in Egypt: Bernand 1969 no. 22. He taught ephebes to win always and not to fall to the ground (i.e. to remain *aptôs*). By extension falling became an image for dying in this epitaph. Hermokrates is said to have fallen by the wrestling tricks of Death. The famous wrestler Milo is brought in as an example of how no one can cheat death. He, though stronger than a tree, fell like a tree in the wind.

8. *AP* 11.316 might be taken to contradict this epigram. There Milo falls on his back when he comes up to accept the wreath because no wrestler was willing to fight him. When the crowd calls out that he should not be crowned, he retorts that it takes three falls to lose a match. Robert 1968: 246-7, has shown that this is not a reference to the historical Milo but a joke in which 'Milo' stands for a generic wrestler at some unidentified festival. More apropos is the story that Milo could stand on a greased discus and not be pushed off (Paus. 6.14.6). Milo was active just before the period in which athletes began to create a range of terms to mark out particularly accomplished athletes. Pindar is the first source we have for both *aptôs* (*O.* 9.93, for a festival other than the Olympics) and *Olympionikes*, 'Olympic victor' (e.g. *O.* 5.21). The term *akoniti*, used of athletes who won because no other athlete was willing to compete against them (essentially what happened to the generic Milo), also first appears in inscriptions at this date. For details on this term, see Brunet 2010: 115 n. 3.

9. Young 1996b. The sources for these athletes are discussed in Moretti 1957 (*Olympionikai*) 25-7 (Pantakles), 40, 42-7 (Chionis), 142-4 (Phanas), 178-9, 186-7, 196-8, 219 (Astylos), 618-20, 622-4, 626-8, 633-5 (Leonidas), 796-8 (Polites). On Chionis and Polites, also see below.

10. See Strasser 2004b, who also proposes emendations for Pausanias' description of Polites in 6.13.3-4 and notes the risk Polites took in trying to win long and short distance races at the same festival.

11. Christesen 2010.

12. Olympia: *Inscr. Olymp.* 219. Miletos and Didyma: Rehm 1958 (*I. Didyma* 2) no. 201, but also see Robert 1949 and Moretti 1953 (*IAG*) no. 59. The Olympia inscription lists only a victory in the *diaulos*. Thus Robert was right to give this runner only one victory (the *diaulos*) in the Didyma inscription in contrast to Rehm's restoration of the *diaulos* and the *hoplites*. Another case that could be added here concerns Claudius Rufus, one of the pankratiasts listed in the first table for having tied the Olympics *anephedros*. Ebert 1998: n. 18, has suggested that the change from 'first and only' in the monument set up during his lifetime to 'first' in the bronze plaque dating much later was made to account for changes in the athletic record books, e.g. the tie earned by Hermagoras in the mid-second

century which is recorded in Moretti 1953 (*IAG*) no. 77. Who made the change is not clear but it shows an awareness of the importance of athletic records.

13. The meaning is not entirely clear. For the options, see Moretti 1953 (*IAG*) no. 59.

14. Harris 1962: 24. The other athlete in question, Demetrios, was even more successful with five total victories in the Olympics. For more on his career, see below. The title *periodonikes* is discussed below.

15. Robert, who had an excellent command of the epigraphical evidence for Greek athletics, likewise noted nothing in his edition of the inscription from Didyma that would disprove the Milesian runner's claims.

16. The original study of records in Greek athletics is Tod 1949. Ramba 1990 does not advance our knowledge much. The adoption of the Greek 'first and only' acclamations in the Roman world is treated by Versnel 1974, especially 396-7 (with useful bibliography). Young's interest in 'firsts' was prompted in part by the influential views of Richard Mandell and Allen Guttman who posited that athletic records are exclusively a modern development. For their and related views, see the survey in Carter and Krüger 1990: 1-11.

17. The opportunities for an ambitious athlete to claim a significant 'first' also become more limited over time. Wrestling is a good example. Dionysides, with his victory *aptôs*, *amesolabêtos*, and *anephedros*, had achieved everything that a wrestler could hope to accomplish. Athletes, however, did not give up their interest in earning a 'first' but the results were less impressive. So with Damas, we get the claim of being the only one to gain twenty victories in sacred contests as a boy. Menander, a second-century CE pankratiast with a less spectacular record than Damas, prides himself of being the first and only one to win all three age groups in three years: Moretti 1953 (*IAG*) no. 72 = Roueché 1993: 91 *ii* b.

18. Miller 2004b: 205, on Moretti 1953 (*IAG*) no. 68 which honours T. Flavius Archibios who won the Olympics twice as a pankratiast early in the second century CE.

19. Şahin 1991 no. 1, with Kassel 1991, Merkelbach 2003; now Hagel and Tomaschitz 1998 no. Sel 147. While the combination of a poem and a victory catalogue is not common, there are parallels, e.g. *SEG* 19 589 (Chios) and the example below for a Magnesian pankratiast. Herz 1996 has argued that based on his name, he received his Roman citizenship from a victory in the Kapetolia in 150, 154, or 158 CE. Grossardt 2002 maintains that this Maron is the Maron mentioned by Philostratus in *Gym.* 36 as well as the pankratiast with the nickname 'Halter' in *Her.* 14.4. The identification with the wrestler is virtually certain. The identification with the pankratiast, originally raised and dismissed by Jüthner 1909 ad loc., is to be rejected. While wrestlers sometimes also competed as pankratiasts, this inscription makes it very clear that Maron was solely a wrestler.

20. The role of athletics in Greek cities during the Roman period has been a particular focus of Onno van Nijf's work: especially van Nijf 1999, van Nijf 2001, van Nijf 2004, and van Nijf 2005. He has treated the specific question of citizenship and Greek athletics, especially how athletes obtained citizenship in other cities, in van Nijf (forthcoming).

21. Also see the Rhodian runner discussed above for his use of the Attic dialect. He noted prominently that he was the first Rhodian to win the *dolichos* at the Olympics and the Pythian games twice.

22. Roueché 1993 no. 91 *i* a (lines 15-20).

23. For bibliography on the office of *xystarchs* and numerous examples of competitors who held it, see Şahin 1991: 146-7 nn. 27-31.

24. Sayar 2000 (*I. Anazarbos*) no. 25. Virtually the same language occurs in Petzl 1982-90 (*I. Smyrna*) 2.1 no. 667/2.2 p. 376 and Şahin 2004 (*I. Perge* 2) no. 314.

25. On this inscription and the *periodos teleios*, see Frisch 1991. Also see Kennell 1988. The athletic title *Olympionikes* occurs as early as Pindar (e.g. *O.* 5.21) but these titles proliferate in the Roman period as athletes sought ways of summing up their different triumphs.

26. The term grand slam has undergone a similar process of specialisation: e.g. a career grand slam (not winning the four tournaments consecutively) and gold grand slam (winning a grand slam in tennis plus the Olympics).

27. Moretti 1953 (*IAG*) no. 79 = Moretti 1968-1990 (*IGUR*) no. 240. Asklepiades is known from nearly as many sources as Damas; other aspects of Asklepiades' career are discussed by Strasser 2004-05. Damas could only claim to be unbeaten as a boxer, a sport he practised in a very small number of festivals. A similar case is Gaius Licinius Inventus who competed in three sports but was unbeaten only as a boxer: Poljakov 1989 (*I. Tralleis* 1) no. 113.

28. *Inscr. Magn.* no. 181 and p. 296 = Moretti 1953 (*IAG*) no. 71b.

29. Examples of winning three events in one day and two festivals in succession can easily be found in Moretti 1953 (*IAG*) e.g. no. 59 (the Milesian runner discussed above) and 67. A very explicit claim of having won two age categories at one time occurs in Petzl 1982-90 (*I. Smyrna* 2.1) no. 661.

30. The term was coined by Ramsey MacMullen: MacMullen 1982 and the phenomenon has been the subject of numerous studies. Two of the more helpful are Meyer 1990 and Woolf 1996, especially the bibliography in n. 1.

6

Gilbert West and the English Contribution to the Revival of the Olympic Games[1]

Hugh M. Lee

In 1749 Gilbert West (1703-56) published his *Dissertation on the Olympick Games*. This treatise, 207 pages long, is 'prefixed' to his verse translations of selected *Odes of Pindar*, namely *Olympians* 1, 3, 5, 7, 12, 14, *Pythian* 1, *Nemeans* 1, 11, and *Isthmian* 2.[2] In the seventeen chapters or 'sections' of the *Dissertation*, West discusses the origin and history of the Olympic Games, the religious ceremonies, the calendar, the officials, the individual events, the athletes, and the prizes and rewards. A final section is devoted to the topic of the 'Utility of the Olympick Games'. Elegantly written, the *Dissertation* still provides a useful description of the ancient Olympics, although it must be supplemented and corrected by subsequent scholarship, especially in the areas of archaeology, art history, and epigraphy.

Yet among sports historians and in Olympic circles, West is almost unknown and his *Dissertation* unread. He is not, however, an obscure figure, for his portrait resides in the National Portrait Gallery in London, where he is listed as an 'author'.[3] He had some reputation as a poet, for Samuel Johnson includes him in his *Lives of the English Poets* and praises the translation of the first *Olympian Ode*: 'A work of this kind must in a minute examination discover many imperfections, but West's version, so far as I have considered it, appears to be the product of great labour and great abilities.'[4]

West's lack of recognition even on his home soil is all the more curious given England's significant place in modern Olympic history. Following Athens (1896), Paris (1900), and St Louis (1904), London in 1908 became the fourth city to host the modern Games, a role which she replicated in 1948. Furthermore, even before Coubertin's inaugural Olympics of 1896, 'Olimpick' or 'Olympian' Games had been held on English soil.

In 1612 Robert Dover, perhaps reviving an earlier festival, held his Cotswold Olimpick Games. The programme consisted of events such as wrestling, horse-racing, dancing, stick fighting, jumping in sacks, and shin-kicking. This celebration was intended as a repudiation of Puritan austerity. Dover's Games, with periodic interruptions, have continued over the centuries on an annual basis.[5] The *Annalia Dubrensia*, a collection of thirty-three poems compiled by Matthew Walbancke to honour

109

Dover and his Games, was published in 1636. Among the contributors were Ben Johnson (*sic*) and Michael Drayton. The poems reveal an enthusiasm for the spirit of the ancient Games even if their modern counterpart was not an attempt to create a historically accurate revival.

In 1850 the physician William Penny Brookes held his first Olympian Games in the town of Much Wenlock in Shropshire county. Events included cricket, football, quoits, and a 50-yard race with the contestants hopping on one leg, but also footraces, a high jump, and a long jump. Like the Cotswold Olimpicks, the Much Wenlock Games continue to be celebrated annually.[6] The original Wenlock contests had a limited focus and were aimed at improving the lives of the local residents, but Brookes' Olympic vision grew over time. He also was involved in the founding of the Shropshire Olympian Games, which were held in 1860 (in conjunction with the eleventh Much Wenlock Games), 1861 (in Wellington), 1862 (in Much Wenlock), and 1864 (in Shrewsbury). Brookes was also a founder of the National Olympian Games held in London in 1866-8, 1874, 1877, and 1883. Elsewhere in England, National Olympic Festivals were also held in Liverpool (1862-7) and Morpeth in Northumberland (1871-1958). Brookes was a friend of John Hulley, who, together with Charles Melly, founded the Liverpool Olympics.[7]

Not only did these nineteenth-century games foreshadow the 1896 Olympics, but Brookes was also a major influence on Coubertin. He corresponded with the Frenchman and convoked a special autumn observance of the Much Wenlock Games, usually held in the spring, for his visit in October of 1890. To Brookes is owed the concept of recurring international Olympics. He also introduced the pageantry into his Games which were later adopted by the modern Olympics. For more than three decades he was involved in the international dialogue which eventually bore fruit in the Games of 1896.[8]

In the twentieth-century scholarship of Greek athletics, England has contributed E. Norman Gardiner and H.A. Harris, who in their books have introduced many to the subject.[9] Gardiner, however, merely lists West in a bibliography, reserving the lion's share of his praise for the German scholar J.H. Krause (1802-82), who is the most eminent scholar of Greek athletics in the nineteenth century and who seems not to have read West.[10] Harris makes no mention of West.

Yet West's *Dissertation* had been read by his younger contemporary, the artist James Barry (1741-1806). In 1777 Barry undertook the pictorial decoration of the Great Room of the Royal Society for the Encouragement of Arts, Manufactures, and Commerce in London (Royal Society of the Arts or RSA). Six murals encircled the chamber, unified by theme of the Progress of Human Culture; the primary focus, however, was the painting entitled *Crowning the Olympic Victors at Olympia*. This subject is discussed by West in section 16, which is entitled 'Of the Olympic, Crown, and other Honours and Rewards conferred upon the conquerors'.[11]

6. Gilbert West and the English Contribution to the Olympic Games

To understand West's contribution to the revival of the Olympics, it is necessary to distinguish between sports for exercise and sports as competitive spectacle. Greeks ran, boxed, wrestled, jumped, and threw the javelin and discus in the gymnasium, the best of them winning the wreath at the great Panhellenic contests. Competition in the games was an extension of the sports practised in the gymnasium. Yet support for physical education has not always been synonymous with approval of the Games. Even in ancient Greece, there were critics of career athletes who sought prizes in the games. For example, as early as the sixth and fifth centuries BCE, Xenophanes (fragment 2) and Euripides (*Autolykos* fragment 282) had complained that athletes were overvalued and contributed little of real value; in the third century CE, the physician Galen (*Exhortation on Medicine* 9-14) likewise criticised athletes, but at greater length.[12]

This dichotomy between sports undertaken for exercise and sports as a means to win prizes and support a career is mirrored in the first modern comprehensive treatments of ancient athletics and the Olympics in the sixteenth century. In 1569 the Italian physician Girolamo Mercuriale (Hieronymus Mercurialis in Latin) published the first modern scholarly study of ancient on Greek exercise and athletics, a work which in all later editions was entitled *De Arte Gymnastica (On the Gymnastic Art)*.[13] By gymnastics he does not mean the modern sport of gymnastics, but rather the exercises like running, boxing, and wrestling, which the Greeks performed while naked (*gymnos*), whether in the gymnasium or stadium. Admiring the twofold goal of ancient education, which called for the training of both mind and body, Mercuriale urges the Holy Roman Emperor Maximillian II to champion the revival of the gymnastic art.[14]

Mercuriale distinguishes three forms of the gymnastic art. The first is the *ars gymnastica medica* or *legitima*, whose goal is the health of the body. The second is the *ars gymnastica bellica*, whose function is to make soldiers fit for war, *bellum* being Latin for 'war'. The third is the *ars gymnastica athletica* – the athletic gymnastic art. This is the gymnastic art of the elite athletes who performed in competitions like the Olympic Games. Mercuriale also calls it the *ars gymnastica vitiosa*, from the Latin *vitium* (fault or vice).[15] *Ars vitiosa* is a translation of Galen's term *kakotechnia (evil art)*, for it is from Galen, who lived in the second century CE, that Mercuriale principally derives his hostility to athletics. Since the goal of physical exercises is to promote health, not to win prizes, Mercuriale, in calling for the revival of physical education, was not advocating a rebirth of the Olympic Games. Subsequent editions of *De Arte Gymnastica* were published in 1573, 1577, 1587, 1601 and 1672, giving some indication of the popularity and influence of the work. The growing interest in physical education and sport in the centuries after Mercuriale is not to be construed as synonymous with a corresponding interest in reviving athletic spectacles like the Olympics.

Given his hostility to the *ars athletica*, Mercuriale writes very little

111

about the Olympic Games. It may not be a coincidence that we do not find the name of Pindar in the lengthy roster of classical authors proudly listed at the beginning of *De Arte Gymnastica*, although he quotes Pindar once and on three occasions cites the ancient commentators on Pindar called the *scholia*.[16] A new *editio princeps* of Pindar by Aldo Manutius had been published in Venice in 1513, and it is inconceivable that the well-read Mercuriale was not familiar with the author.[17] Whereas, however, Pindar composed odes in honour of the victors in the Panhellenic contests and is therefore a treasure trove of information for anyone writing on the Olympic Games, Mercuriale's limited discussion of the Games suggests that he wished to avoid thus encouraging the evil gymnastic art.

In 1592 the Frenchman Petrus Faber (Pierre du Favre or du Faur) wrote his *Agonisticon*, which is a 306-page account in Latin of the great Panhellenic festivals. A second edition followed in 1595. Like Mercuriale, Faber had indefatigably perused the extant literary sources from classical antiquity. In so doing he provides a complementary study to Mercuriale's treatise.[18]

Pace Mercuriale, Faber argues that contests like the Olympics are a kind of *ars gymnastica bellica*: they encourage military fitness. He writes, 'The Roman emperors, in part to please the populace, in part even for public usefulness ... decided to retain in the republic of the Roman world athletic games already established in Greece of old before the time of Plato himself, in order that, through many exercises of this manner, young men might become quicker and faster for war.'[19] He cites with approval a Roman imperial edict which exempted from civic duties athletes who had won three times in major sacred contests like the Olympic Games.[20]

Mercuriale seems to have read the *Agonisticon*, for he compliments the author, stating that he had read it 'with great profit', lauding the treatise as 'a work full of extraordinary knowledge', and he enthusiastically praises the author as 'the most delightfully learned man in all France'.[21] On the other hand, Mercuriale does not cease to characterise athletics as the *ars vitiosa* in the 1601 edition of *DAG*, the last before his death.

West sees his *Dissertation* as an improvement on the *Agonisticon*. He acknowledges his debt to Faber but with a qualification, stating that he has been 'assisted by the labours of a learned Frenchman, Pierre du Favre, who in his book entitled *Agonisticon*, hath gathered almost every thing that is mentioned in any of the Greek or Latin writers relating to the Grecian Games, which he has thrown together in no very clear order'. West adds, 'In this *Dissertation* I have endeavoured to give a complete history of the Olympic Games: of which kind there is not, that I know of, any treatise now extant; those written upon this subject by some of the ancients being all lost, and not being supplied by any modern, at least not so fully as might have been done, and as so considerable an article of the Grecian antiquities seemed to demand.'[22] West's criticisms of Faber are not unjustified. Indeed, on the title page Faber calls his work an *opus tessela-*

tum, a 'mosaic', and throughout he interweaves discussion of the ancient material with his fervent Christian pronouncements.[23] We can therefore attribute to West the first comprehensive and coherent history of the Olympic Games in modern times.

The musical world of Europe in the eighteenth century lends further context to West's achievement. In the early 1730s at the imperial court in Vienna, the poet Pietro Metastasio (1698-1782) composed *L'Olimpiade*, a pastoral romantic drama set at the ancient site and very loosely based on a passage in the fifth-century BCE historian Herodotus (6.126-31). Over the ensuing decades, 57 composers, the great majority Italian, wrote operas using Metastasio's text, beginning with Antonio Caldara, whose opera had its debut in Vienna in 1733.[24] In 1734 Antonio Vivaldi's *L'Olimpiade* was performed in Venice, and Giovanni Battista Pergolesi's followed in Rome in 1735. Of more relevance, a pasticcio version of Pergolesi's opera featuring the castrato soprano Angelo Maria Monticelli was performed in London in 1742 at the King's Theatre to much acclaim.[25] No evidence has come to light indicating that West attended the performance or knew of it. The same venue subsequently witnessed versions by other composers, including one, now lost, by the Englishman Thomas Arne (1710-78) which was performed on two nights in April 1765, nine years after West's death. Domenico Cimarosa's setting was performed in 1788 and 1789, as were pasticci by other composers between 1770 and 1780.[26]

Metastasio's libretto contains anachronisms and errors of fact concerning the ancient Olympics.[27] Unlike West, he was not primarily concerned with presenting a historically accurate account of the Games. Nevertheless, each in his own way serves as a bridge to the nineteenth-century movement to revive the Olympics, and the many operatic versions of *L'Olimpiade* together with the *Dissertation* provide a measure of the interest in the Olympics during the eighteenth century. Furthermore, each sees in the Olympics something more than mere sporting competitions. Metastasio's *L'Olimpiade* not only enhanced the 'image of majesty' of his Hapsburg patrons but also conveyed that image upon the Games themselves and thus enhanced their dignity. 'Prescient of Coubertin's athletic moral cosmology, *L'Olimpiade* is a chivalric story in which the noble values of patriotism, loyalty, filial love, honor, and the claims of community are verified and extolled.'[28] As will be seen below, West, in discussing 'The Utility of the Olimpick Games', promotes his own transcendent view of what the Olympics can be.

West's enthusiasm for the Olympic Games cannot of course be separated from his fondness for Pindar. As noted earlier, the *Dissertation* serves as the preface to his translations of the Greek poet, whom he describes effusively, 'Of all the great writers of antiquity, no one was ever more honoured and admired while living, as few have obtained a larger portion of fame after death, than Pindar.'[29] West may have inherited his love of Pindar from his father. Dr Johnson speculates: 'He was the son of the reverend Dr. West; perhaps him who published Pindar at Oxford about the beginning of this century.'[30] In 1697 the Oxford press had published an edition of Pindar co-edited by Richard West (1671-1716) and Robert Welsted (1670/71-1735). The paternal link is affirmed by the *Oxford Dictionary of National Biography*, which calls him the eldest son of Richard West.[31] Gilbert West attended Eton and Oxford. Unlike his younger brother, Vice-Admiral Temple West, he attained no comparable eminence in public life. He was, however, friendly with William Pitt the Elder and the poet George Lyttelton, a member of Parliament. They used to visit West at his Wickham estate in Kent, and to them West dedicated his translations of Pindar.

Another contemporary, no less than Sir Isaac Newton (1643-1727), is also cited by West. Like other learned men of his time, Newton had received a classical education. Although best known for his scientific and mathematical works, he also wrote extensively on myth, religion, and history.[32] Concerning the earliest Olympics and the adoption of four-year Olympiads, West refers to Newton's *The Chronology of Ancient Kingdoms Amended*, posthumously published in 1728. The *Chronology* consists of six chapters, of which the first is entitled 'Of the Chronology of the First Ages of the Greeks'.[33] Coincidentally, both Newton and West died on the same day, 20 March, in 1727 and 1756 respectively.

West had also read Mercuriale.[34] He may well be referring to Mercuriale's criticism of athletes when he remarks: 'There is still another prejudice against Pindar, which may rise in the minds of those people, who are not thoroughly acquainted with ancient history, and who may therefore be apt to think meanly of Odes, inscribed to a set of conquerors, whom possibly they may look upon only as so many prize fighters and jockeys. To obviate this prejudice, I have prefixed to my translation of Pindar's Odes a *Dissertation on the Olympick Games*: in which the reader will see what kind of persons these conquerors were, and what was the nature of those famous Games.'[35]

West's final chapter on the 'Utility of the Olympick Games' is by far the longest section, comprising one-fourth of the total length of the work. It is an extended attempt, *pace* Mercuriale, to make the case for the *ars gymnastica athletica*.

West echoes Faber in asserting that games like the Olympics, by offering rewards like exemption from public duties, can inspire young men to become more physically fit and thus better soldiers. West not only had referred to the law of Diocletian cited by Faber.[36] Like him he also mentions Plato's approval of gymnastic exercises: 'Of this Plato himself was so sensible, that he delivers it as his opinion that every well constituted republic ought, by offering prizes to the conquerors, to encourage all such exercises as tend to increase the strength and agility of the body, as highly useful in war.'[37] It is no accident that in this part of the *Dissertation*, West includes his translation of Lucian's *Anacharsis*, in which the character of

Solon states: 'You may be able to form some judgement to yourself, what sort of men they are to prove in arms, and fighting for their country, their wives, their children, and their gods, who for the sake of an olive or a laurel crown contend even naked with so much eagerness for the victory.'[38]

West, however, believes that the athletic art, beyond encouraging martial fitness, can also have moral or spiritual benefits. First, he claims that the Olympics encouraged morality because 'no one who was guilty of any flagrant or notorious crime, or who was depraved in his morals, could compete at Olympia'.[39] He also asserts that the Games, since the olive wreaths which were the prizes had no monetary value, would lead athletes to understand that honour and glory, not compensation, should be the reward for meritorious deeds.[40] Furthermore, the Games promoted 'concord and union' among the Greeks by providing them with a sense of their common nationality, by replacing armed conflict with sporting competitions, and by providing mediation for quarrels between Greek states.[41] Again, inasmuch as Olympia over the centuries had become the repository of public monuments, trophies, and dedications, it was a source of pride and inspiration to the Greeks as well as a means of historical instruction. Thus a Greek would be 'reminded of the glorious exploits of his ancestors and countrymen, and excited to imitate their virtues, in hopes of acquiring one day the like honour to himself and his country'.[42]

To the above advantages of holding Olympic Games, West adds yet another, the commercial and economic benefits. Here he hearkens back to the legendary King Iphitus of Elis who, according to Pausanias (5.4-5-6), at the behest of the Delphic Oracle, revived the Olympic Games in the eighth century BCE. West states that Iphitus

> ... also instituted a fair, to be held at Olympia at the same time; with a view, doubtless, of uniting the several people of Greece still closer to each other, in a friendly intercourse of mutual commerce, which can only flourish in times of peace; and which, by the many advantages it brings along with it, as well to the public as to the particular persons engaged in the various branches of trade, naturally tends to call off the attention of mankind from war and violence, and, what perhaps is still worse, the stupid and lazy indolence of an uncivilized and savage life, to the more pleasing methods of polishing and enriching themselves and their countries, by cultivating all the useful arts of civil and social industry.[43]

In his concluding paragraph, West proposes that the athletic gymnastic art can be useful to society as a whole, and to citizens of all classes and occupations:

> A wise and prudent governor of a state may dispose the people to such sports and diversions, as may render them more serviceable to the public; and that by impartially bestowing a few *honorary prizes* upon those, who should be found to excel in any *contest* he shall think proper to appoint, he may excite in the husbandman, the manufacturer, and the mechanic, as well as in the

soldier, and the sailor, and men of superior orders and professions, such an emulation, as may tend to promote industry, encourage trade, improve the knowledge and wisdom of mankind, and consequently make his country victorious in war, and in peace opulent, virtuous, and happy.[44]

West depicts a utopian vision of society in which the athletic gymnastic art plays an integral role. Far from being evil or perverse, it can be a force for good for society as a whole. By expounding on the widespread utility of the Olympic Games, West thus goes beyond Faber's limited argument that athletics can encourage military fitness and presents a more far-reaching refutation of Mercuriale's blanket condemnation of athletics. The modern Olympic movement, which sees the Games not simply as a sporting competition but as a means to promote world peace and international brotherhood and sisterhood, likewise embraces a wider view of the Games' potential.

Crucial to West's salutary athletic gymnastic art is the stipulation that the prizes be limited, or 'few' and 'honorary'. Following Galen (*To Thrasyboulos* 33) he believes that the gymnastic art became perverted shortly before the time of Plato when athletes, rather than exercising for health or military fitness, began to pursue physical training excessively in order to win valuable prizes and rewards. Physical training thus became an end in itself, a profession.[45] West adds that this abuse of athletics became 'vicious excess' under the Macedonian conquest in the fourth century and the Romans in the second, when 'the Greeks, lost together with their liberty, every sentiment of true virtue and glory, and were left to compete only for the prizes themselves'.[46] By means of this restriction on prizes, West intends to rescue athletics from Mercuriale's criticism.

West thus anticipates the amateurism of the modern Olympics, which, beginning in 1896, banned professionals for almost a century while espousing an anachronistic amateur ideal.[47] In Greek antiquity, there was no stigma attached to the collecting of valuable prizes in athletic competitions.[48] In the nineteenth century the hostility to professionals becomes intermingled with social elitism, which played no role in West's concept of the Olympics.[49] Since 1992 participation in the Olympics has been opened to all professionals, and we can only speculate what West would have thought of this decision.

A direct line thus runs from Mercuriale and Faber to West. Can we connect them, and especially West, to William Penny Brookes? At present there is no direct evidence indicating that Brookes had read those authors. Rather than being an antiquarian or scholar, Brookes lived his life in the public sphere. In 1841, he founded the Wenlock Agricultural Reading Society, which was a lending library open to local farmers. West's book was not in this library.[50]

Brookes had, however, studied medicine in Paris and Padua, and so must have read Latin.[51] Indeed, the *Oxford Dictionary of National Biogra-*

phy asserts: 'A polymath, Brookes was fluent in French, Greek, and Latin.'[52] The Padua connection is intriguing, both because Mercuriale had been a professor there in 1569, and because the 1601 and 1672 editions of *De Arte Gymnastica*, along with Faber's *Agonisticon*, are listed in the library catalogue as *libri antichi*, 'old books'. West's *Dissertation* is not listed in the Padua catalogue. Nevertheless, it was not a rarity in England, and was known, as we have seen, to Samuel Johnson and James Barry. Later editions of the *Dissertation* were published in 1753 and 1766, and it was also reprinted in 1824 to accompany a later prose translation of Pindar.[53]

There are, however, thematic similarities connecting Brookes to West. In 1850, as a branch of the Wenlock Agricultural Reading Society, Brookes founded the Wenlock Olympian Class (WOC) 'for the moral, physical and intellectual improvement of the inhabitants of the town and neighbourhood and especially of the working classes, by the encouragement of out-door recreation, and by the award of prizes annually at public meetings for skill in athletic exercises and proficiency in intellectual and industrial attainments.' Is there an echo of West in the references to 'moral … and intellectual improvement' and to 'proficiency in intellectual and industrial attainments'? The first of these 'public meetings for skill in athletic exercises' was the 1850 Much Wenlock Olympian Games. In 1860 the WOC was separated from the Wenlock Agricultural Reading Society and became the Wenlock Olympian Society, perhaps to better enable Brookes to pursue his expanding Olympic vision.[54] If Brookes had not read the *Dissertation*, he certainly shared West's view that athletics could foster benefits to society as a whole.

Indeed, Brookes' life was one of dedication to the well-being of his community. As a country doctor, he may have covered as much as seventy miles a day on horseback. He was a Justice of the Peace for forty years, and a Commissioner of Roads and Taxes. As Chairman of a gas company he was involved in bringing improved gas lights, and he also became a Director of the company which brought new rail lines to Much Wenlock. As a philanthropist he contributed most of the funding for the town Council Chamber. He advocated physical education in the schools.[55] The Wenlock Games are a natural extension of his concern for the well-being of all his fellow citizens, including the working classes. Whether Brookes had read West remains to be established. We can say, however, that whereas West wrote eloquently about the utilitarian features of the Olympic Games, Brookes was a man of action who actually implemented them.

In summary, between Robert Dover in the seventeenth century and William Penny Brookes in the nineteenth stands the eighteenth-century figure of Gilbert West, whose *Dissertation on the Olympick Games* was, when published, the best account of the subject. Against Mercuriale's condemnation of the athletic gymnastic art, including Panhellenic competitions like the Olympic Games, he not only repeats Petrus Faber's argument that athletics can be conducive to preparing the youth of the nation for military fitness but also enunciates a more expansive vision of an Olympics which can contribute much to the moral and spiritual welfare of society as a whole. It is a vision which he shares with Brookes, Coubertin, and the modern Olympic movement, even if the precise nature of West's influence, especially on Brookes, requires further study. The concept of a dignified, transcendent, even majestic Olympics is also one which is to be found in the eighteenth century in Metastasio's *L'Olimpiade*, even if at present we have no knowledge whether West was aware of the operatic versions or witnessed the 1742 London performance of the Pergolesi pasticcio.[56] Of West's connection to James Barry we have no doubt. The *Crowning of the Olympic Victors* in the Great Room of the Royal Society of the Arts is not only a visual realisation of a passage from West's *Dissertation* but also captures the spirit of the work. Rather than being confined to relative obscurity, Gilbert West deserves to be crowned among England's Olympic champions.

I wish to thank Chris Cannon and Helen Cromarty of the Wenlock Olympian Society for their helpful responses to my inquiries. Their gracious assistance in no way implies agreement with the points made in this paper, and any errors are my own responsibility.

Notes

1. An initial version of this paper entitled 'Gilbert West and the Revival of the Olympic Ideal' was presented at the 8th International Conference of the European Committee for Sport History on 27 August 2003, in Olympia, Greece, and subsequently published in the conference proceedings; see Lee 2004.

2. The complete title is *Odes of Pindar, With several other Pieces in Prose and Verse, Translated from the Greek. To which is prefixed a Dissertation on the Olympick Games*. It should be noted that West employed Roman numerals for the page numbers in the *Dissertation*, Arabic for the pages of the translations. For all page references to the *Dissertation* in this paper, I have converted the Roman numerals into Arabic. The *Dissertation* is itself preceded by a preface of 21 unnumbered pages. The translations of Pindar total 121 pages, making them less than half the length of the *Dissertation*. In addition to the Pindaric odes, West also provides translations of Horace, *Odes* 4.4; Euripides, *Iphigenia in Tauris*; Lucian, *The Triumphs of the Gout*; *Apollonius Rhodius*, selections from the *Argonauticks* (*sic*), namely the *Song of Orpheus* and the *Setting out of the Argo*, and the *Story of Phineus*; *The Hymn of Cleanthes*; and Plato, *Menexenus*. The translations, including Pindar, comprise 315 pages. In the *Dissertation*, 156-80, West also translates Lucian's *Anacharsis*.

3. The portrait, a line engraving by Edward Smith (active 1823-51) after an unknown artist, is accessible from the website of the National Portrait Gallery, London, 2009, accessed 27 August 2010: http://www.npg.org.uk/collections/search/largerimage.php?sText=West%2C+gilbert&submitSearchTerm_x=0&submitSearchTerm_y=0&search=ss&OConly=true&firstRun=true&LinkID=mp60617&role=sit&rNo=0.

4. Johnson, *Lives of the English Poets*, vol. 3, 328-33. For the assessment of West's translation of *Olympian* 1, see 332.

5. For book-length treatments of the Dover Games, see both Whitfield and Ruehl 1975. A more concise account can be found in Ruehl 2004: 4-5, 14.

6. Both the Cotswold and Much Wenlock Games maintain websites. For Robert Dover's Cotswold Olimpicks, accessed 27 August 2010, see http://www.olimpick-games.co.uk/. For the Wenlock Olympian Games, see the website of the Wenlock Olympian Society, accessed 26 August 2010, at http://www.wenlock-olympian-society.org.uk/. I have not seen Neumüller's diploma thesis, *Die Geschichte der Much Wenlock Games 1850-1895*.

7. Ruehl 2004: 8-11, 14; Young 1996a: 8-12, 24-41. See also Challis in this volume.

8. Young 1996a: 8-12, 59-62, 70-95, 121-2, 168-9. See also Anthony 2004 for the correspondence between Coubertin and Brookes.

9. Gardiner, *Greek Athletic Sports and Festivals* (1910), *Olympia* (1925) and *Athletics of the Ancient World* (1930); Harris, *Greek Athletes and Athletics* (1968) and *Sport in Greece and Rome* (1972).

10. Krause's works on athletics include his *Theagenes* (1835), *Olympia* (1838), *Die Pythien, Nemeen und Isthmien* (1841a), and *Die Gymnastik und Agonistik der Hellenen* (1841b). See Gardiner (1910) vii and x for his comments on Krause, and 511 for his reference to West.

11. West 1749: 29-52. The mural is the subject of the next chapter in this volume, entitled 'James Barry's *Crowning the Victors at Olympia*: Transmitting the Values of the Classical Olympic Games into the Modern Era' by William Pressly. The murals can be viewed online in a panorama, accessed 24 September 2010, at http://www.willpearson.co.uk/virtual_tours/james_barry/james_barry-001.php?format=fpp

12. The English translations of Xenophanes, Euripides, and Galen are readily available in Miller 2004a: 173-4, 182-3.

13. The first edition actually bears the title *Artis Gymnasticae apud Antiquos Celeberrimae Nostris Temporibus Ignoratae Libri Sex*. In the second and later editions, the title becomes *De Arte Gymnastica Libri Sex*. References here are taken from Mercuriale 2008.

14. Mercuriale 2008: 2-7. The dedication is made in the second edition of 1573. In the first edition of 1569 the dedicatee had been Cardinal Alessandro Farnese, Mercuriale's patron in Rome to whom he also served as a physician; see 781-4 for the Latin text.

15. Mercuriale 2008: 170-85.

16. Mercuriale 2008: 248-9, cites Pindar fragment 148 (= Athenaeus Epitome 1.40.22B). References to the *scholia* are to be found on 280-1, 292-3, and 340-1.

17. Sandys 1964: 98, 104.

18. For a catalogue of references to the Olympic Games from 393 to 1896 CE, see Lennartz 1974, to which should be added a Byzantine reference discovered by Decker 2008. Lennartz also does not mention either Petrus Faber or Natalis Comes (Natale Conti), who, in his *Mythologiae*, 131-4, first published in 1567, gives a brief account of the Olympic, Pythian, Isthmian, and Nemean Games.

19. Faber 1592: 4. The translation from the original Latin is mine.

20. Faber 1592: 2, 4. The edict is a rescript of the Emperors Diocletian and Maximian, preserved in the *Codex Justinianus* X.54.1.

21. Mercuriale 2008: 138-9. The new 2008 edition is based on that of 1601.

22. West 1749, the twelfth and thirteenth (unnumbered) pages of the Preface

to the *Dissertation* and translations. For other references to Faber, see 115, 116, 120, 128, 132, 135, and 190. In this and subsequent quotations from West, I have eliminated the more frequent capitalisation of nouns which was a feature of eighteenth-century orthography.

23. See also the criticisms of Faber in Krause 1835: xvii-xx.

24. For a list of the composers who used Metastasio's libretto of *L'Olimpiade*, see Sadie 1992: 356 under the entry 'Metastasio, Pietro'; for Caldara's version, 662-3.

25. Sadie 1992: 663 under the entry 'Olimpiade, L' (ii)'. See also the entry 'Monticelli, Angelo Maria', 1992: 455, which states: 'Monticelli had a lyric, agile voice and was a great actor, praised by Burney, Walpole and others. He was responsible for much of the popular dispersion of Pergolesi's *L'Olimpiade*, whose arias for Megacles he often sang.'

26. See Segrave 2005: 7-13 for an excellent account of Metastasio's libretto and the various composers who set it to music. For performances of *L'Olimpiade* in London, see 2005: 9-12; on 25 n. 93 there is an interesting discussion, including a comment by Charles Burney (1726-1814), concerning the apparent lack of success of Arne's version.

Complete CD sets of Vivaldi's *L'Olimpiade* exist: on the Naive label conducted by Rinaldo Alessandrini with the Concerto Italiano orchestra, and on Nuova Era by the Clemencic Consort (no libretto provided). A DVD of Baldassare Galuppi's version of 1747 is available on the Dynamic Italy label with Andrea Marcon conducting the Venice Baroque Orchestra. A three-CD set of Pergolesi's *L'Olimpiade* with the Academia Montis Regalis conducted by Alessandro De Marchi is now available on the Sony BMG label.

27. Lee 2003b: 167-8.

28. Segrave 2005: 13; also 2010: 118.

29. West, the unnumbered first page of the Preface to the *Dissertation* and translations.

30. Johnson 1968 vol. 3: 328.

31. Wilson 2005, 'Gilbert West'.

32. Manuel 1963: 1-64.

33. West 1749: 6, 10, 28, 29.

34. West 1749: 155.

35. West, the unnumbered twelfth page of the *Preface* to the *Dissertation* and translations.

36. West 1749: 150.

37. West 1749: 181.

38. West 1749: 178.

39. West 1749: 191-2. See, however, Young 1984: 73-4 n. 70, who states, 'There was absolutely nothing in the Olympic regulations about athletes being "irreproachable personally" ... Nor is there any ancient source for the notion that Olympic athletes were required to be "without a criminal record".' I should add that Young here is not addressing West, but rather later scholars and proponents of the Olympic movement.

40. West 1749: 193-5.

41. West 1749: 197-202.

42. West 1749: 205.

43. West 1749: 202-3.

44. West 1749: 206. The italics are West's.

45. See West 1749: 183-6, 192. The reference to Galen is on 184; he uses the word 'profession' on 184-5.

46. See West 1749: 184 and 191 for his criticism of athletics as a profession, and 186 for the decline into 'vicious excess' after the Macedonian and Roman conquests.

47. See Segrave 2005: 8, and Lee 2003a, especially 15-16; I am mistaken when I state, 16, that West does not mention Mercuriale.

48. For the 'myth of amateurism' in the modern Olympics, see Young 1984, who, however, does not discuss West.

49. Young 1996a: 30-41, 45-7, 87-8, 92, 99, 107, 130-1, 141, 154, vividly recounts how the socially elitist form of amateurism evolved and then became a part of the modern Olympic movement.

50. Chris Cannon, archivist of the Wenlock Olympian Society, informs me that in the Wenlock Agricultural Society's catalogue of books compiled by Brookes, West's book is not listed.

51. Brookes was not enrolled as a student at the University of Padua but studied 'beside' it, and in all likelihood had access to the library, as Helen Cromarty of the Much Wenlock Society informs me.

52. Cromarty 2004, 'Brookes, W.P.'

53. *The Odes of Pindar in English Prose, with Explanatory Notes: to Which Is Added West's Dissertation on the Olympic Games, in Two Volumes* (Oxford: Munday and Slatter, 1824). The translator's name is not given.

54. Young 1996a: 8-9. 28. To be consistent with modern conventions, I have, in the quotations from Brookes, eliminated his more frequent capitalisation of nouns and adjectives.

55. Drury 2007-8: 24-5.

56. Concerts featuring the entire opera or selections from different versions of *L'Olimpiade* took place in Montreal before the 1976 Olympics, and in Athens in 2003 as a prelude to the Games of 2004; see Segrave 2005: 17-18. It goes without saying that neither city has London's eighteenth-century links to the opera.

Fig. 7.1. James Barry, *Crowning the Victors at Olympia*, 1777-84. Oil on canvas, 11 ft. 10 in. x 42 ft., Royal Society of Arts, London.

122

James Barry's *Crowning the Victors at Olympia*: Transmitting the Values of the Classical Olympic Games into the Modern Era

William Pressly

James Barry's mural *Crowning the Victors at Olympia* (Fig. 7.1) is the first major, modern depiction of the Olympic Games.[1] Barry, an Irish painter who was born in Cork on October 11, 1741, began this picture in 1777 as part of a larger series. In that year he undertook to decorate the Great Room of the Society for the Encouragement of Arts, Manufactures, and Commerce, which three years earlier had moved into its new building in the Adelphi, London, constructed by the Scottish architect Robert Adam. The artist demanded and received complete control over the subject matter, creating six murals he entitled *A Series of Pictures on Human Culture* (1777-84). These six works form an almost continuous band around the walls of the room. Each is approximately 12 feet high; four are 15 feet wide; and the remaining two measure an impressive 42 feet in length. The first three paintings are devoted to Greek civilisation. The series begins on the west wall with a painting of Orpheus instructing a savage people. The next stage of Greek civilisation depicted is *A Grecian Harvest-Home*, showing the benefits of an agrarian society. The 42-foot-long painting *Crowning the Victors at Olympia*, which occupies the entire length of the north wall, provides the grand climax to this depiction of the advancement of Greek culture. The two works on the east wall, *The Triumph of the Thames* and *The Distribution of Premiums at the Society of Arts*, are concerned with aspects of contemporary British civilisation, while the series closes with *Elysium and Tartarus*, another monumental painting which is opposite *Crowning the Victors at Olympia*.[2] *Crowning the Victors*, however, was from the beginning intended as the room's primary focus: it was the first work one saw on entering the room, and as can be seen in the Pugin and Rowlandson print (Fig. 7.2), the Society's president sat beneath this mural with all the seats facing in this direction.

In gazing on the mural, the room's occupants witness an idealised version of a procession of the victors at the Olympic Games with its protagonists drawn from different periods. Two painted statues flank the

Fig. 7.2. *The Great Room of the Society of Arts*, designed and engraved by A.C. Pugin and T. Rowlandson, aquatint by J. Bluck. Hand coloured etching and aquatint, from R. Ackermann's *Microcosm of London*, vol. 3, 1809, Yale Center for British Art, New Haven.

entire composition, with Hercules trampling the serpent of envy on the left and Minerva on the right, representatives of physical virtue and mental excellence. Barry cites as his textual source Gilbert West's book *Odes of Pindar, with ... a Dissertation on the Olympick Games*, first published in 1749 with new editions appearing in 1753 and 1766. The artist introduces himself at the lower left in the character of the Greek painter Timanthes, holding his recreation of Timanthes' painting of the satyrs approaching a sleeping cyclops as described by Pliny. Hiero of Syracuse is the winner of the chariot race, and he is accompanied by Pindar, who sings of Hiero's glory. Next comes the winner of the horse race. The procession itself turns around one of the stadium pillars, inscribed with the Greek word 'ΑΡΙΣΤΕΥΕ', which West had translated as courage.[3]

Farther to the right is the painting's principal focus, showing the former victor, Diagoras of Rhodes, being carried on the shoulders of his sons. A little over a decade earlier, J.J. Winckelmann had written in his *Thoughts on the Imitation of Greek Works in Painting and Sculpture*, 'To be like the God-like Diagoras*, was the fondest wish of every youth'.[4] Pindar's *Seventh Olympic Ode* celebrating Diagoras' victory in the cestus [boxing] was held

7. *James Barry's* Crowning the Victors at Olympia

Fig. 7.3. James Barry, *The Diagorides Victors at Olympia*, 1792. Etching and engraving, British Museum, London.

'in such Esteem among the Ancients, that it was deposited in a Temple of *Minerva*, written in Letters of Gold'.[5] Fittingly for the painting's theme, physical prowess is reverenced within a temple for the goddess of wisdom. Barry, however, does not show Diagoras' moment of victory but that of two of his sons. Although he compresses the action by introducing the showering of flowers on the victors upon their approach to the judges, he chooses the following moment as described by Gilbert West: 'This venerable *Conqueror* [Diagoras the Rhodian] is said to have accompanied his two Sons, *Acusilaus* and *Damagetus,* to the *Olympick Games*, in which the young Men coming off victorious, *Acusilaus* in the *Cœstus*, and *Damagetus* in the *Pancratium* [boxing and wrestling], took their Father on their Shoulders, and carried him as it were in Triumph along the *Stadium*, amid the Shouts and Acclamations of the Spectators; who poured Flowers on him as he passed, and hailed him happy in being the Father of such Sons.'[6] This moment was so central to the painting's meaning that *The Diagorides Victors at Olympia* became the title for the artist's 1792 print reproducing the painting (Fig. 7.3).

In his notes to Pindar's ode, West offers an even lengthier account of this moment, one which is indebted to Pierre Bayle's *The Dictionary Historical and Critical of Mr. Peter Bayle*:

Mr. *Bayle* in his Dictionary has an Article upon this *Diagoras*, in which he relates from *Pausanias* a famous Story of him, *viz.* That *Diagoras* having attended his Two Sons *Damagetus* and *Acusilaus* to the *Olympick* Games, and both the young Men having been proclaimed Conquerors, he was carried on the Shoulders of his Two victorious Sons through the midst of that great Assembly of the *Greeks*, who showered down Flowers upon him as he passed along, congratulating him upon the Glory of his Sons. Some Authors (adds Mr. *Bayle*) say, he was so transported upon this Occasion, that he died of Joy. But this Account he rejects as false, for Reasons which may be seen at large in the Notes upon this Article. *Tully* and *Plutarch*, alluding to this Story of

125

Fig. 7.4. James Barry, *Detail of the Diagorides Victors* (1795), state III with inscription, *c.* 1798-1800. Etching and engraving, British Museum, London.

Diagoras, add, that a *Spartan* coming up to him said, 'Now die, *Diagoras*, for thou canst not climb to Heaven.' Which Mr. *Bayle* paraphrases in this Manner: 'You are arrived, *Diagoras*, at the highest Pitch of Glory you can aspire to, for you must not flatter yourself, that if you lived longer you should ascend to Heaven. Die then, that you may not run the Risk of a Fall.' Which is certainly the meaning of this famous Saying of the *Spartan*.[7]

This Spartan, an old man in shadow who stands on tiptoe in his red-strap sandals, grasps Diagoras' right hand while showering him with flowers with his left.

7. *James Barry's* Crowning the Victors at Olympia

Diagoras had three sons who won Olympic crowns,[8] although only two of them are shown supporting him on their shoulders. The young man to the left of this group is surely the third son, who, while throwing flowers with one hand, touches his brother's hand with the other. Diagoras' grandson Pisidorus also was to be an Olympic victor,[9] and the boy at the right of the group is he, Barry asserting in his description to the print detail of 1795 (Fig. 7.4) that three generations are present in his sculpturesque grouping of the Diagorides: 'These Diagorides afford a subject of such peculiar felicity for a group in sculpture, that I have often complimented myself by supposing that there must have been (notwithstanding the silence of Pausanias) something like those of mine set up in the Altis at Olympia; the characters of the men in their different stages of life – father, sons, and grandsons, such a race of heroes, where the naked occurred with such peculiar propriety, and so gloriously connected with ethics, and with all the duties of the good citizen, that I can recollect nothing remaining of the ancients, where the subject matter is more exemplary, more impregnated with the unction, spirit, and *venustas* [grace], which are the inseparable characteristics of Grecian genius.'[10] This 'race of heroes' is not based on an exceptional gene pool but rather on the inculcation of the highest ethical standards, the promotion of virtuous conduct to which all can aspire.

At the right, a lesser judge crowns the winner of the foot race while handing him a palm with the three enthroned, principal judges looking on. Behind the winner of the footrace is the winner of the armed foot race, whom a bandaged opponent is congratulating. Barry emphasises all of these athletes' physical beauty, a visual testament to the Greek ideal uniting beauty and moral understanding. In his composition Barry follows West's description of the moment when each victor is recognised: 'The *Conquerors* being summoned by Proclamation, marched in Order to the Tribunal of the *Hellanodicks*, where a *Herald*, taking the *Crowns* of *Olive* from the Table, placed one upon the Head of each of the *Conquerors*; and giving into their Hands *Branches* of *Palm*, led them in that Equipage along the *Stadium*, preceded by *Trumpets*, proclaiming at the same Time with a loud Voice, their Names, the Names of their Fathers, and their Countries; and specifying the particular *Exercise* in which each of them had gained the Victory.'[11] Barry, following West's lead, writes of the victors being crowned with olive, but in the painting the crowns appear closer to laurel, an even more common classical symbol of victory and one that also celebrates Apollonian creativity. West offers an explanation, based on Plutarch, of the meaning of the palms: they represent, 'the unsuppressive Vigour of their [the victors'] Minds and Bodies, evidenced in their getting the better of their *Antagonists*; and surmounting all Opposition, like those Plants, whose Property it was, according to the Opinion of the Ancients, to rise and flourish under the greatest Weights, and against all Endeavours to bend or keep them down.'[12]

127

Pockets of spectators give witness to Greek intellectual achievements. Between the rearing horse and the group of Diagorides victors appears a cluster of celebrated intellectuals, all drawn from Athens' glorious past. The most prominent, with his left arm raised, is the Athenian statesman Pericles, to whom Barry has given the features of the late William Pitt, the Earl of Chatham, Britain's great statesman. Pericles is in conversation with Cimon, the general and statesman who had been his opponent. Between them are two heads, and the older of the two is perhaps the philosopher Anaxagoras, who looks to Pericles, one of his pupils. The Athenian comedic playwright Aristophanes is seen between Pericles' head and upraised arm, mocking the head's inordinate length. The first figure in the group to the right of Pericles is presumably the tragedian Euripides. At the far right of this group stands a pensive Socrates with his arms folded beneath his toga. The boy next to him, unidentified in the artist's text, is probably Plato, Socrates' most famous pupil.

A highlighted line of spectators recedes between the lesser judges and the scribe. The first is the Greek philosopher Philolaus with a scroll depicting his speculation on the solar system. He is followed by the Greek physician Hippocrates and the melancholy philosopher Democritus, who is also known as the laughing philosopher, here his slight smile exposing his bottom row of teeth. After naming this third figure, Barry concludes with an etcetera. It seems unlikely that he simply became bored with naming the participants but rather invites the viewer to project his or her own list of worthies, forcing one to interact with the painting rather than passively receiving the artist's choices. Behind the scribe registering the Olympiads is the historian Herodotus, who is most famous for his histories of the Greco-Persian wars, battles from which are commemorated on the throne. Herodotus is in shadow, head on hand, and the scroll with his name rests at the feet of the principal judges, his right hand lightly touching it.

The impressive marble base of the judges' throne has ornate relief carvings. Along the bottom are palm trees, between which are smoking altars flanked by amphorae. Each tree supports a shield with the names in Greek of three major military victories, which, from left to right, are Marathon (490 BCE), Thermopylae (480 BCE), and Salamis (480 BCE). In contrast to the others, this last was a naval victory, and Barry introduces a ship's prow behind the palm supporting the shield. Winged Victories holding wreaths gracefully ascend to the front of the throne decorated with a cartouche presumably intended for an inscription. Above the Victories are facing portrait medallions of Solon, the great lawgiver of Athens, and Lycurgus, of Sparta. In Barry's account, their names are followed by another etcetera, and there is an unseen medallion that continues on the throne behind the column. Since a similar arrangement is presumably to be found on the other side of the throne, there are still more opportunities for naming.

7. *James Barry's* Crowning the Victors at Olympia

Gilbert West describes how the Olympic Games demonstrate that sports can serve a public good. He argues that the nature of the contests can be expanded with prizes bestowed on those who excel in a wide variety of endeavours such as agriculture, manufacture, the armed services, and the professions, leading to the promotion of the national welfare.[13] Like West, Barry sees the games as offering the optimal social institution for promoting excellence. Despite the strife that competition engenders, the judges ensure that the playing field remains a level one, with only the truly deserving being rewarded. In addition, the occasion fosters a strong sense of community. In the background, the sacrificial procession proceeding toward the Temple of Jupiter gives witness to the importance of religion and ritual within this structured system. Public rather than private interests are being served.

Barry's depiction celebrates factors that are part of the modern Olympic Games, at least in terms of its aspirations. He embraces the concept of the purity of sport which rewards discipline and dedication within prescribed rules. He too lionises the idealised male form that can result from intensive training, although, as was the case with many of his contemporaries, his is an androgynous conception. Seeing the games as a promoter of unity, he of course opposes any notion that they offer a measurement for the success or failure of competing political ideologies, and the commercialisation of sports never entered his head. But in adding up the score as to those qualities that Barry perceives in the Olympic Games and their presence or absence in the modern version, there is a glaring difference, one that is the primary subject of this essay.

In the early eighteenth century, the French historian Charles Rollin pointed out for the general public the close association between classical sporting events and religion: 'Games and combats made a part of the religion, and had a share in almost all the festivals of the ancients.'[14] The Olympic Games were the most important of four Panhellenic games, the others being the Delphian, Isthmian, and Nemean. However, the Great Panathenaic Festival, held in Athens, was unofficially on their same level.[15] All these games (and there were numerous other minor ones throughout Greece) were centred on religious worship, the athletic contests being performed in the gods' honour, and this religious dimension pervaded all parts of the festivals, including the elaborate processions, the athletic competitions, and the sacrifices. Underlying the procession depicted by Barry in *Crowning the Victors at Olympia* is more than a hint of the Panathenaic Procession as depicted in the sculpture of the Parthenon: in his mural the procession at Olympia is conflated with that of Athens. The direction of the procession from west to east is the same as that of the Parthenon frieze, where the twin processions both begin at the temple's southwest corner, one moving eastward along the south side to turn the corner to end in the centre of the east side and the other proceeding along the west side to turn eastward along the north side to end again above the centre of the eastern entrance. Barry's rearing horseman also echoes elements of the graceful cavalcade in the Parthenon frieze, even if the horse's attenuated foreleg and the rider's long, wavy hair are Barry's own invention. Then too the artist gives Pericles, the instigator of the building of the Parthenon, a prominent position, and Pericles' pointing upward directs one's attention to the procession accompanying the sacrificial bull, another recurring motif contained in the Parthenon frieze. Finally, Minerva appears twice in the mural, most prominently in the 'statue' on the right, where she is in full armour as Minerva Polias, the same type as in Phidias' grand statue in the cella of the Parthenon. This is how she appeared when she sprang from the head of Jupiter, the subject of the sculpture on the Parthenon's eastern pediment. Her other appearance in the mural is on the side of Hiero's chariot, where the subject is the naming of Athens, the same subject of the sculptural decoration on the Parthenon's western pediment. The Parthenon's religious solemnity and noble grandeur informs Barry's design.[16]

At the same time he was executing his mural, Barry was also intimately involved in another attempt to 'recreate' a classical game in London. His close friend Giuseppe Baretti was doing the same thing in another venue.[17] Baretti had hit on the idea of commissioning music for performances of Horace's *Carmen Seculare*,[18] which the Latin poet had composed for the Secular Games held by the Emperor Augustus in 17 BCE. The meaning of 'secular' in this context requires explanation, as this festival, which over a three-day period consisted of sacrifices, performances, and athletic competitions, was profoundly sacred in nature. Baretti himself offers clarification:

> *Carmen Seculare* means a Poem, or a Song, made at the beginning of a *Seculum*; that is, of a Century, to hail it in auspiciously. It was the custom of the Romans to celebrate the foundation of their city at the beginning of every century by a great festival; in which, among a variety of games and diversions, a Song was introduced, made in honour of Apollo and Diana, the tutelar Deities of their town, to implore a continuance of their favour and protection. The Song was sung in a temple dedicated to those Deities, by seven and twenty boys, and as many girls, all born of their noblest families.
>
> The recurrence of a new century happened to fall in the reign of Augustus, who built a temple on the Palatine-Hill for the purpose of that festival, and ordered Horace to compose the Song.[19]

Baretti required time to find a suitable composer, finally settling on the Frenchman François-André Danican Philidor with the London performances being held at the Freemasons' Hall on 26 February, 5 and 12 March 1779. Thus during those years Barry was considering his recreation of the Olympic Games, Baretti was considering his of the Secular Games, and the two friends surely discussed at length their related projects, each fuelling the passion of the other and sharpening their perceptions of the value of these recreations to modern culture.

130

Fig. 7.5. James Barry, *Ticket of Admission for Horace's 'Carmen Seculare'*, 1779. Etching, Royal Academy of Arts.

Barry was even directly involved in Baretti's project, executing for his friend the ticket of admission (Fig. 7.5). Horace's poet opens with the injunction, 'STAND off, ye Vulgar', and Barry's image is remarkable for its compression of the foreground, denying the viewer easy access and thereby keeping him or her at a respectful distance. The poet himself is the administering 'priest'. His inscribed bust is backed by a slanting architectural feature bearing the print's title, beyond which is seen a simplified version of the Pantheon and in the distance the Temple of Apollo on the Palatine Hill. Above in the clouds the primary deities addressed in the poem, Diana and Apollo, are portrayed in intense concentration: they are

William Pressly

not so much Horace's inspiration as they are the poet's creation, appearing like a thought balloon above his head. One is again reminded of the hymn's opening stanza, which bears the title '*The* POET *to the* PEOPLE':

> STAND off, ye Vulgar, nor profane,
> With bold, unhallow'd Sounds, this festal Scene:
> In Hymns, inspir'd by Truth divine,
> I Priest of the melodious Nine,
> To Youths and Virgins sing the mystic Strain.[20]

Higher still in Barry's print is Apollo's sun chariot, with four women, representations of Hours or of the Seasons, harnessing the horses. The women in relief on the chariot itself (only four can be seen) may be intended for the Nine Muses. Barry's print is an image of Horace as a potent cultural hero, not just a celebrant at a sacred festival but a shaper of mystic values that the profane hold in awe.

Barry also links the Roman Secular Games with his depiction of the Greek Olympic Games. In the case of the ticket of admission, the image is framed in the same palm fronds, references to eternity, that not only permeate the mural but also originally surmounted each of the pictures (see Fig. 7.2), an important decorative motif that did not survive nineteenth-century alterations.[21] Furthermore, in the mural the chorus of young boys accompanying Pindar on his lyre harks back to Horace's hymn. The viewer witnesses here Barry's version of Baretti's and Philidor's boy-chorus performing Horace's sacred song in the Freemasons' Hall. Both Baretti's version of the Secular Games and Barry's of the Olympic Games have something to teach the modern audience about sacred, communal values and the important role played by creative men in advancing civilisation's highest goals.

While the ethos of classical religion animates the spirit of Barry's mural, the artist was also concerned with the Christian tradition that borrowed from the classical games the idea that the athlete possesses a religious dimension. In his First Epistle to the Corinthians, the Apostle Paul had made the analogy between pagan contests and the Christian's journey through this world, when he compared the crowning of the winner of the footrace and the crowning of the boxer or pancratist to that of a Christian victor:

> Know ye not that they which run in a race run all, but one receiveth the prize? So run, that ye may obtain.
> And every man that striveth for the mastery is temperate in all things. Now they *do it* to obtain a corruptible crown; but we an incorruptible.
> I therefore so run, not as uncertainly; so fight I, not as one that beateth the air: But I keep under my body, and bring *it* into subjection: lest that by any means, when I have preached to others, I myself should be a castaway.
> (1 Corinthians 9:24-7)

132

In his history, Rollin refers to Paul's analogy, but he goes on to point out how Tertullian, an early church father, had extended it to apply as well to martyrs:

> St. Paul, by an allusion to the Athletæ, exhorts the Corinthians, near whose city the Isthmian games were celebrated, to a sober and penitent life. *Those who strive*, says he, *for the mastery, are temperate in all things: Now they do it to obtain a corruptible crown, but we an incorruptible.* Tertullian uses the same thought to encourage the martyrs. He makes a comparison from what the hopes of victory made the Athletæ endure. He repeats the severe and painful exercises they were obliged to undergo; the continual anguish and constraint, in which they passed the best years of their lives; and the voluntary privation which they imposed upon themselves, of all that was most affecting and grateful to their passions.[22]

For St Paul and Tertullian, the spiritual values embodied in classical games also illuminate the course and conduct of the Christian life.

One could not only look to the traditional analogy between the classical athlete of virtue and the committed Christian, but Gilbert West also provides an extended comparison between the Olympic Games and the foundations of the Roman Catholic Church. After mentioning how 'the great Dignity and Authority of the *Hellanodicks* was founded solely upon this Power of Excommunication', he writes, 'Whether the Thunders of the *Vatican* [i.e. the power of excommunication] were forged in Imitation of those of *Olympian Jupiter*, I will not determine; tho' I must take notice, that many of the Customs and Ordinances of the *Roman* Church allude most evidently to many practised in the *Olympick Stadium*, as *Extreme Unction*, the *Palm*, and the *Crown* of Martyrs, and others; which may be seen at large in *Faber's Agonisticon*.'[23] In citing Petrus Faber's sixteenth-century book *Agonisticon*, West is at pains to ground his observation within a larger Renaissance tradition. In citing West as his source, Barry in his turn signals his awareness of this argument that the Olympic Games could be interpreted as having laid the foundations for the Catholic Church. A closer look at the artist's imagery places it squarely within this tradition.

Barry's interpretation of the lesser judge handing a palm to the foremost victor at the same time he places a laurel crown on his head alludes to the imagery of Italian Baroque art, inspired by the Counter-Reformation, where martyrs are frequently shown being awarded palms and crowns. Nicolas Poussin's well-known *Martyrdom of St. Erasmus* (Fig. 7.6), executed for St Peter's Basilica in 1628-29, is one such example, where an angel hovers overhead holding a palm branch and a laurel crown.[24] It is no accident that one of the artist's preparatory studies for his athletes was in the twentieth century misidentified as an Ecce Homo, an identification that, while technically incorrect, gets to the heart of his conception.[25] In addition, in the mural by facing the crown or chaplet

133

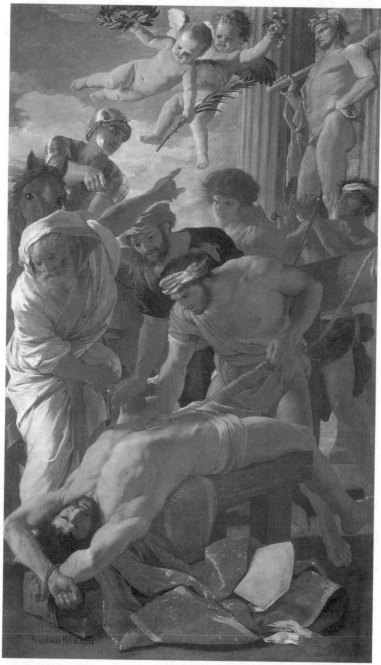

Fig. 7.6. Nicolas Poussin, *The Martyrdom of St. Erasmus*, 1628-9. Oil on canvas, Pinacoteca, Vatican.

134

downwards, Barry differentiates it from the laurel crown Pindar wears as a poet.

In his writings as well as his art, Barry connects Olympic practices with Catholic ones, extending the analogies made by Gilbert West. On two occasions, first in 1793 and again in 1798, he makes comparisons between the sacred territory of the Eleans, where the games were held, and the papal territories.[26] The same 'truce of God' that had protected those who participated in the Olympic Games, regardless of which Greek states might then be at war, should extend to the Pope's domains. For him, the papal government, modelled on Olympic practices, was that modern institution that could best humanise society in its unparalleled success in the promotion of the arts. He makes explicit the continuity between this classical culture and the Catholic one in his later print detail focusing on Diagoras (see Fig. 7.4). The following is the English translation of the print's Italian inscription: 'This group of Diagoras and his children taken like a little bouquet of flowers from the painting of the Olympic victories and in testimony of the deepest and most affectionate veneration and thanks is painted to adorn the exemplary and triumphant course of the papal government of Rome, mother and gracious protectrice of the praiseworthy creative arts by James Barry.'

Stepping back and viewing the composition as a whole, the full extent of Barry's bold scheme becomes clear: in terms of the Christian narrative the classical procession is to be seen as a papal progress. Such a connection between Olympic and papal processions would have come naturally to him in light of West's linkage of Olympic rituals with Catholic ones. The pope carried in his *sedia* is the central motif for numerous illustrations of papal processions, and little imagination is required to associate images such as that of Pope Gregory XI (Fig. 7.7) being carried along in his *sedia* supported by graceful attendants with that of Diagoras borne aloft by his sons.[27] There is also a close visual analogy between Barry's Diagoras borne in triumph on his sons' shoulders and Pope Julius II in Raphael's Vatican fresco *The Expulsion of Heliodorus*, where the pope is supported in his *sedia* by young male attendants, one of whom is no less than Raphael himself (Fig. 7.8). Given Barry's constant citing of the Vatican frescoes as the closest forerunner of his own attempt, he intends the viewer to make this connection.

Barry's inscription in the margin of his 1792 print (see Fig. 7.3) records that Diagoras was descended from a still greater antecedent: 'The famous Diagoras of Rhodes carried on the shoulders of his two Victorious Sons amidst the joy & exultations of the Nations assembled at Oly[m]pia. Pausanias relates that this illustrious family the Diagorides were descended from ARISTOMENES the Messenian, whose whole life appears a brilliant texture of the noblest Services rendered to his Country & whom the Delphic Pythia pointed out as the best & most distinguished Man of all the Greeks.' In the classical narrative, Diagoras looks back to Aristome-

Fig. 7.7. Giorgio Vasari and Workshop, *Pope Gregory XI Returns to Rome from Avignon in 1376*, 1573. Fresco, ICCD/fondo fotografico, GFN E 73640, Sala Regia, Vatican.

nes; in the Christian narrative he looks back, as do all the popes, to St Peter. In one sense on entering the Great Room, the dominate focal point is Pope Diagoras, the Holy Father who is borne in triumph on the shoulders of his children, the sons of the Church.[28]

Within the long history of the games, the number of judges varied from one to a maximum of twelve, but no source gives the number as three.[29] Barry's three enthroned judges are no less than a reference to the Trinity: a commanding Christ is the principal figure and to the left (Christ's right)

136

Fig. 7.8. Raphael, *The Expulsion of Heliodorus*, 1511-14. Fresco, Stanza di
Eliodoro, Vatican.

is the white bearded profile of God the Father, while a sublimely pensive
Holy Spirit sits at the right. In the classical account, the central judge
instructs the attentive scribe to inscribe the victor's name into the Olympiad; in the Christian account, Christ directs that the saint's name be
recorded in the Book of Life. A reference to Christ appears as well in the
exact centre of both the painting and the 1792 print. This spot is occupied
by Socrates, who is frequently seen as a classical counterpart to Christ:
both died for the highest principles after refusing to reject the cup placed
to their lips. Again, in *Crowning*, Barry discreetly embeds another hidden
Christian analogy. Although Socrates/Christ's placement is central, his
presence is still understated: in terms of modern life his importance and
centrality are, as here, too often and too easily overlooked.

The procession of the Olympic Games, which brings together all of
Greece, transforms into the establishment of its heir, the Roman Catholic
Church, which, in the modern world, is that institution that can best unite
all mankind. The Olympic Games established a model in terms of both
physical and mental pursuits for a meritocracy in which the games' judges,
by ensuring the promotion of excellence, prevented the envious mediocre,
who were the scourge of modern English society, from suppressing true

merit. While the Catholic Church was no longer in the business of overseeing sporting events, it still nurtured the concept of the virtuous spiritual athlete, and it, at least according to the artist, applied the same competitive principles, governed by fair play, to the arts, thereby promoting cultural progress and happiness. When one perceives that the painting's meaning is that the classical world forms a foundation for Christianity with the Roman Catholic Church, properly understood, embodying the finest aspects of that tradition, one can understand why Barry placed so much emphasis on this picture and why he needed as well to disguise its overarching significance. Had the membership of the Society of Arts understood his intent, it would have expelled both him and his murals. One might recall that the Gordon riots occurred in 1780, while he was still at work on the murals. This, the worst riot of the eighteenth century in England, was sparked by anti-Catholic sentiment.

Barry was not suggesting that the Olympic Games should be reconstituted in eighteenth-century London. What he was attempting to resurrect was the games' religious and social underpinnings, which in his view meant a return to the Catholic Church. As long as England was outside this cultural mainstream, the English would be unable to achieve their full potential. Few would have recognised Diagoras as a classical prototype for the papacy. Yet for the discerning, at civilisation's apex is the artist's celebration of the Roman Catholic Church as the true heir of those spiritual values embodied in the Parthenon sculptures of Periclean Athens and in the awe-inspiring solemnity of the Olympic Games.

Notes

1. For my earlier essay on this painting, see Pressly 2010. My fullest account will appear in the book I am now completing on Barry's murals at the Royal Society of Arts.

2. Barry (1783) wrote a description of the paintings for the first exhibition of his series, which opened on 28 April 1783. The section on the picture of the Olympic Games is found on pp. 50-8. This section is reprinted in Fryer 1809, vol 2: 328-31.

3. See Gilbert West 1749: lxxxvi. I am grateful to Professor Hugh Lee for his suggestion that 'excel' would be a more accurate translation. Prof. Lee's essay on West is happily in this same volume.

4. Winkelmann 1765: 5.

5. West 1749: 47.

6. West 1749: cxxxvii.

7. West 1749: 63-4 n. 11. For Cicero's and Plutarch's accounts, see *M. Tully Cicero's Five Books of Tusculan Disputations* (London, 1715), 56; and *Plutarch's Lives*, 6 vols (Edinburgh, 1763), 2: 356.

8. See West 1749: 63 n. 11.

9. See West 1749: 63 n. 11

10. See James Barry, *A Letter to the Dilettanti Society* (London, 1798), in Fryer 1809. 2: 576.

11. West 1749: cxxxii.

12. West 1749: cxxxi-cxxxii.

13. See West 1749: ccvi.

14. Rollin 1774: xlix.

15. For an introduction to these five major games, see Valavanis 2004.

16. Although Barry never went to Greece, he was on intimate terms with Athens' antiquities. His first employer when he arrived in London as a young man was James 'Athenian' Stuart, who had been to Athens and co-authored *The Antiquities of Athens*, which was eventually to number three volumes. The use of Roman terminology in this essay can grate, particularly when using 'Minerva' for 'Athena' in the case of the Parthenon, but even 'Athenian' Stuart employed this nomenclature.

17. Barry had already painted Baretti's portrait, a work that he exhibited at the Royal Academy in 1773 (reproduced in Dunne 2005-6: 101). Each man had a volatile temper, and their friendship was eventually to rupture over one of Barry's outbursts. Fanny Burney refers to this occasion when writing her sister Susan on 11 November 1781: 'The History of the quarrel of Barry & Baretti was really frightful – how can Barry appear again amongst you? – I am very sorry indeed he has given this glaring specimen of that violence & ungovernable rage which from Time to Time he has even himself hinted at' (Rizzo 2003. 4: 503).

18. I am using the spelling employed by Barry and Baretti rather than '*Sæcu-lare*'.

19. Baretti 1779: 9.

20. Francis 1749.1: 485. Baretti mentions using Francis' translation for his own work.

21. Barry presumably would not have classified the beribboned palm borders as frames. He had said his solution of a continuous frieze of paintings would save the Society the necessity of purchasing frames, but from the beginning he must have envisioned some type of surround.

22. Rollin, 1: liv. Gilbert West also quotes St. Paul's exhortation to the Corinthian converts at length (see West 1749: clxxxix-cxc).

23. West 1749: xl-xli.

24. In the first half of the eighteenth century the painting was replaced by a mosaic after it, but Barry would have known both the mosaic and the picture itself, which was removed to the Vatican's Pinacotecca.

25. This drawing is reproduced in Dunne 2005-6: 213, DR60.

26. See James Barry, *A Letter to the Right Honourable the President ... of the Society for the Encouragement of Arts ...* (London, 1793), in Fryer ed. 1809. 2: 435, and *A Letter to the Dilettanti Society* (1798), in Fryer ed. 1809. 2: 526.

27. Images of papal processions are numerous. Multiple examples are reproduced in Maurizio Fagiolo dell'Arco 1997. See in particular Giovanni Orlandi's 1605 print of the procession of Pope Leo XI (199) and Giovan Battista Falda's 1676 print of the procession of Pope Innocent XI (506). J.I. Van Swaneburg's painting *Ceremonial Procession of the Pope in St. Peter's Square* of 1628 also gives a good sense of the colourful pageantry observed on such occasions (reproduced in colour in Garms 1995: 43).

28. Possibly Barry intended to show the pope held up by two churches, the Roman Catholic Church, which looks up with reverence at him, and the Greek Orthodox, which has been distracted from full acknowledgment of its true leader. The third of Diagoras' sons, seen at the left holding one of his brother's hands, is perhaps representative of the Protestant churches, which stand even further apart from the papacy.

29. The number of judges was at first one, then two, and in the 103rd Olympiad, it was increased to twelve in accordance with the number of the tribes of Elis. (In this essay on classical and biblical parallels, the symmetry between the twelve tribes of Elis and the twelve tribes of Israel should not go unnoted.) But in the next Olympiad the number of judges was reduced to eight, and after that increased to nine and finally to ten. See Potter 1706. 1: 447-8. Gilbert West gives a slightly different account, having the number go from one to two, then nine, followed by ten, with twelve in the 103rd Olympiad. After that it dropped to eight but settled at ten in the 108th Olympiad. See West 1749: xxxiv. The only time three judges are cited is in the context of the judging of a single contest.

The Race for a Healthy Body: the Ancient Greek Physical Ideal in Victorian London

Debbie Challis

A bronze replica of the fifth-century BCE Greek sculpture Diadoumenos by Polykleitos is in the park around the Lausanne Olympic Museum. It is displayed alongside contemporary sculptures by artists who have interpreted 'sport, the athlete and the Olympic ideals' to illustrate 'the synergy between the worlds of art and sport to which Pierre de Coubertin so keenly aspired'.[1] The museum tells the story of the modern Olympics and traditions, paying homage to its ideals. A section 'The Ancient Games' stresses the importance of sport in ancient Greece with information on various games and sporting ceremonies, including, of course, Olympia. It emphasises the importance of the arts to the ancient games, from the sculptors who memorialised athletes as kouroi to the poets who immortalised victors in verse. This artistic view is reflected in the collection of casts of sculpture at the museum as well as the red-figure vases that act as 'objets d'art' illustrating 'the games and the beauty of the scenes that they inspired'.[2]

The copy in the Olympic Park of the ancient Greek athlete crowning himself is, as Nigel Spivey points out in his review, 'inevitable'.[3] Greek sculpture acts as a physical ideal as well as an artistic representation of athletic prowess with wider connotations around the body, fitness and race.[4] This last connotation is unrecognised in the museum, as is the question of the authority through which perfect physical fitness is determined. On the athletics field, competition determines the victor, but the representation of an idealised human body in Greek sculpture does not necessarily resemble the bodies of athletes, ancient or modern, or of people working out on gym equipment (as 'the Life Room' exhibition at Chelsea School of Art in Autumn 2009 illustrated). Rather, Greek sculpture represents an ideal, and in turn has been idealised. Fae Brauer argues that the ideal body was 'established through canonisation of the Apollo Belvedere and Borghese Gladiator', which had an impact on the 'measurement of man' and 'ranking of race'.[5] Brauer points out that this body culture based on classical antiquity was part of the modern Olympic movement. Photographs of naked athletes in the pose of classical sculptures abounded in photography studios in the late nineteenth century, and at the 1900 Paris Olympics the Olympians were even photographed nude by Richer and

Etienne-Jules Marey.[6] The origin of the modern Olympics in the nine-teenth century can be traced to anxiety about a degenerating race, linked to a perception of healthy and unhealthy bodies.[7] The first Olympic Games in Athens in 1896 represented a culmination of international Hellenism, recognition for sport and emulation of the physical ideal represented by ancient Greece.

These connections between the healthy body, national strength and the ancient Greek physical ideal had their roots in earlier movements; argu-ably such connections could be traced back to the writings of Johann Joachim Winckelmann in the mid-eighteenth century. This chapter will consider the more obvious emergence of these connections in mid-nine-teenth century Britain. The idealised form of a healthy body was based on perceptions formed by classical sculpture and literature, as can be seen in the first-class silver medal designed for the 1868 Wenlock Olympian Games, which had a winged figure of Nike on a Maltese Cross holding a crown of olive leaves with an inscription from one of Pindar's Olympian odes above: 'There are rewards for glorious deeds'.[8] Athletics in Victorian Britain was heavily indebted to the Greek physical ideal as embodied in sculpture and literature, and this chapter considers how an idealised healthy body was also positioned with regard to anxieties around class, race and urban living. The formation of athletic clubs and festivals illus-trated a practical method of dealing with the perceived crisis of unfit bodies, particularly in urban centres. Charles Kingsley's lectures on health and sanitary reform, in particular his arguments for physical exercise for both men and women, illustrate some of the anxieties and the ideals underpinning the athletics movement in the mid-nineteenth century. Kingsley belonged to a group of writers, educators and reformers described by the term 'muscular Christianity'. This term has continued to be applied to Kingsley and much of his work. Kingsley was deeply concerned by the lack of opportunity for physical exercise for people in Britain and the impact this had, particularly in London and other urban areas. It is no accident that Kingsley's concern was simultaneous with an emerging, if mainly amateur and upper class, athletics and gymnastics movement in Britain.

Olympians in the park

An advertisement under the heading 'Crystal Palace' appeared in the *Pall Mall Gazette* on 11 July 1866:

> The great gymnastic gathering from all parts connected with the National Olympian Association, will be held at the Crystal Palace on Wednesday 1st of August. Entries received up to July 28 by the Hon. Secretary, Gymnasium, Old St Pancras Road, King's Cross. Tickets for Reserved Seats and the Banquet 5d each, may be had at Crystal Palace, Exeter Hall and the usual agents.[9]

This advert was repeated in the *Pall Mall Gazette, Daily News* and the *Morning Post*, among other newspapers, in the run up to 1 August 1866. The three-day sports festival organised by the National Olympian Association (NOA) signalled the start of Crystal Palace's reputation as a centre for athletics.[10] The principal organisers were Dr William Penny Brookes of the Wenlock Olympian Games in Shropshire, John Hulley of the Liverpool Gymnasium and E.G. Ravenstein, President of the German Gymnastic Society in London. These three men and eight others had formed the National Olympian Association at the Liverpool Gymnasium on Myrtle Street on 7 November 1865. The 1866 sports festival was their first national Olympic Games.[11]

There had been a flurry of activity around sport and physical education in the years leading up to 1866, in which Brookes, Hulley and Ravenstein were intimately involved. Brookes had set up Olympic Games at Much Wenlock and sent £10 for prize money to the Olympian Games in Athens in 1859, the earlier Greek festival which inspired the 1866 event.[12] In 1859 Britain's first gym club, the German Gymnastic Society, was established with Ravenstein as founding Director, and in 1864-5 the first purpose built gym was erected at 26 Pancras Road (where applicants for the 1866 sports festival were invited to apply).[13] The NOA had its offices in Liverpool due to Hulley's work at organising sports festivals for men in Liverpool, Manchester and North Wales. In early July 1866 the *Liverpool Mercury* carried an advertisement for an Olympic Festival at Llandudno at the end of the month, which was organised by Hulley for youths under 15 years of age.[14] The Olympic festival at the Crystal Palace was preceded by a juvenile athletes' festival in Wales at which nearly 4,000 people attended and 27 young men competed.[15] Hulley believed in the importance of exercise for all, and in 1861 he gave a lecture on 'Physical Education' in which he outlined his belief in the importance of individual physical fitness for the health of the nation and of 'the race':

> Each man and woman should take as much pride, in the cultivation of the bodily as of the mental faculties, feeling deeply that the grand truth, that the interests of our race are just as much bound up in the right development of the ones as of the other. We should not be content until the thoughts and sinews, the powerful bodied and manly minds of our ancestors become prevalent among us and are blended with the advantage of our advanced civilisation, with our greater enlightenment and refinement, and a longer average of life, we should cultivate all those sports and manly exercises which promote bodily health and vigour, just as sedulously as we cultivate any other branch of education, for no amount of mental cultivation, intellect, or wealth will ever make up to a community for the lack of manly ability and pluck.[16]

Crystal Palace was a popular venue on the edge of London. Home to the expanded building of the Great Exhibition, with its fine arts and industrial courts and a large park, the Crystal Palace had had its busiest year yet in 1865-6 with a substantial rise in visitor numbers and season ticket holders.[17] The Palace and Park had been constructed with the intention of hosting sports activities and its cricket pitch was adapted as athletic tracks for the festival. Since the National Olympic Festival was held on a 'shilling day', the cheapest fee for admissions to the Crystal Palace, more people could afford to attend. The first day of the festival was in fact a swimming contest which was held at Teddington Lock in the Thames. (This was now able to happen in a relatively clean River Thames due to Joseph Bazalgette's new pumping station and massive new sanitary system in London.) Various swimming and sports clubs took part at Teddington, while the second and third days of the Olympic Festival took place at Crystal Palace. The sports activities included running, leaping, climbing, putting a 36-pounder, steeple chasing, hurdle-racing, vaulting, throwing the javelin, wrestling, boxing, fencing, sabre and sabre against the bayonet, as well as gymnastic competitions.[18] Although entry to the competition was free, entrants needed to be members of NOA. This event attracted around 10,000 spectators and competitors, including the eighteen-year-old cricketer W.G. Grace who won the 440 yard hurdle race.[19] Entertainment was part of the festival, with the Coldstream Guards providing accompanying music, and a banquet and torch lit parade in the Palace and Park to conclude the event. Commenting on the toasts at the end of the evening to Ernst Ravenstein and the German Gymnastic Society, the *Penny Illustrated Paper* proclaimed:

> And an equally long life (the printers are waiting or I would say more) to the National Olympian Association, which has for its motto the appropriate Latin saying of 'The strength of the citizens is the strength of the state!'[20]

Health and fitness were about more than just personal well-being; they bore on society and the nation.

Although the National Olympic Festival in 1866 did not actually award money as prizes, it awarded medals and other incentives:

> The object of the association is to promote physical education and public games generally, and to encourage skill and strength in manly exercises, by the award of medals or other prizes, money excepted.[21]

William Penny Brookes presented the prizes. The object of the games was to encourage physical fitness by emulating the manner of ancient Greece in order to preserve the strength of the nation. Yet not all were happy with the formation and activities of the NOA. The founding of the Amateur Athletic Club in the same year was an attempt to ensure that British sport remained in the hands of gentleman athletes from Oxbridge and public schools. Based in London, this group grew in influence over the next decades, in part due to the romance attached to the amateur athlete believed to have taken part in the ancient Olympic Games. There were six national Olympic festivals between 1866 and 1881. The cult of the amateur athlete embodied in the AAA vied with NOA attempts to bring sport to the masses, and, while being rivals, both organisations raised awareness and interest in sport in Britain during the nineteenth century.

The 1866 festival was about more than sport. The venue of Crystal Palace was itself important, and not just due to its popularity (it had 300,000 visitors in July 1866).[22] The grounds had been designed for 'manly sports' and the official guide to the Crystal Palace described the 'ennobling' effects of walking through the park past various neoclassical sculptures in the open air:

> On every side, a soothing and ennobling contemplation, in which he may find rest from the fatigues, and strength for the renewed labours of an active, a useful, and an enjoyed, if transitory existence.[23]

One doctor went further, describing Upper Sydenham air as the purest and cleanest around London. Alfred Beaumont Maddock, a former physician of Malling Lunatic Asylum who had a practice in Mayfair but lived in Upper Sydenham, recommended visiting or staying in the vicinity of the Crystal Palace for its air and sanitary arrangements. At that point Upper Sydenham was in a green belt that surrounded London. Maddock contended that the English people outside of London had greater longevity than any other European nation due to the use of the countryside for sport:

> The pedestrian, the sportsman, the racer and the athlete of various other kinds evince not only the healthy nature of their pursuits, but the bracing effects of air, climate and diet by which their bodily, ay and in many instances even their mental powers are sustained, invigorated and developed.[24]

Healthiness was connected to the air and environment as well as exercise, and correspondingly, the English countryside, and its use for sport, were linked to the classical past. Interest in competitive sports was encouraged by the idea that the Greeks lived out a more pastoral existence and were closer to nature. Matt Cook has considered how Hellenism and pastoralism helped to form a clearer idea of national identity; central to this was 'the muscular body as a symbol of health, vitality, personal endeavour and self restraint'.[25] The healthy body was associated with the countryside, while London was often seen as a corrupt degenerate city.

Muscular Hellenists

This emphasis on health, the purifying effects of the countryside, and physical exercise, with its connection to ancient Greece, had vocal advocates in the literary and pedagogic world. Athleticism in Victorian Britain was based on a number of competing traditions and influences, of which

145

the Homeric ideal of the 'strongest and the best' was important. This idea influenced the competitive nature of the games industry at public schools and Oxbridge. Thomas Hughes' novels *Tom Brown's Schooldays* (1857) and *Tom Brown at Oxford* (1861), in which Tom combines 'academic prowess and brilliant athleticism', illustrate the ideal.[26] Hughes, a founding member of the Working Men's College with Charles Kingsley and a fellow Christian Socialist, expounded a form of 'muscular Christianity' and social reform in the late 1850s and 60s.[27] Hughes' fictional work illustrating the invigorating benefits for young men of competitive sport influenced Pierre de Coubertin in his thinking about physical exercise that led to the foundation of the modern Olympic Games.[28]

Thomas Hughes and Charles Kingsley expounded particular points of view in their fiction. Many of their novels were 'social problem' novels, in which they applied their own brand of religious faith as well as political and social convictions on leading issues. James Buzard has argued that if we read nineteenth-century social realist novels as performances of 'metropolitan autoethnography', we can use the literary form as a rich and significant kind of historical evidence.[29] Studying the writers' personal views as immersed within the culture they are writing for or about, while informed by the cultural and ideological framework of the imperial metropolis to which the writers belong, is useful here to unpack perceptions of health, fitness and the Greek physical ideal. These novels are fiction but are carefully constructed to advocate certain points of view. In the case of Kingsley, such an analysis also illustrates how his fictional work and non-fictional campaigns are closely connected.

The term 'Muscular Christianity' was coined in the *Saturday Review*'s review of Kingsley's novel *Two Years Ago* (1857). Although Kingsley at first disliked the term, he later embraced it. It is not hard to see why the term was deployed. *Two Years Ago* is set against the backdrop of the major cholera epidemic of 1854-55 in a small fishing town in the west of England and the start of the Crimean War. Tom Thurnall is the flawed hero who has travelled the world and is a healthy and intelligent, though too worldly wise, doctor. Thurnall expounds on the perfect ingredients for a healthy life to the opium-addicted poet Elsley Vavasour (Vavasour's unhealthy duplicity is emphasised by his use of an exotic name and fake identity to disguise his past as simple John Briggs). Vavasour acts as an unhealthy (in mind and body) foil to the bracing Thurnall:

> Believe me, it may be a very materialist view of things: but fact is fact – the *corpus sanum* is father to the *mens sana* – tonics and exercise make the ills of life look marvellously smaller. You have the frame of a strong and active man; and all you want to make you light-hearted and cheerful, is to develop what nature has given you.[30]

Thurnall is athletic, practical and intelligent but lacks a spiritual Christian faith, which he later finds through his love for Grace Harvey and his suffering in the Crimean war. Vavasour, on the other hand, is an effete unhealthy intellectual whose deceit and vanity cause him to spiral out of control. Thurnall's continual manliness and activity become rather irritating to a reader and his character is a perfect example of Kingsley's typical hero as 'a masculine, charismatic and authoritative Englishman who stands as a representative of a resolutely Anglo-Saxon and Protestant nation empire'.[31] Both *Two Years Ago* and Thomas Hughes' *Tom Brown's Schooldays* were published in the same year, 1857, and helped to set the tone of the first national Olympic Games in 1866. A combination of energy, physical exercise, pure air and manliness can invigorate the nation.

This celebration of sporting manliness and physical hardihood was soon parodied and inverted.[32] Wilkie Collins in his novel *Man and Wife* (1870) casts the villainous Geoffrey Delamyn as an avid athlete obsessed with training his body to physical perfection. One of the highlights of the novel comes when the dastardly Delamyn runs a foot race at Fulham in front of crowds of spectators. Collins imagines a foreigner following the crowds only to find out that everyone is gathered to watch 'a pair of strong young men':

> ... run round the enclosure for a given number of turns, with the object of ascertaining which could run the fastest of the two. The foreigner lifted his hands and eyes to Heaven. Oh, multifarious Providence! who would have suspected that the infinite diversities of thy creation included such beings as these?[33]

Collins suggests that such an interest is peculiarly English. Collins is supported by the French writer Hippolyte Taine in *Notes sur l'Angleterre* (1872) who wrote of the peculiar passion aroused by competitive sport at school and university, particularly among the upper classes. This emphasis on sport and the upper classes is again illustrated by the comment of the painter Mr Phoebus in Benjamin Disraeli's later novel *Lothair* (1881) that the English aristocracy 'most resemble the old Hellenic race; excelling in athletic sports, speaking no other language but their own, and never reading'.[34] Disraeli ironically comments on the traditional upper-class embrace of athletic sports while neglecting the improvement of the mind, thus only fulfilling one half of the Olympian ideal.

The emphasis in readings of muscular athleticism has usually been placed on the male athletic body, with good reason due to the history of the Olympics in Greece and the competitive sports ethos of public schools in Britain. The Greeks and their sports were believed to hold wholesome and rational masculine virtues.[35] Deeply influential on the ideal of the perfect male body was Greek statuary, whether as an object of athletic virtue for the 'muscular Hellenists' or for veiled homoerotic imaginings. Athena Leoussi has vividly shown how important for ideas of 'national regenera-

147

tion' was the 'transformation of the male form along classical lines', based on the Pheidian ideal as embodied in the Parthenon sculptures, and how influential this was on contemporary artists in England.[36] This sculpture-led imagining of the perfect healthy body was also influential on perceptions of female beauty and the physical fitness of the breeders of the future nation. In his lecture 'The Science of Health', Kingsley addresses the question of whether the 'Whether the British race is improving or degenerating?' and considers the poor breeding of British 'stock' in un-healthy conditions amongst unhealthy people. He argues that both men and women should emulate the athleticism of the Greeks:

> Therefore I would make men and women discontented, with the divine and wholesome discontent, at their own physical frame, and at that of their children. I would accustom their eyes to those precious heirlooms of the human race, the statues of the old Greeks; to their tender grandeur, their chaste healthfulness, their unconscious, because perfect might: and say – There; these are tokens to you, and to all generations yet unborn, of what man could be once; of what he can be again if he will obey those laws of nature which are the voice of God.[37]

The use of Greek sculpture to describe ideal physical characteristics is reflected in fiction, usually with regard to describing beauty. By the time of Disraeli's *Lothair* it was almost a stock description; for example the beautiful Theodora Campian is described as 'pale, but perfectly Attic in outline, with the short upper lip and round chin'.[38] Kingsley uses this descriptive conceit much earlier in his 1850 novel *Alton Locke* when the hero first sees Lillian, the subject of his ill fated infatuation, and describes her as:

> Beautiful, beautiful, beautiful beyond all statue, picture, or poet's dream. Seventeen – slight but rounded, a masque and features delicate and regular, as if fresh from a chisel of Praxiteles … skin of alabaster … stained with the slightest flush.[39]

The heroine Grace Harvey in *Two Years Ago* is described as having a brow 'like that of a Greek statue'.[40] Ideal female beauty in Kingsley (and elsewhere) was related to ideas about class and femininity as well as physiognomy. An alabaster skin signifies an upper-middle-class young woman beyond the reach of the working class Alton Locke (though Lillian is ultimately portrayed as somewhat insipid and facile). Again, this conceit was open to parody, or at least gentle humour. For example, Anthony Trollope describes Madeline Staveley in *Orley Farm* (1862) as having an oval face though 'some might say it was almost too thin' and a Grecian nose but perhaps too wide 'at the nostrils to be considered perfect in its chiselling'.[41] Trollope mocks the conventions of female beauty – his heroine is clearly pretty but in fashionable terms would not be found beautiful as she is not perfectly chiselled and Grecian enough. Particular perceptions of class, gender and race were interrelated in Kingsley's work. Yet, what these novelists described, even if half in jest, was the idealised physical characteristics of a middle-class woman in Victorian Britain. Kingsley pushes the comparison of female bodies to sculpture beyond beauty in his non-fiction, considering Greek sculpture not just to embody beauty but also bodily perfection and physical fitness.

Nausicaa playing ball

The Olympic Games at Crystal Palace in 1866 were for male competitors only. Charles Kingsley was unusual in arguing that physical education should be for both men and women. In his lecture 'The Two Breaths' on the importance of pure air for breathing, which was published among in *Sanitary and Social Lectures* in Britain (and in the US in *Health and Education*), Kingsley rails against the practice of making girls sit up right and straight, commenting that 'lolling around' is as graceful as 'every reposing figure in Greek bas-reliefs and vases'. His main contempt was, however, reserved for 'stays' which did not allow women to exercise and made the female figure unnatural:

> I spoke just now of the Greeks. I suppose you will all allow that the Greeks were, as far as we know, the most beautiful race which the world ever saw. Every educated man knows that they were also the cleverest of all races; and, next to his Bible, thanks God for Greek literature. Now, these people had made physical as well as intellectual education a science as well as a study. Their women practised graceful, and in some cases even athletic, exercises. They developed, by a free and healthy life, those figures which remain everlasting and unapproachable models of human beauty: but – to come to my third point – they wore no stays.[42]

Kingsley was concerned in his novels with social issues and was a reformer on education, sanitation and the work of the clergy of the Church of England. Considered radical by many, especially in the established church, Kingsley towards the end of his life concentrated on public talks dedicated to sanitary reform, health and physical education.[43]

Kingsley gave his lecture 'Nausicaa in London: Or, The Lower Education of Woman' in 1873 and it was repeated on his US tour a year later (shortly before he died).[44] He had used the image of Nausicaa in *Two Years Ago* to describe Grace leaving Tom Thurnall on an eventful evening 'like Nausicaa when she left Ulysses'.[45] In his lecture, Kingsley's interest in women's education is intertwined with his concern about health and the breeding of a fit race. It has often been cited as an example of anxiety over degeneration, particularly in London, among more recent writers on perceptions of the body in nineteenth-century Britain.[46] It is useful to précis the essay and consider some of the language used in order to illustrate more thoroughly its relevance to the ideals of the ancient Greek body and physical fitness. Kingsley begins by recounting how he had left visiting the Greek sculptures at the British Museum and walked the streets of London with his head 'still full of fair and grand forms' whose limbs and attitudes 'betokened perfect health, and grace and power':

> For I had been up and down the corridors of those Greek sculptures, which remain as a perpetual sermon to rich and poor, amid our artificial, unwholesome, and it may be decaying pseudo-civilisation; saying with looks more expressive than all words – such men and women can be; for such they have been; and such you may be yet, if you will use that science of which you too often only boast. Above all, I had been pondering over the awful and yet tender beauty of the maiden figures from the Parthenon and its kindred temples.[47]

This set him to musing on the passage in the *Odyssey* in which Nausicaa is playing ball with her female attendants and friends. Quoting the relevant part at length, Kingsley argues that Nausicaa's father Alcinous was not a king in the modern European sense but more likely a wealthy man of property or a trader. This makes Nausicaa, in Kingsley's reading, middle class rather than aristocratic, perhaps like the audiences at whom the lecture was directed. After thinking about the part Nausicaa plays in the *Odyssey*, Kingsley dwells on the 'healthfulness' of the scene and considers physical sports in the liberal education of the Greeks and Romans.[48] Kingsley then contrasts this with modern ideas of education and the emphasis on literacy, declaring that a 'wise man would sooner see his daughter a Nausicaa than a Sappho, an Aspasia, a Cleopatra, or even an Hypatia'.[49]

Kingsley walks through the London streets with this on his mind and starts to look at the women around him. He criticises fashion, singling out the Grecian or 'S' bend produced by corsets, and the way heels, hats and corsets make women look unnatural. He considers the science of physiognomy lost in the modern world when even the fashions worn for sea bathing are ugly and unnatural. From such reflections Kingsley moves on to consider the education of women, which he argues needs to include physical exercise:

> If, in short, they will teach girls not merely to understand the Greek tongue, but to copy somewhat of the Greek physical training, of that 'music and gymnastic' which helped to make the cleverest race of the old world the ablest race likewise: then they will earn the gratitude of the patriot and the physiologist, by doing their best to stay the downward tendencies of the physique, and therefore ultimately of the morale, in the coming generation of English women.[50]

Otherwise, Kingsley warns, there will be a huge impact on the fitness of and future of the country since women will develop 'into so many Chinese dwarfs – or idiots'.[51] Kingsley equates certain races, physical and mental health issues as sinister symptoms of poor inheritance.

Kingsley talks about and gazes at middle-class women, making clear not only his obsession with hygiene but also with the physical consequences of health and fitness for women's bodies, particularly with regard to sexual attraction and successful pregnancy. In Kingsley the interests of sex and hygiene 'effectively roll into one'.[52] The implication is that women need to have healthy physical bodies in order to get pregnant with and give birth to a healthy race. Kingsley extols physical activity and general awareness about health to combat the threat of degeneration with which he ends his lecture ('so many Chinese dwarfs – or idiots'). Kingsley's use of 'ablest race' is a reference to Francis Galton's 1869 book *Hereditary Genius*, which explained human history and achievement through ideas about race and ancestry. Galton argued that the ancient Greeks were 'the ablest race of whom history bears record; with Athens being the ablest' and contended that 'the average ability of the Athenian race is, on the lowest possible estimate, very nearly two grades higher than our own – that is, about as much as our race is above that of the African negro'.[53] This view accords with that of Kingsley, who alienated himself from many of his Christian Socialist friends, such as Thomas Hughes, by backing Governor Eyre over the Jamaican uprising and subsequent massacre in 1866. The sub plot of *Two Years Ago* is about an actress with part African-American slave ancestry and how this taints her relationship with an American man from the North. Although the plot ends happily and reflects anti-slavery ideas, racialised descriptions and assumptions litter the novel. The actress is passionate and volatile due to her racial background as 'part Negro'. Kingsley frequently used racial and racist explanations for issues in society, arguing, for instance, that suffrage in England should be extended to the working classes, but that Irish Celts and Black people 'lacked the historical experience and racial endowment for self government'.[54]

The issues around physical inheritance and physical exercise for women that Kingsley considers were widely discussed in late Victorian intellectual and artistic circles. Leoussi has suggested that Kingsley's arguments may have influenced 'unconventional subjects' in Victorian art such as Edward Poynter's *Nausicaa and Her Maidens Playing Ball* (1879) and Frederic Leighton's *Girls Playing Ball* (1889), which starred the 'Athenian looks' of his model Dorothy Dene.[55] Kingsley also had theoretical antecedents. For example, the surgeon and racial theorist Robert Knox, like Kingsley, took the sculptures from the Parthenon to be the highest forms of perfection in beauty and depiction of anatomy in *A Manual of Artistic Anatomy for the use of Sculptors, Painters and Amateurs* (1852).[56] Knox proclaimed that 'Woman, full-grown, beautiful woman is the standard of all excellence, all beauty, all perfection' and in the figure of the Greek Venus 'all nations and races must yield the path to Greece'.[57] As we have seen, the use of Greek sculpture in descriptions of female beauty had become commonplace to the point of parody in novels by the 1860s. Kingsley's lectures on Nausicaa, Greek sculpture, higher education for women and the implications for health and race in nineteenth-century London reflect more general ideas about female beauty, Greek sculpture and breeding. These concerns echo those voiced by members of the NOA with regard to athletics, male fitness and the Olympic ideal.

Athleticism became popular at about the same time in the mid-nineteenth century as racially deterministic thinking permeated culture and intelligentsia. The two became intertwined and, though this is complex, there were some clearly overlapping areas of interest. One of these was the high regard for the classical world, as illustrated by the dual belief that the Greeks were the 'ablest race' and that their sculpture reflected this physical reality of the perfect body from good breeding toned by athletics and exercise. The 'condition of England' question asked by radicals in the 1840s and 50s shifted, in times of more economic prosperity and less social disorder, to focus on the condition and health of the nation's body and how this was related to social problems. The 1860s saw the growth of athletic clubs, sporting festivals and gymnasiums, which harnessed athletics and physical fitness in the fight against physical and moral degeneration amongst men. The NOA's slogan 'The strength of the citizens is the strength of the state!' reflected the idea that exercise would improve the strength of the nation. Kingsley opened this out to include women as well and positions himself as an authority on what constitutes the fit female body through his knowledge of the classics. In 'Nausicaa' Kingsley drew on an idealised vision of ancient Greek literature and sculpture to illustrate the need for physical exercise and racial determinism to combat decay in the metropolitan centre of the British Empire.

Conclusion: exercising art

In his review of the display of sculptures related to sport in the park of the Olympic Museum at Lausanne, Nigel Spivey comments that, though the professionalism of the athlete has grown under the modern Olympic movement, the power of the artistic representation of athleticism has not.[58] It is likely that artistic representations of the athletic human body will be forever overshadowed by the use of certain kinds of bodies as vehicles for perceptions of physical and racial fitness. An exhibition, 'the Life Room', at the Chelsea Art School in November to December 2009, was a contemporary response to combining art and sport, which allowed people to exercise on gym equipment and other people to draw them exercising, alongside a cast of the Venus de Milo and images of life drawing sessions. The exhibition interrogated what was meant by 'life drawing' as well as the historical and contemporary values of the Olympic Games, using the modern popularity of the 'gym' as a tool:

8. The Race for a Healthy Body

In the late 20th and early 21st century the rise of the fitness gym represents a new realisation of the Olympian ideal and classical beauty; a place where people work on and observe the human form and where individuals can recreate themselves by sculpting/modelling their bodies through exercise. The gym presents an ideal site for the artist to observe the human form and create images – a place to see and be seen and to contemplate the intricacies of the human form.[59]

Alongside the gym equipment, materials for drawing and the photographs and prints of life room was information on the Ancient Olympics and Olympia. (Interestingly, Donald Smith, the curator of the exhibition, said that in an open library of books related to the exhibition the only two to be stolen were the site guides to Olympia.)[60] It is clear that people have used the Ancient Olympics and Olympic ideals as an authority to determine what, or rather who, is physically fit and a physical ideal, and who is not. Who has had this authority and who has not should be considered in any wider history of sport, the Olympics and its relationship to Ancient Greece. These issues have not disappeared though they have shifted. If 'the Life Room' is a recent example of the interaction of sport, art and Ancient Greece, greater interrogation of who has access to gym technology and how corporate sponsorship operates within art and sport in society is needed. Kingsley and the NOA stressed the importance of athletics and sport to the health of the nation and, in different ways, pointed out the need for wider distribution of access to better health and well-being among diverse social classes. 'The Life Room' exhibition was itself sponsored by a commercial gym (Techno-Gym and Village Hotels). Debate over the legacy of the 2012 London Olympics, especially in a time of economic uncertainty, taps into some of the same concerns raised in the nineteenth century. The first national Olympic Games in Crystal Palace in 1866 was free to enter and cost a shilling to watch. London 2012 will be different. Both were sold as strengthening the nation.

Notes

1. *Olympic Park, Lausanne* Information Sheet, obtained in 2002.
2. *Olympic Museum Lausanne. Visitor's Guide* (2002), 29.
3. Spivey 1997: 3.
4. See also Simpson in this volume.
5. Brauer 2008: 9.
6. For more on this see Brauer 2008a and Callen 2008.
7. Pick 1989: 131.
8. Furbank et al. 2007: 7.
9. 'Crystal Palace', *Pall Mall Gazette*, 11 July 1866 (Issue 443).
10. The National Recreation Centre opened in Crystal Palace Park in 1964, the grounds of the former Crystal Palace, and was the only part of an envisaged £10 million scheme for a National Youth and Sports Centre to be completed.
11. Toohey and Veal 2007: 32.

12. Ashrafian 2005: 969.

13. Taines 2005: 113.

14. *Liverpool Mercury*, 6 July 1866, front page.

15. 'Juvenile Olympic Festival', *North Wales Chronicle* (Bangor Wales), 28 July 1866, Issue 2071.

16. The speech in full is available on the website dedicated to John Hulley by Ray Hulley, www.johnhulley-olympics.co.uk [accessed 8 August 2010].

17. 'Crystal Palace', *The Times*, 14 June 1866 (Issue 25524), 9 col. C.

18. 'National Olympic Festival', *Penny Illustrated Paper* (London), 11 August 1866 (Issue 254), 81.

19. Furbank et al. 2007: 5.

20. 'National Olympic Festival', *Penny Illustrated Paper* (London), 11 August 1866 (Issue 254), 81.

21. 'National Olympian Association', *Morning Post*, 2 August 1866 (Issue 28905), 3.

22. *Daily News*, 31 July 1866 (Issue 6314).

23. Phillips 1854: 163.

24. Maddock 1860: 17.

25. Cook 2003: 124.

26. Jenkyns 1980: 212.

27. In *Tom Brown's Oxford* (1861), Hughes even includes a chapter entitled 'Muscular Christianity' in which he defends this combination of spiritual development, intellectual inquiry and healthy sporting activity.

28. Coubertin 1888.

29. Buzard 2005: 3-17.

30. Kingsley 1901: 201.

31. Wee 1994: 67.

32. Vance 1985: 15.

33. Collins 1995: 488.

34. Disraeli 1881: 25.

35. Stevenson 2005: 199. The term 'muscular Hellenists' is borrowed from Stevenson 2005: 207.

36. Leoussi 1999.

37. Kingsley1880: 44.

38. Disraeli 1881: 34.

39. Kingsley 1983: 71.

40. Kingsley 1901: 44.

41. Trollope 1985: 185.

42. Kingsley 1880: 27.

43. Kingsley1877: 419.

44. Vance 2004.

45. Kingsley 1901: 259.

46. Cook 2003: 133, Stevenson 2005: 208, Pict 1989: 195, Leoussi 1999: 88.

47. Charles Kingsley1874: 70.

48. Kingsley 1874: 74.

49. Kingsley 1874: 77.

50. Kingsley 1874: 87.

51. Kingsley 1874: 88.

52. Fasick 1994: 92.

53. Galton 1869: 341-2.

54. Lorimer 1978: 155.

55. Leoussi 1999: 88. Poynter's painting was one of four (since destroyed), which also included *Atalanta's Race*, for Edward Montagu Stuart Grenville for his Billiard Room at Wortley Hall in Yorkshire.

56. Knox 1852.

57. Knox 1852: 100 and 164.

58. Spivey 1997: 6.

59. Chelsea School of Art, 'the Life Room: press release', 03/11/2009, http://www.chelseaspace.org/archive/theliferoom-pr.html [accessed 15/08/2010].

60. Conversation at The Chelsea School of Art on 12.12.2009.

Nervi's Palazzo and Palazzetto dello Sport: Striking a Delicate Balance between Past and Present in 1960 Rome

Ann M. Keen

When Rome hosted the Summer Olympic Games in 1960, what could have been a fairly simple, yet spectacular, two-week sporting event, instead escalated into a defining moment in the city's history, a tangible illustration of the city's ambitions as it emerged from the shadow of World War II. From the decision to bid for the Games through the planning stages, to the presentation of the Games from 25 August to 11 September, organisers knew they had a valuable opportunity to help dictate the course of the public perception of Rome and they utilised every means available to them to support their efforts. Fully cognizant that, for the first time, millions of people would be watching on television, the host committee orchestrated what amounted to a two-week-long postcard from Rome, complete with stops at famous ancient landmarks as well as newly constructed venues. Serving as a backdrop for the drama inherent in the athletic contests, the buildings highlighted the city's architecture, from its classical tradition to its cutting-edge post-war modernism. Pier Luigi Nervi, a practising architect and engineering professor at Sapienza – Università di Roma at the time, was charged with designing two indoor arenas for the Rome Games, the Palazzo and the Palazzetto dello Sport. These buildings garnered much attention and international acclaim for both the architect and the city because their forms were able to echo Rome's classical past without resorting to nostalgia, and their construction utilised innovative methods and materials, necessities in the aftermath of World War II.

As an applicant to host the 1960 Games, Rome had a number of intangible elements working in its favour with the International Olympic Committee (IOC). Perhaps most important, Pierre de Coubertin, father of the Modern Olympic movement, had wanted Rome to host the Olympics since 1904: 'I desire Rome only because I wanted Olympism, after its return from the excursion to utilitarian America [St Louis in 1904], to don once again the sumptuous toga, woven in art and philosophy, in which I had always wanted to clothe her.'[1] For various reasons, including the eruption of Mount Vesuvius in 1906 and the World Wars, Rome had never

Fig. 9.1. Palazzo dello Sport, view looking southwest.

Fig. 9.2. Palazzo dello Sport, view looking northwest.

hosted the Games since their reintroduction in 1896. But finally, in the early 1950s, there were a number of factors that came together. For the IOC, it was essential to show the world that an Olympics in the heart of Europe did not have to be draped in politics, as it was in 1936 Berlin. Also,

157

Fig. 9.3. Palazzetto dello Sport, view looking north.

Italy would be celebrating its centennial as a unified country in 1960. And for Italy, hosting these Olympics only fifteen years after the end of World War II could provide a tremendous opportunity to help rehabilitate the global standing of both Rome and the entire country.

For the 1960 Summer Olympics, there was a new benefit to hosting the Games as well: beyond the usual media exposure generated leading up to and during the Olympics, the Games would be the first televised worldwide. Live feeds were provided to one hundred television channels, recorded broadcasts televised in eighteen European countries, and delayed broadcasts in the United States, Canada, and Japan. The number of people seeing the Games, the host city, and its architecture thus increased far beyond city inhabitants and two weeks' worth of on-site attendees into the sphere of millions of people worldwide (Giacomini 1960: 382-3).

In assembling an application to host the 1960 Summer Games, the Italian Olympic Committee faced a number of problems, not the least of which was the lack of appropriate buildings to host the competitions. Upon assessing the existing sports venues in Rome prior to submitting its application to the IOC, the Italian Olympic Committee determined that Rome possessed only one venue that met Olympic standards, the Stadio dei Cipressi, built in 1936-37 under Mussolini's order for potential Olympic bids in the 1940s.[2] Located in the Foro Italico, known as the Foro Mussolini during his rule, the stadium had been renovated in 1952-53. It held 82,000 and would serve as the main stadium for the Games, thus acquiring its new name: Stadio Olimpico.

In its application, the Italian committee detailed its plan to hold the Games in two main areas in the city: the North Olympic Centre (Foro Italico Zone) and the South Olympic Centre (EUR Zone). The committee, in concert with Rome's Ministry of Public Works, decided several existing buildings, like the Stadio dei Cipressi, could be modified to host events, but a number would need to be built. Unlike common practice for prior Olympics, the venues constructed for the 1960 Summer Games would be permanent structures. After the Games, Rome organisers conveyed their goal in opting to build permanent venues: 'But perhaps the greatest satisfaction afforded those responsible for the sports venues was that once the Games were over, the venues that had been prepared for the event today become an ever-increasing attraction to Roman youth which frequents them with great enthusiasm, filled with the memories of the success of the Rome Olympiad.'[3]

Given the expanded platform of television, Rome organisers saw the opportunity to reinforce visually the continuity of Rome's history and to validate the city's re-emergence onto the global stage. The organising committee intended to highlight Rome's storied past while simultaneously refocusing the world's attention on Italy's ability to move beyond its recent war history. After Rome's bid to host the 1960 Summer Games succeeded, Giulio Onesti, president of the Italian Olympic Committee, underscored this goal in a February 1957 letter to all presidents of National Olympic Committees:

> It is a cause of great pride for the Italian Olympic Committee to prepare an enterprise defined by all as extremely arduous and which will prove even more difficult in this Rome which, in the 2,700 years of its history, has seen so many projects, friends, enemies and so many people pass through it ... The holding of the Olympic Games is indeed one of the greatest honours for a nation which wishes to illustrate its considerable advance in sport and to document its aspirations through such an aesthetic and moral ideal as is sport (Giacomini 1960: 35).

In hosting the Olympic Games, organisers hoped to galvanise both Italians and visitors alike to appreciate the larger scope of Rome's narrative. They wanted to communicate clearly that Rome's recent past would not overshadow the city's history nor suppress its future potential. Former press chief of the Italian Olympic Committee Donato Martucci said it best, when summarising the overall goal for the hosts of the 1960 Summer Games in Rome: 'We wanted to show that we were a free country, a new progressive nation, one that had left fascism behind' (Judah 2008: 46). The facilities plan for the Games, then, incorporated both known historic landmarks as well as modern, new arenas.

Two venues and the marathon course were chosen to represent the eternal grandeur that was Rome's enduring legacy. The Baths of Caracalla (212-219 CE) and the Basilica of Maxentius (303-313 CE) were selected to host the gymnastics and wrestling competitions, respectively. The marathon course was designed to begin at the steps of the Capitol, taking runners through the streets of Rome to the finish line at the Arch of Constantine (315 CE), in the shadow of the Colosseum (70-82 CE) (Giacomini 1960: 80). These sites unabashedly exemplified the immortality of Rome's classical past and its integral role in the development of Western culture. Olympic sports history worked in concert with the city's history, visually associating centuries' worth of Olympic contests at ancient Olympia with the grandeur of the Roman Empire.

Rome's classical past, however, was not the only moment in its history embraced by the Games. Buildings in the EUR district played an essential role in determining the context for new structures built for the Games. This area southwest of the city centre was originally intended to host the Esposizione Universale Roma (EUR), a Mussolini-planned festival to celebrate the twentieth anniversary of Fascism in Italy in 1942, which never took place. The Palazzo dei Congressi (designed by A. Libera, 1938-54) was chosen as the site for the fencing events (Giacomini 1960: 68), and other buildings of the EUR, including the Palazzo della Civiltà Italiana (designed by G. Guerrini, E.B. Lapadula, and M. Romano, 1938-43), provided visually and architecturally impressive statements regarding the artistic and technical prowess of living Italian architects who incorporated classical elements with modern style. While celebrating Italy's re-entry to the mainstream via the 1960 Summer Games on two sites developed by the Fascist regime (Foro Italico and the EUR district) may strike observers as ironic, the interplay between 'old' and 'new' Rome, the resounding grandeur of the buildings, and the quality of the original site designs apparently ruled the committee's decision (Gordon 1983: 67; Giacomini 1960: 55, 68). At this specific moment in time, with the end of the war only fifteen years in the past, the committee wanted to instil in athletes, visitors, and television viewers alike the power to participate in this singular ritual, re-establishing the continuity of the Games' collective celebration of youth, skill, and dedication (Giacomini 1960: 35, 47).

Thus in 1956, with full knowledge of the Rome organising committee's high expectations and the potentially daunting task of complementing these iconic landmarks of the Eternal City, Italian architects submitted proposals to design the new Olympic venues. Entries were reviewed by members of Rome's organising committee and a subcommittee called 'Rome Olympic Constructions', comprising organising committee members with specific architectural and engineering qualifications, as well as outside consultants, primarily engineers serving at public institutions like the Ministry of Public Works and the National Institute for the Housing of State Employees. Designs and all large-scale construction projects were also examined by the Inter-ministerial Committee for Sports Venues, the Rome Municipality Building Committee, the Superior Council of the Ministry for Public Works, and the Superintendent's Office for Rome

Monuments and Fine Arts (Giacomini 1960: 55). In short, winning an Olympic commission was no small feat.

Pier Luigi Nervi, well known throughout Italy and beyond as a specialist in designing cost-effective large-scale buildings, was awarded commissions to build three new venues for the Rome Games. In the EUR district, he worked with Marcello Piacentini, the original planner of the district, on the Palazzo dello Sport, a large indoor arena designed to seat 17,000-plus spectators. The Palazzo would host basketball and boxing events at the Olympics. Working with architect Annibale Vitellozzi, Nervi designed the Palazzetto dello Sport in the Flaminio district just east of the Foro Italico. Host to basketball and weightlifting events, the Palazzetto was designed to seat 3,500 for basketball and 5,600 for weightlifting. Nervi worked with his son Antonio, also an engineer, on Flaminio Stadium, an outdoor stadium designed specifically for soccer located just to the south of the Palazzetto (Giacomini 1960: 58). While Flaminio Stadium was recognised as a significant building at the time (and still is), the Palazzo and the Palazzetto were the focus of the popular press covering the progress of the Rome Games.

With so much at stake for the city and the country, Rome organisers entrusted Nervi with the Olympic commissions after careful consideration of his experience and past accomplishments. Pier Luigi Nervi (1891-1979) was born in Sondrio, Italy, in the northern region of Lombardy. He was graduated from the Civil Engineering School of Bologna in 1913 and soon after joined the Society for Concrete Construction. After serving with the Corps of Engineers in World War I, Nervi returned to his engineering practice and began executing large-scale structural designs throughout Italy.[4] Relevant to sports architecture, his first major project was the 35,000-seat Giovanni Berta Stadium in Florence. Nervi won the competition for the stadium in 1929 and the project was completed in 1932. It features a 55-foot cantilevered roof and dramatic exterior exposed cantilevered spiral stairs.

Between 1935 and 1942, Nervi won a series of commissions to build airplane hangars in locations throughout Italy. The first two, built in 1936, used reinforced concrete poured in place. The inherent difficulty of using that process for large-scale buildings prompted him in 1939 to design the rest of the hangars using precast concrete sections, which would become his hallmark. Retreating Germans destroyed all of the hangars in 1944, but Nervi utilised similar processes in constructing his Olympic venues. According to the architectural historian Terry Kirk, restrictions that were placed on wartime commissions like the airplane hangars helped force Nervi's hand towards the use of prefabricated systems. Emphasis on labour efficiency and minimised use of materials, especially steel in reinforced concrete, along with the truthful expression of structure (i.e. making the building's structure visible), helped garner Nervi a reputation as one who achieved functionality without sacrificing aesthetics (Kirk

161

2005: 191). The interior ceiling of his Orvieto hangar featuring a lamella truss vault (a barrel vault with a diamond-patterned rib structure), with its seemingly simple geometry and rhythmic repetition, is clearly an antecedent for the domes of the Palazzo and the Palazzetto.

An exposition hall in Turin, another large-scale project, bolstered Nervi's reputation for efficiency and structural beauty and provided him with necessary experience using a new material he developed, ferrocement. Nervi's ferrocement process called for the use of a steel-mesh netting with liquid concrete applied to it. Instead of having steel reinforcing the concrete element in one location (a rod through the centre), the concrete is essentially reinforced throughout the entire form. The architecture critic Ada Louise Huxtable called Nervi's Salon B at the Turin Exposition Hall (1948-49), 'one of the most impressive interior spaces of this century' (Huxtable 1960: 25). Like the strict timeline necessary for Olympic construction, the Turin building was constructed in a very short time (eight months), so the fact that the construction of parts of the building could take place simultaneously was extremely advantageous. Manufacture of roof forms occurred at the same time as floors and walls were being assembled, all independently. Again, Nervi delivered cost effectiveness on a large-scale project (Salon B's roof spans 330 feet), with critically acclaimed results. Huxtable and others appreciated the aesthetics and structural clarity of the lines of force articulated across the vaulted ceiling, gathering at buttresses along the walls to distribute pressure from the ceiling down to the ground. The architectural historian R. Stephen Sennott describes the ceiling as an 'undulating concrete canopy' (Sennott 2004: 417). All this was achieved through Nervi's inventive processes with prefabricated elements due to the limited resources available in post-war Italy, especially wood for formwork that would have been required for poured-in-place concrete. To be sure, organisers judging the Olympic designs had a long list of Nervi's successes on which to evaluate him.

City officials and Rome's Olympic organisers hoped to complete the city's as-yet unfinished EUR district with a crowning architectural and cultural achievement: the Palazzo dello Sport. While the Esposizione Universale Roma that Mussolini planned never happened because World War II intervened, Olympic organisers deemed it a perfect place to continue the cutting-edge modern architecture for which the district was already known (Giacomini 1960: 67-8. It appears the organisers were unfazed by the district's overt association with Mussolini, as they recounted their selection in the official report of the Games:

> The modern garden city of the E.U.R. became an ideal centre for a group of sports venues which had been constructed not only because of the XVII Olympiad but also to meet the ever-increasing sports requirements of the capital ... Buildings, villas, trees, stairways, ornamental work, porticoes, terraces, parks and artistic fountains completed the modern quarter of the

E.U.R. which, having been created for the Olympiad of Civilisation was soon to offer the magnificent resources of its artistic decor to the Games of the XVII Olympiad (Giacomini 1960: 67-8).

No mention is made of any residual political context associated with the site.[5] With the location selected, designers were challenged to create an arena that would match the modern grandeur of the Palazzo della Civiltà Italiana, the Palazzo Congressi, the Palazzo delle Scienze, and the Church of Saints Pietro e Paolo.

From the early planning stages of the Games in Rome, organisers were prepared to spare little expense for this new arena. In reports to both the Italian Olympic Committee and the International Olympic Committee, the host committee described its approach to venue renovation and construction for the Rome Games: 'Improvements of luxury or of high cost were to be avoided and the aim was to create functional venues to be run at a minimum cost. One exception was made, i.e. for the Palazzo dello Sport because of the type of events to be held there and the particular area where it was to be built' (Giacomini 1960: 54). The total cost for the project was approximately two billion lire.[6]

Nervi's proposal for the Palazzo dello Sport was submitted in collaboration with architect Marcello Piacentini (1881-1960), known as one of Mussolini's favourite architects and a primary planner of the EUR district.[7] Kirk mentions that the teaming of older with younger designers for the Olympics highlighted their shared classical foundations, yet prevented the projects from displaying the 'rhetorical classicism of Fascist Romanità' (Kirk 2005: 194). Piacentini, given his role in the planning of the EUR district, likely approached the Palazzo as a capstone to his modernist triumphal district. But in pairing Piacentini with Nervi, Olympic organisers effectively counteracted Piacentini's potential for political rhetoric with Nervi's emphasis on structure and function.[8] Nervi clarified his approach to architecture during the construction of the Palazzo:

> But if one is to master structural problems, he must thoroughly understand the laws of statics and strength of materials; even so completely that physical and mathematical knowledge become structural intuition – the only true source of inspiration in creative structural design. When, as it so often happens, structural invention derives only from formal sources, the result can hardly be other than unnatural, uneconomical, and unlovely.[9]

Nervi approached architecture from the perspective of the tangible, rather than the rhetorical, which suited everyone involved in the overall planning of the Rome Games.

As Olympic organisers had hoped, the design took into consideration the context in which the building would be set: the plan called for the building to serve as an anchor for one end of the EUR district, with Via Cristoforo Colombo encircling it. This setting proved to be a crucial element in establishing the Palazzo as a significant monument in post-war Rome. Whether specifically verbalised to the builders or not, the organising committee clearly expected the Palazzo dello Sport to serve as a new landmark for the city, and happily declared, upon its completion, that it 'dominated the whole of the E.U.R. zone' (Giacomini 1960: 68).

The approach to the arena was planned to inspire awe and, I would suggest, to convey a sense of ritual. Thousands of people would make their way daily to the Palazzo for basketball and boxing events during the Olympics. With the building's placement at the top of a steep grade, visitors would ascend a series of steps in a manner that can only be interpreted as processional before reaching the building's entrances, spread equidistantly around the perimeter. From the top of the hill, the entirety of the EUR complex is visible, complete with lush, exotic vegetation around a man-made lake.

The building design is a combination of glass exterior walls and a concrete interior structure, a mix that was not met with uniform praise by architecture critics. Over the years there has been much discussion concerning the Palazzo's glass envelope, and most critics see it as an unhappy compromise between Nervi and Piacentini. The drama inherent in the majority of Nervi's other buildings is still present, but visible only from inside the building or by looking through the glass walls at night when the building is lit from the interior. Huxtable notes that Piacentini was adamant in having a columned building, and the uniformity of the glazed panels in the curtain wall may have satisfied his aesthetic demands. Huxtable's taste, however, was not satisfied: 'The effect from the outside is of an almost neo-classic blandness that conveys little visual excitement' (Huxtable 1960: 29). The Olympic architectural historian Barclay Gordon concurred: '[Piacentini] settled in the end for a circular curtain wall that packages the whole building in glass, reducing Nervi's grand dome to a visual null and giving back almost nothing in return' (Gordon 1983: 69). Criticism centres on the issue of the glass curtain wall obfuscating the interior concrete construction. Unlike the International Style's use of the curtain wall to unmask a building's skeleton, the Palazzo's exterior appears rooted in the formal, rather than in a strong cohesion between form and structure.

Despite the envelope's perceived shortcomings, a number of renowned historical references influenced Nervi's design in addition to his own earlier works. Architecture critics have called the building 'Pantheonic', most clearly evident in the design of the dome (Kirk 2005: 194). The structure comprises precast ribs dispersing stress from the dome down to 48 joints that sit on a 300-foot ring forming the uppermost of three seating sections in the arena. The network of ceiling ribs springs from a central tension ring, visually echoing the Pantheon's oculus. Lighting, acoustic, and air conditioning systems are located in this central space, which is raised above the dome's aluminium shell and features clerestory windows for additional natural light.

164

Nervi employed a variety of methods in creating his concrete structure (Huxtable 1960: 29). In addition to the ceiling sections, seating areas were prefabricated as well. Supporting columns were poured in place using reusable moulds, and joints throughout were grouted *in situ*. By this time, Nervi had developed an efficient method, both in terms of time and cost, allowing for simultaneous construction on various parts of the building. The processes used to construct the Orvieto airplane hangar and Salon B in Turin proved integral to the construction of the Palazzo.

The architect G.E. Kidder Smith raised another association between Nervi's domes and the Roman architectural tradition. He discussed Nervi's structural technique for allowing natural light into his domed structures as being reminiscent of Hagia Sophia, having the effect of 'making the solid roof float in air' (Kidder Smith 1955: 228). The interplay of light and shadow, form and space at the base of the dome strongly influences the visitor's experience. The near-overwhelming grandeur of the structural presentation resonates in both buildings. However, the mystical moodiness of the sixth-century Byzantine church has been replaced in the twentieth-century Palazzo with the human-centred drama of Olympic competition.

The symmetry and clarity of the Palazzo's plan supports comparisons to Nervi's historical influences. The three-tiered, circular plan features openings at regular intervals, rooms of similar sizes independent of their use, and centralised services for athlete and spectator alike. Specialised areas for television coverage, Olympic honoured guests, and warm-up for the athletes were all incorporated seamlessly. Perhaps most important for the public, there are no obstructions between spectators and the competition area, making every seat worth its ticket price.

Nervi often claimed to engineer buildings, rather than design them, allowing him to avoid aesthetic objectives that he felt often encumbered architects (Kirk 2005: 193). Barclay Gordon addresses the question of Nervi's engineering outlook versus the public's perception of his work: 'Though all the spaces are shaped to satisfy the needs of structure, this is by no means an arid landscape of engineering necessity. The spaces within are strongly modeled and richly animated by expressive concrete forms' (Gordon 1983: 73). Interior corridors are a mixture of open spaces punctuated by heavy structural members, but the balance is delicately struck. It is this balance in the passageways that affects the visitor aesthetically, whether Nervi intended it or not. Huxtable says that the combination of the angular geometry of the support columns and the reticulated under-surface of the seating section is 'one of the building's most striking effects' (Huxtable 1960: 30).

Nervi's examination of the structural issues inherent in a large-scale sports facility resulted in a building that not only resolved the requirements necessary for the fortnight of Olympic events, but also satisfied the prescribed goals of the Rome organising committee. The Palazzo, especially the interior, embodied the potential of post-war Italian architecture, asserted itself as a new monument in the EUR district, and provided a bridge between Rome's classical past and its modern present, on display to a global audience.

As discussed, the one thing critics did not praise about the Palazzo dello Sport was its glass exterior walls. Whatever the reason for the predominance of glass on the Palazzo's exterior, the primary criticism is the lack of harmony between the building's façade and its interior. There was no such problem with Nervi's Palazzetto dello Sport.

In spite of its relatively small size (5,000 fixed seats), the Palazzetto dello Sport also serves as a modern monument for post-war Rome. Everything critics found successful in the design of the Palazzo is reiterated in the Palazzetto, with the added consideration that the Palazzetto's exterior appeared to critics more in keeping with Nervi's design objectives than the Palazzo's glass curtain wall. Accolades for the Palazzetto are primarily directed towards Nervi's exploration of and emphasis on the distinctly modern use of concrete on the outside of the Palazzetto. What is hidden behind the glass curtain wall in the Palazzo – the concrete structural skeleton and dome roof supports – is instead clearly celebrated on the exterior of the Palazzetto dello Sport. The glass wall is present, but recessed.

Nervi partnered with well-known Italian architect Annibale Vitellozzi (1906-91) to build the 'Small Sports Palace' in the North Olympic Centre, next to the Olympic Village and across the Tiber River from the Foro Italico. Vitellozzi supervised many of the Olympic installations for the organising committee and is the architect of record for the Olympic Stadium, the swimming stadium, and the Acqua Acetosa training facility, in addition to his contribution to the Palazzetto. Vitellozzi's most famous project prior to the Olympics was his design for the new façade and concourse at Termini Station in Rome (1947-50). With the number of projects Vitellozzi was working on for the Olympics, it is unclear how involved he was with the design process of the Palazzetto. Contemporary critics range from omitting any mention of him at all to crediting him with requesting the building's circular plan. The official Olympic Report states that the Palazzetto was built 'in accordance with a general plan' by Vitellozzi, with Nervi responsible for the reinforced concrete portion (Giacomini 1960: 60).

The organising committee required a multipurpose facility with a flexible seating plan at the lowest cost with minimal construction time. Given Nervi's past successes, it is no surprise that the 5,000-seat arena was built in just over a year and proved to become a standard against which other Olympic buildings were measured. One important factor in keeping design costs to a minimum was Nervi's use of a competition entry he had submitted for a sports facility in Vienna in 1953. Records of this submission are the likely source for many critics' assessment of the level of Vitellozzi's participation in the Palazzetto's final design (and perhaps Piacentini's in the Palazzo as well). The interior of the Palazzetto features a modification of the Vienna submission's interior lamella dome and a steeper seating layout, and the Vienna exterior dome configuration falls somewhere between the Palazzetto and the Palazzo. The Vienna competition, while won by local architect Roland Rainer, allowed Nervi to work out many of the details for this type of sports facility prior to submitting his designs to the Rome organisers.[10]

After adapting the Vienna submission for the Palazzetto, Nervi set to work refining the construction process for prefabrication that he had been using since his airplane hangars project in the 1940s. Typically, ferroconcrete shells required large wooden forms to cast the roof in place, and these large frames could account for nearly half of the construction budget on a given project (Gössel and Leuthäuser 1991: 251, 253). To minimise both cost and turnaround time, Nervi prefabricated many structural elements for the Palazzetto, most notably, the 1,620 polygonal plates that comprise the dome's exterior. Assembly of the roof elements was rapid, as workers did not have to set up wood frames, pour the concrete, wait for the concrete to set, remove the frames, and then move them a short distance to begin again. The roof was assembled much like a jigsaw puzzle, with work in other areas able to take place simultaneously.[11] In post-war Rome, there was plenty of available labour, but building materials were prohibitively expensive. Nervi's plan for multitasking on the construction site shortened the construction timeline significantly, keeping labour costs to a minimum, and his limited use of steel and wood also reduced expenses. In conceiving not only the design of the Olympic buildings but the entire construction process, Nervi was able to draw on his background as both an engineer and a builder. In addition to the Palazzetto's impressive cost-effectiveness[12] and rapid construction timeframe, the building's form contributed to new standards being set for arenas of this size.

Nervi's particular ability to bridge the past and the present was essential to his success with the Olympic buildings, particularly the Palazzetto. Nervi designed and executed the small-scale facility with many of the same elements that he incorporated into the Palazzo. The Palazzo is basically a large-scale version of the Palazzetto, minus the Y-shaped supports and roof edging. And as is true for the Palazzo, comments can be found in the critical literature referring to the Palazzetto's Pantheonic debt and its Hagia Sophia-esque floating roof. Kirk discusses its structure in terms of the Pantheon: 'Light slips in around the entire perimeter and illuminates the low dome from below, inverting the experience of mass and light in the Pantheon model' (Kirk 2005: 193-4). Janson and Janson describe the effect of light entering around the dome: 'A marvel of engineering it seems to float effortlessly, like the dome of Hagia Sophia, in a pool of light without visible support' (Janson 1995: 860). Visitors were even reminded of medieval building methods when seeing the Palazzetto. Describing preparations made in advance of the Olympics, the *New York Times* reported: 'Outside the building [the Palazzetto], concrete supports rise from the ground in handsome original lines. There seems nothing to call them but flying buttresses – the ultimate use of an idea conceived by the builders of the great cathedrals' (Daley 1959).

In remaining true to his engineering principles, however, Nervi was able to move people beyond nostalgia for a lost Rome and bring them face to face with Rome's burgeoning future using those same features: the building's concrete dome and exterior structural elements. *LIFE* and *Look* magazines editor John Peter notes how Nervi's innovative processes with concrete move him beyond the reaches of traditionalism and didactic quotation: 'Today, with Nervi, for example, we see how one can exploit reinforced concrete in a plastic way without resorting to these old solutions which date back to the use of stone' (Peter 2000: 19). Nervi's use of columns and domes may be considered traditional, but his methods freed him to express these elements using a distinctively modern vocabulary.

Nervi's use of the traditional dome form and the visible structural supports provided critics, visitors, and television viewers with a glimpse of the ancient world that the Rome organising committee was anxious to evoke, but at the same time, gave them an opportunity to appreciate innovation and the modern aesthetic. Visually associated with organic forms ranging from a mushroom to a beetle, the Palazzetto features 36 Y-shaped piers supporting a 'flute-edged roof', as Huxtable calls it (Huxtable 1960: 29). While many elements of the Palazzetto are repeated in the Palazzo – the glass wall, circular plan, lamella interior dome – the roof and the structural supports are unique to the Palazzetto, and are often highlighted as the key to the Palazzetto's impact on its visitors. Critics and visitors generally agree that the Palazzetto was the 'most delightful building these Games produced' (Gordon 1983: 63).

In his designs for the Olympic venues, Nervi stayed true to the design standards he established in his earlier work: every element in the buildings is functional and essential. In discussing one of his earlier works, Nervi stated: 'The esthetically satisfying result of the interplay of ribs placed in this way is a clear reminder of the mysterious affinity to be found between physical laws and our own senses.'[13] Nervi maintained that the success of his efficient designs lay in their simple structural expression, where force lines are emphasised, natural mathematical curves are employed, and repetitive patterns create rhythmic harmony. Huxtable theorised that Nervi never set out to create architecture, but rather to solve a structural problem (Huxtable 1960: 28). And yet in the Palazzo and Palazzetto dello Sport, his structural solutions were asked to rise above mere architecture into the lofty realm of enduring landmarks in a city already crowded with extraordinary sights and attractions.

Now that the circumstances in which these buildings were erected and the expectations that were placed upon them have been discussed, the questions remain: Were they successful? Did they achieve the lofty goals set out for them by Games organisers, the city, and the entire nation? Architecturally speaking, the buildings have been considered largely successful from the time they were built through to the present day, especially the Palazzetto, which has garnered international praise in myriad books on architecture of the twentieth century. But in terms of Rome's vast history, these buildings are mere babies, nearly sixty years old. What all Olympic host cities know, however, is that the longest era in the life of any Olympic building is its life after the Games. Since 1960, both buildings have been in continuous use, the Palazzo still as a sports arena but also as a concert hall, and the Palazzetto as an arena for local sports.

Can it be measured whether the buildings and the Olympics helped the city regain its place on the world stage? Could this architecture have actually lifted the spirits of the city's inhabitants? Could it have truly inspired those who, for the first time, were watching from around the world? Obviously, this type of success is impossible to measure quantitatively. What is undeniable is the fact that these buildings stand as physical testaments to the massive effort undertaken by the city to rejuvenate itself and restore its international reputation. This effort was duplicated almost identically in the next Olympics, held in 1964 in Tokyo, Japan, a city and a country also intensely affected by World War II. Japan, like Italy, had experienced the resultant hardships of its participation in World War II and was in the process of recovering its economic, cultural, and political footing when it hosted the 1964 Summer Games. New venues built for the Games, especially those built by Japanese architect Kenzo Tange (who had toured Nervi's Olympic buildings in 1962), played an important role in bridging the gap between historic and modern Japan, both physically and in spirit (Sacchi 2004: 63). Tange delivered architecture for the Tokyo Games that lived up to the precedent established by Nervi in 1960 Rome, creating venues that served as modern, apolitical monuments in another city that was intent on rebuilding itself and rehabilitating its international reputation.

Perhaps more than the sincerest form of flattery, Tokyo's imitation of Rome's plan for the 1960 Games was likely simply a recognition of what worked. In more recent years, many cities have followed in Rome's footsteps in trying to create new, apolitical landmarks to generate tourism and revive urban areas, including Bilbao's Guggenheim Museum, and in 2008, Beijing's Bird's Nest and Water Cube for the Summer Olympics. The 1960 Rome Games created a legacy of its own, comfortably ensconced within the city's enormously rich heritage, a brief chapter but essential nonetheless to understanding how the Eternal City regained its title in the wake of World War II.

Notes

1. P. de Coubertin, as quoted in Guttman 2002: 28.
2. Giacomini 1960: 55. While Rome had made applications to host the Games in 1940 and 1944, Mussolini had been thwarted in his quest by Tokyo (1940) and London (1944). Neither of these Games took place due to World War II.
3. Giacomini 1960: 54. Many buildings erected for past Olympics had been temporary installations in an effort to minimise overall costs.
4. For more information on Nervi's life and early works, see Huxtable (1960) and Kidder Smith (1955).
5. The political implications of the organising committee's site selection did not go entirely unnoticed, however. Just prior to the opening of the Games, inscriptions honouring Mussolini and other Fascist symbols were chiseled away from buildings in the Foro Italico by order of the Italian Parliament, as noted in 'Fascist Symbols Go for Rome Olympics', *New York Times* 9 August 1960, 2.
6. Two billion lire in 1958 would equal approximately $3.2 million U.S. dollars in the same year. Despite the organisers' claims, new venue construction costs were not necessarily minimised at the Games. The Olympic Stadium cost 3.4 billion lire, the Olympic Velodrome cost just over 1 billion, and Flaminio Stadium cost 900 million. The Palazzetto dello Sport, at a cost of 263 million lire, was lauded for its cost-effectiveness.
7. Official documentation issued by the Rome organising committee and the Italian Olympic Committee and most notices in architectural journals credit Nervi and Piacentini as the primary design team, while the majority of information provided in newspapers and magazines name only Nervi.
8. The extent of Piacentini's participation in the design of the Palazzo dello Sport continues to be debated by critics. The fact that Piacentini was 78 when the Palazzo was built (he died in 1960), contributes to the belief that Piacentini's role as co-designer of the building may have been limited, making his tendency towards political rhetoric in architecture largely moot in the case of the Palazzo.
9. 'Nervi's Views on Architecture, Education, and Structure' in *Architectural Record*, December 1958, 118.
10. For sketches and additional information on Nervi's Vienna submission, see Huxtable (1960) and 'Hall des sports de Vienne' in *Architecture d'Aujourd'hui* 1954, July-August, vol. 25, 72-5.
11. For a discussion of the architect's building processes, see Kidder Smith (1955) and Nervi (1956).
12. The Palazzetto cost approximately $475,000 to build in 1956-57.
13. Nervi as quoted in Huxtable 1960: 27.

Trailing the Olympic Epic: Black Modernity and the Athenian Arena, 2004

Michael Simpson

The highlight of the BBC's extensive coverage of the Athens Olympics in 2004 was the BBC's promotion of that coverage. In two trailers that initially heralded and then accompanied the broadcasts, a lone athlete was shown, either running with a torch or using his sporting prowess in hostile encounters with various mythical beings. 'Awesome', for once, is plausible. Yet my opening claim may look at best mischievous, and at worst grossly unfair. Surely the events themselves, not to mention the athletes, must eclipse both the BBC's coverage of these events and the mere advertising of it? After all, both coverage and promotion depend logically and materially on what they cover and promote, respectively: without the cast, no broadcast. But this sensible caveat reckons without the liberties available to the BBC's advertising of its Olympic broadcasts. The events themselves, like all sports when spectated rather than executed, are attended by a degree of repetition, mechanism and sheer tedium. The coverage, meanwhile, though increasingly compelling because of technological advances in filming and editing, is ultimately constrained by the nature of the events represented. The promotion of the coverage, however, is largely untaxed by such mundane considerations of reference and can employ those technological resources more creatively, adding fiction to fact, by way of computer animation, and thus dramatising the events as myths. Even protests, as we shall see, can be covered by this dramatisation.

This is the BBC: announcing Athens

Scintillating rather than slick, the BBC's promotion consisted of two separate trailers related by the common factor of the runner, played by the same actor. I shall concentrate on the longer of the two, describing it in some detail, before analysing it as part of my larger argument. The shorter of the two trailers traces the progress of a male athlete, trimly bearded, dark-skinned, and wearing a white leotard featuring the Olympic logo, as he runs bearing an Olympic torch across diverse but recognisable Greek landscapes, natural and cultural, until he reaches an elongated Greco-Roman stadium and lifts the torch, under the five rings of the Olympic logo, as though he might light the Olympic flame.

The longer trailer is structured round a series of dramatic confrontations. It begins with a close-up of two running shoes worn by an unseen figure, as one of them is stamped on the ground. The camera zooms out to reveal the same athlete, identically attired, standing on a white square on a vast chessboard, behind which is a white mountain or mountains constructed like crystalline columns. Disclosed there, in a palace, are figures resembling Hera and Zeus in Don Chaffey's film *Jason and the Argonauts* (1963), as they manipulate mortals through chess pieces, for their own amusement.[1] Taking up the athlete's challenge, Zeus deploys on the board a chess piece bearing the word 'Hercules', and the camera reverts to the athlete's location, as a partly ruined statue dissolves into rocks which then recompose themselves before him into a monstrous, or heroic, figure. This creature hurls a rock, like a discus, which crashes through the columns in the side of a Greek temple on a mountainside, making a hole through it. The athlete makes his throw, and his projectile flies through the hole already made and thereby exceeds Hercules' pitch. With a satisfied smile, back on Olympus, Hera flicks Hercules' chess piece over, and on the ground he duly crumbles into a heap of boulders.

Now the athlete runs into a city composed largely of futuristic white columns which resemble Olympus, where Zeus mobilises a chess piece signifying Hermes. In the city, the athlete duly encounters Hermes, and the two race together until Hermes takes flight in order to traverse a chasm between buildings. Short-circuited, the athlete responds simply by running further and faster, to compensate for Hermes' stratagem, and catches up with him before pulling ahead and winning. Zeus responds by angrily sweeping the pieces off the chessboard while Hera looks on, horrified. As the pieces are scattered, one remains on the board, bearing the name Poseidon. The athlete has reached a cliff above the sea and is confronted by a colossal and monstrously amphibious Poseidon rising from the water. Diving into the sea, the athlete swims away, and Poseidon pursues him before being obstructed by rocks which allow the much smaller athlete to escape between them. Game over.

Throughout this action, there has been an insistent soundtrack featuring an instrumental riff from a garage rock song, complete with pounding bass line and heavy electric guitars.[2] Back on Olympus, Zeus walks peremptorily away from the game, Hera smiles triumphantly, and the athlete attains his destination, which is a crowded stadium, with vaguely Roman contours, in which he victoriously raises his left arm to universal applause. Meanwhile, the very English male voiceover intones, 'The Olympic Games, starts 13th of August on the BBC. Legends will be rewritten.'

But why do these trailers and their shared and distinct features matter? After all, the running time – literally – has been sixty seconds for one and ninety for the other. The classical references are obviously relevant to the agenda of this volume, but what is the larger import of the trailers, as a preface to the BBC's Olympics coverage? The answer is that this coverage of the greatest show on earth, by perhaps the most respected broadcasting organ on the planet, is an exercise in global communication, and that the trailers, prefacing and contextualising the sport itself, serve to inscribe it with meaning. Such meaning was sustained by the fact that different segments of the trailers, of varying duration, regularly interpolated the BBC's coverage. The short trailer was a segment unto itself, while the long one was sometimes screened in full and sometimes in parts. Broadcast so often and displaying such creativity and technical gloss, these trailers may have even been instrumental in augmenting the UK television audience for the opening ceremony, which was 8.6 million viewers, as compared with 3.5 millions for the Sydney Games in 2000.[3]

My overall argument is as follows. The broadcasting ambit of the BBC potentially addresses the globe, through proliferating channels centred on the internet. Meanwhile, the Olympics potentially represents the world, as a metonym of it. But there is a limit on all this cultural globalisation, not least on the BBC's Olympics coverage, which was confined at the time to the UK. Despite the Olympian nature of the BBC's address, further-more, virtually to the world about the world, this address, in the trailer, promotes a quite particular worldview. Although the political geography of this worldview is given more historical depth in the trailer, by way of the classical figures, the worldview itself remains ideologically narrow, cinematically framed, as it is, within an allegorical epic of the triumph of Western values. Purveyed here is only the dominant model of globalisa-tion. It is, indeed, the familiarity of this story and model that permits the trailer to make sense as it is segmented differentially throughout the BBC's Olympic coverage. Without knowing the epic already, we wouldn't be able to give these segments meaning and so permit them to impart that meaning to the Athens Olympics. This epic is dramatically interrupted, however, by its own resources, as both African modernity and the tragic mode of classical Greece contradict this story; the very resourcefulness of the epic, faithfully presented by the trailer, is what prevents the trailer from controlling its associations. In constructing this argument, I shall subscribe to the broad methodology of classical reception studies, which will be supplemented by the theoretical orientation of sports studies and the coordinates of that field shared with cultural studies. My analytical method, meanwhile, will be derived chiefly from literary studies, especially as inflected by a dramatic and theatrical concentra-tion adapted to film.

To develop this substantive argument, I shall elaborate an analysis of the longer trailer, which is a worthy text for this theme not only because of its ideological complexity but also because of its sheer cinematic virtu-osity.[4] It is a systematic interpenetration of present and past, of ancient and modern, in the modelling of Olympus, the styling of the amphitheatre, and in the relationship between marvellous Greek epic and the ingenious techniques of animation and film-editing. The Athens Olympics are thus cast as a realisation of ancient promise, as testimony to the globalisation of an originally Greek enlightenment, now returning to source to be tested and celebrated against that ideal. How we got here, however, was via a largely linear epic plot, coursing progressively through history, and occasionally, as now, recurring to Greek sources for a fix of authentication. This historical epic is recounted as a series of mythical trials, notably the contests between the mortal athlete and three apparently immortal counterparts. There is also another dimension of conflict constituted by Zeus and Hera, who are engaged in the game of chess. Chess was, of course, one proxy arena in which the Cold War was fought, especially in the highly charged contest between Bobby Fischer and Boris Spassky in 1972, which coincided with the Munich Olympics.[5] Substantiating this allegorical equation between the chess game in the trailer and the Cold War is the status of Hera and Zeus, as higher powers who might thus represent the superpowers, each investing their champions with a larger import. What is at stake historically, then, between the athlete and his opponents, is, in the terms of the allegory, the conflict between the West and Communism, between the First World and the Second. Since the victory has already been won, however, the contest between Hera and Zeus can be recoded comically as the war of the sexes, in which, as the cliché goes, women have always already won. Hera and Zeus are clearly not Shakespeare's Miranda and Ferdinand in *The Tempest*. Indeed, the citation of Chaffey's *Jason and the Argonauts* gestures to Hollywood and thereby invokes this American medium to affirm, jovially, the victory of the West.[6]

Given that the Olympics are a global media event and that this trailer is a small element therein, some relevant comparison is in order. It should be said straight away that spectacular trailers promoting broadcast coverage of the Games are by no means specific to the BBC or to Athens 2004. NBC fielded a vivid trailer in 2004, and such devices, in varying forms and magnitude, have been a feature of most coverage since Rome 1960, which was the first Olympics to be televised in any meaningful sense.[7] These spectacles appear to have increased in ambition, complexity and duration in a correlation with developments in the opening ceremonies of the Games. Inflating the pageantry significantly was the Moscow Olympics of 1980, and Barcelona in 1992 seems to have marked a more self-conscious orientation towards television, perhaps reflecting the wider availability of video recording technology from the mid-1980s onwards.[8] Coverage can now be recovered, for future delectation.

Yet, for all the resources and inventiveness expended on these sequences promoting this coverage, there is not necessarily a story of progressive advance to tell about the BBC's efforts. While 2004 featured the stunner of the runner, the BBC's offering for the Beijing Olympics in 2008 was an animation incorporating a monkey, a pig and a green monster. Notwithstanding the differences, there are some common factors: they feature characters from Greek and Chinese myths, respectively; they dramatise an epic plot, culminating in arrival at the Olympic stadium; as trailers, they are knowingly reflexive, conveying us vicariously to the stadium, by tracing the characters on the same trajectory; and they both figure arrival there as a redemption.[9] Watch the BBC and get so close that you feel like an Olympian. In being televisually delivered to the Olympic stadium in Athens, moreover, we were first being included as privileged observers of a certain history of civilisation, and hence of ourselves: as preparation for spectating and then identifying with the athletes as they competed, we were installed as witnesses to the opening ceremony and, within it, a massive pageant representing the process of civilisation, encoded as the history of Greek art. The variety of cultural styles paraded in the succession of tableaux-vivants addressed a potentially wide, even multicultural audience, provided that the audience was prepared to respond to this invitation in terms that favour Greek culture and its supposed recruitment of some other cultures towards the telos of Western modernity.[10] Though direct collusion with the BBC was ruled out by the official secrecy surrounding the planning of the opening ceremony, the BBC trailer had rehearsed us well for it, and the ceremony effectively reciprocated. The pageant, after all, was titled 'allegory'.

Small screen, big picture

There is another instalment in the triumph of the West vibrating quite discernibly within the epic trailer. This one turns on the mortal athlete himself, and particularly on his ethnic profile as contrasted with that of other characters.[11] Though his ethnic identity is opaquely unspecific, there is the distinct possibility that he is characterised as being of African descent, and it is this figuring that I shall assume and address. Corroborating this reading, in a binary opposition, is the fact that his second opponent is an immortal, blonde, Aryan Hermes, or superman, backed by a stereotypically white Zeus, who resembles a very Anglo-Saxon, patriarchal Hollywood producer, equipped with distinguished short white hair and beard, and, if he spoke, probably an English accent, to bespeak the sinister. The athlete, meanwhile, is sponsored by a conceivably 'oriental' Hera, though categorically not a black Athena (Fig. 10.1). Hercules, in the first contest, has no ethnic profile, but, like Hermes and Zeus himself, he is cast as constitutionally superior to the mortal athlete, who is therefore supposed to lose (Fig. 10.2). But he doesn't, and this scene of heroically thwarted expectations, which were predicated on an assumption of inferiority, recalls the Berlin Olympics in 1936, where Jesse Owens triumphed in four events.[12] Famously detonating the Nazi ideology of Aryan supremacy and African subordination, along with the pseudo-science that rationalised it, Owens effectively enacted an Homeric epic.[13] In doing so, he was

Fig. 10.1. Zeus and Hera with chess board.

Fig. 10.2. Athlete confronting Hercules.

one of a number of cultural agents who helped to project African peoples into the frame of classical Greece. It is to this compatibility that the BBC's short trailer gestures in showing an African-descended athlete picking up the torch of Greece and, like Prometheus, taking light and civilisation into a world implicitly benighted.

So, the BBC's epic trailer allegorically recounts famous victories over Fascism, in the athlete's performance, like Jesse Owens in track and field, and over Communism, in the conceit of the chess game, which is both an arena within and a metaphor for the competition of the Cold War. But what exactly does this allegory valorise? Who wins? Is it merely some idealised notion of the Olympic tradition or is it a bigger and more numinous concept of 'the West'? I think it is both, at least.[14] What consolidates the Olympics and the West into a single ideological manifold within the trailer is especially visible in the athlete's encounter with Hercules. This contest is highly charged in any case because it involves a modern athlete being pitted against the founder of the Olympic Games, after he has become immortal. By desecrating, with his discus, one of the gods' own temples, Hercules signifies the damage that is done to the ideal of Greece by efforts to stage-manage the contest and thus appropriate that ideal to another agenda; neither Zeus nor Hitler can be allowed to dictate the outcome and significance of the Olympic Games, which in 2004, as in 1936, will be determined not by a conspiracy of higher powers but by a competition between individual mortals, and the higher powers that they represent respectively. It's the athlete stamping his foot, not Zeus, that starts the competition. Zeus' trafficking with Hermes and Hercules is an attempt to fix the contest and its agenda, whereas Hera's relationship with a mortal African athlete is a contrary effort to open the contest and its agenda, potentially to all comers, including those who might not be conventionally identified with the glory that was Greece. To do so is, of course, more consonant with the Greek ideal of competition, and so the athlete becomes more Greek than Zeus himself, precisely in the act of winning this competition between conspiracy and competition. Once the athlete, as a modern Olympian, challenges Zeus' old role as the deity to whom the ancient Olympics were dedicated, and Zeus responds by entering the meta-competition, the latter puts in play, and at risk, his right to make up the rules rather than abide by them. By triumphing in this strategic competition, for the principle of competition, the African-descended athlete, like Jesse Owens, restores Greece to itself, in the very year when the Olympics returned there. The circle is complete, and one plausible name for this historical trajectory, and what it encompasses culturally and economically, is 'the West', though some related terms will also be canvassed in what follows.

What the allegorical epic of the trailer thus valorises, in particular, is the principle of competition. It also explains why. Competition, as instantiated metonymically in the Olympic Games, beginning in Greece and asserting itself thereafter, is represented as the efficient working of history itself, as it sorts the more sustainable forms of social life from the less sustainable. Thus, Fascism and Communism, in turn, perish before a stronger competitor. The validity of the latter's success, and of this Hegelian model that describes how it achieves it, is demonstrated in the very characteristics of this winning social form: liberal democracy and capitalism share, inter alia, the property of competition. Ancient Greece,

Michael Simpson

in its investment in competition, thus formulates the iron law of history aright, at the beginning, and so is continuous with modern capitalist liberal democracy.

The premium placed on competition is legible in the specifically Homeric episodes that feature in the epic within the trailer. While the short trailer, as we have noted, invokes the mythical figure of Prometheus, in the torch relay, the long trailer can be seen as resonantly Odyssean. The quests of Herakles and Jason also reverberate here, though in a minor key. As this Hercules pitches his discus through the temple, and as the athlete exploits this opportunity by throwing his own discus through the gap, thereby surpassing the first cast, the scenario of Odysseus confronting the Cyclops comes into focus: it is Polyphemus who, in accordance with Odysseus' plan, rolls away the great stone from the mouth of the cave, after he has been blinded, whereupon Odysseus and his men slip past him. Unlike Odysseus, the athlete does not plan for this advantage, as his facial expression clearly indicates, and he merely capitalises on the opening in the temple as it arises. The outcomes of the two contests are very similar, however, as the human protagonists turn the strength of their non-human antagonists to their own account.

The succeeding two encounters, with Hermes then Poseidon, follow this pattern. Hermes resorts to the trick of flying, but this device merely provokes the athlete to go 'faster, higher, stronger', until he wins. There may well be a broad parallel between this event and Odysseus' brief competition in the games hosted by the Phaeacians, where he is provoked by Euryalos to throw the discus victoriously. But precise equations with Odysseus' feats throughout the epic seem to be almost deliberately thwarted by the trailer, since he declares to the Phaeacians:

> Of the others I say that I am far superior, of all the men who are now upon the earth, eating bread. I would not wish to contend with the men of old, nor Herakles, nor Eurytos of Oikhalia, who rivalled even the gods at the bow ... Only in running do I fear lest one of the Phaeacians surpass me, for I have been tamed too shamefully in many waves.[15]

Unlike the athlete, he can neither run so well now nor compete, retrospectively, with Herakles, at least in archery. Diverging more radically from the *Odyssey*, however, is the ending of the trailer, where the athlete arrives 'home', even as a returning champion, like the Games themselves as they recur to Greece, but unlike Odysseus whose homecoming is infinitely more complex. Although the scenes within the trailer only gesture towards the *Odyssey*, they are consistent with one another in respect of the property discussed above: competition, no matter how adverse or unfair, improves the athlete's performance and his progress towards the Olympics themselves. Hercules and Hermes, as we have seen, merely inspire the athlete to defeat them, effectively by their own strength. In the

10. Trailing the Olympic Epic

event, Poseidon pursues the athlete through his own element of water using his colossal strength, yet his sheer size not only prevents him from closing the chase beyond the rim of rocks but also serves to propel the athlete forwards, ahead of him, on the very wave that his pursuit generates before him.

What this paradigm asserts, within the allegorical epic of the trailer, is the supremacy of competition in global history, crucially informed by Western civilisation, of which the Olympic tradition forms a part: competition can convert unfair or bad competition into fair or good competition, and so validates itself. Since this argument is articulated in a representation of the Olympics, moreover, the geographical dimension of the history assembled here is accentuated: to the extent that the Games are a global phenomenon, they associate, in this account of them, the principle of competition, and capitalist liberal democracy which it shapes, with the process of globalisation by which that economic and political system is propagated.[16] In syllogistically establishing these successive linkages, the trailer factors ancient Greece into the sequence, at the very beginning, where it functions as an origin of competition, democracy, capitalism, globalisation, and of course, history itself, which is here represented as the working out of these forces through the founding principle of competition.

In telling and showing this rather standard *grand récit* so impressively, the trailer achieves something else. It reconciles the two opposed conceptions of the Olympics that are paraded ritually across international public culture: on the one hand, the Olympics are cast as pure, formal competition, as that lonely, empty 'tunnel' described by one of the runners in the British film *Chariots of Fire* (1981); on the other hand, they are represented as saturated with politics, as a pulsing content. The trailer reformulates these opposed perspectives not only as a dichotomous single model of the Olympics but also reconciles them, while preserving the integrity of each. The Olympics here really is pure competition, but what results from this rigorously formal exercise is a selection among polities which, in their time, possess immense substance. Sporting form and political content are coordinated beautifully by the trailer.

Breaking records, bending rules

Yet the trailer is smarter, even, than this, since it seems to be able to anticipate and incorporate, at least as complications, a historical ghost or two that haunt and contradict this epic of the West. As the athlete raises his arm in the stadium, does he not glancingly trace the 'Black Power' salute of Tommie Smith and John Carlos at the Mexico City Olympics in 1968? Any such equation between the athlete and the two Olympians is complicated by the fact that the athlete raises his left arm in a gesture of triumph, whereas the standard Black Power salute involved the right arm, as did the Fascist salute (Fig. 10.3).[17] Given that the right is the general

179

Fig. 10.3. Athlete salutes in 'Olympic stadium'.

norm in any case, the athlete's gesture would appear to be a designed deflection of this sign of Black Power, as of Fascism. But there is another twist here. While Tommie Smith saluted with his right arm, John Carlos used his left. Decoding the drama of the event shortly afterwards, Smith declared: 'The right glove that I wore on my right hand signified the power within black America. The left glove my teammate John Carlos wore on his arm made an arc with my right hand and his left hand also to signify black unity.'[18] But necessity also mothered invention: the athletes used different hands because Carlos had forgotten to bring his own pair of symbolic black gloves, unlike Smith, and so Smith's pair was divided, or shared, between them.[19] In the event, the athletes give victory with one hand and take it away with the other, as they win the race but refuse to participate in the symbolic relay of Western, and especially American, triumph: capitalist liberal democracy wins out, in the American forms of Tommie Smith and later Bobby Fischer, against all comers, but the African-American figure of Smith exposes, from the inside, the historical cost of that victory. A small part of that cost is the figurative ode of Pindaric praise that Smith would otherwise have garnered; a larger part is the death threats that he and Carlos received on their return to the US, only months after the assassination of Martin Luther King, Jr.[20]

Any such dramatic moment of dissent with and within the epic trailer is recuperated, however, as the athlete in the stadium catches the contours of Martin Luther King at the Lincoln Memorial and so gestures back to civil rights already achieved and forwards to their potential substantiation in Athens 2004 and beyond. Centred against the neo-classical stylings of the Lincoln Memorial in 1963 and invoking a historical memory of victory in the Civil War, King, like the BBC's athlete, addresses an

180

attentive multitude and looks forward, famously, to another victory. Like King, the triumphant athlete has a dream, but it is one that seems to take for granted and follow logically from the historical fulfilment of King's; the athlete can compete and win because the dream of Civil Rights has been realised. So it's OK, the West can cope with its own history. But if the trailer is so smart, in its articulation of the epic, why is it that the ultimate principle of competition, promoted by trailer and epic alike, is nowhere to be seen at the end? The epic has triumphed in its story of competition, and so now there is no competition. There is no competitor against the West, and there is no competitor against this epic story itself. We seem suddenly to be becalmed, in what used to be Francis Fukuyama's post-history (1992). Adroitly manipulating this contradiction between 'now you see it, now you don't', the narrative logic of the trailer, at its conclusion, is that the competition has been sublimated into the sport of the Athens Olympics, which we are now about to watch.[21]

To the degree that the trailer can symbolically overcome the contradictions that it acknowledges, especially within its own ideological thrust, it promotes the hegemonic version of globalisation, as an expansion of economic and political neo-liberalism. It anchors and legitimates that large process historically, as we have seen, by rhetorically plotting a continuity with ancient Greece. The geographical axis of this version of globalisation, meanwhile, is provided by the institutions of international sport, not only in the trailer but in point of fact. Nancy Rivenburgh summarises the scholarly consensus about the channel between sport and globalisation:

> Sport is essential to the globalising structure of media organisations. Sport is a relatively cheap method for filling hours of television time and moves easily across cultural and linguistic borders. Rupert Murdoch called sports the 'cornerstone of our [News Corporation] worldwide broadcasting' (2003: 35).

The institution of the Olympic Games, which the trailer introduces, is thus part of the infrastructure of globalisation; television coverage of the Games is a medium of globalisation; and the sporting events themselves are part of the content, or symbolic capital, of the process.[22] Coordinating these factors, the BBC's trailer advances the received version of globalisation, even as it is resisted by those such as John Hargreaves, who asserts, 'Globalisation is not a myth, but neither is it as significant as is often made out' (2002: 41). Rivenburgh is similarly sceptical about the staying power of the Olympics as a 'global media event' among proliferating alternative spectacles in new channels of communication. She invokes two taxing prerequisites: 'a fundamental allure of media events is that they resonate with human mythology and a fascination with the transcendent' (2003: 47). In mobilising the resource of Greek myth, the trailer both elevates such 'human mythology' within the Olympics and promotes the hegemonic 'myth' of globalisation beyond the critical bounds that Hargreaves realistically, and in my view rightly, tracks.[23] There is much to be gained from actively mythologising globalisation, because this protean process without a settled definition or understanding might be shaped to the advantage of any agency that can successfully narrate it.

In the event, there is more competition behind and around this BBC trailer than it admits, as it deflects the competition onto the Games themselves. The coverage itself is involved in a competition for viewers, within a global market of broadcasting. Though the BBC is constitutionally prevented from advertising other commodities, it is not debarred from advertising itself and its products: the BBC trailer thus advertises BBC Olympics coverage which advertises BBC programmes, which can be purchased, at competitive rates. One index of the commercial stakes here is that the Athens Olympics was the first to be broadcast by the BBC via broadband, including live streaming video. In this context, the internationally scrutable nature of the trailer, largely devoid of language, comes into commercial focus, as does its heroic context and its inclusiveness: who wouldn't want to identify with the hero and winning side here, and who, in the 'developed' world at least, could not?[24] As such, the conceit of the exclusive Cold War chess game is here re-written as the inclusive twenty-first-century computer game. Mythologised classically, and watched via broadband for the first time, the athletes at the Athens Games are framed as mythological action figures in a computer game that 'we' could all play.[25] Although national rights to broadcast coverage of the Olympics are agreed and guaranteed, such that 'rights-holders' in one nation cannot compete directly for viewers with rights-holders in another nation, a quantum of indirect competition with NBC over other products and programming is likely to have borne on why the BBC trailer tells the story that it does. If you like this …

There may be another dimension of competition within which the trailer operates. Telling the triumph of the West in 2004, with reference to the touchstone of Athens, barely three years after the terrorist attacks on the US, and just one year after the invasion of Iraq, may be more than coincidental. This telling thus occurs competitively, in the context of another, imagined epic that is attributed to terrorism in general and an Islamic terrorism in particular. Alien and monstrous, the figure of Poseidon in the trailer may even register a trace of this terrible antithesis. It is this aspiring epic that Tony Blair rejected in casting the 'War on Terror' as an epic struggle not 'between civilisations', or different epics, but 'about civilisation' itself, between narratives that compete to be the one, supreme epic.[26] The assumption here was that the other, attempted epic was too inept and destructive to win the prize. Therefore, the real one must win.

The question of what is the real one, among 'master narratives', has been raised by Fredric Jameson and decided according to some exacting criteria applied in the search for

10. Trailing the Olympic Epic

... an adequate account of the essential *mystery* of the cultural past, which like Tiresias drinking the blood, is momentarily returned to life and warmth and allowed once more to speak, and to deliver its long-forgotten message in surroundings utterly alien to it. This mystery can be re-enacted only if the human adventure is one; only thus ... can we glimpse the vital claims upon us of such long-dead issues as the seasonal alternation of the economy of a primitive tribe, the passionate disputes about the Trinity, the conflicting models of the *polis* or the universal empire, or ... the dusty parliamentary and journalistic polemics of the nineteenth-century nation-states. These matters can recover their original urgency for us only if they are retold within the unity of a single great collective story; only if, in however disguised and symbolic form, they are seen as sharing a single fundamental theme – for Marxism, the collective struggle to wrest a realm of freedom from a realm of Necessity; only if they are grasped as vital episodes in a single vast unfinished plot (1981: 19-20).

Though predating, in 1981, the late phase of the Cold War, this formulation of a philosophy of history possesses considerable coherence, especially since Fukuyama's 'end of history', identified with an international liberal capitalist order, came to such an early end. This formulation is exemplified, moreover, by certain aspects of the allegory that I have read in the BBC's long trailer: the epic form there has embraced, at least gesturally, numerous cultures along both historical and geographical axes and has adopted a critical stance towards a few of them in the process. It has also concluded with an unfinished plot, in delivering its viewers to the 2004 Olympic contest itself. So compelling is this epic narrative of the *longue durée*, even in its cinematic compression and velocity, that it can accommodate certain impediments within its course, as they resist the forces that would breathlessly gloss over them. The 1968 Mexico City Games and the 1972 Munich Olympics were both occasions of hideous political violence: at the former, dozens of people were killed by Mexican security forces, and at the latter, terrorists murdered eleven Israeli athletes. Insisting that they be read and accorded due reflection, these particular Olympics, as they are discerned, resist the narrative sweep of the trailer, force some recursion, and so prevent this sweep from conditioning the audience in merely passive spectating. Rather than being swayed, we may want to stop the record, rewind, rethink, replay.[27]

Shades of tragedy

For all its fresh historical impetus and high production values, the epic of Western values as presented in the BBC trailer competes not only with external factors, such as other broadcasting networks and the imagined terrorist counter-narrative, but also with its own internal resources. Beyond the general references to the 1968 and 1972 Games, which the trailer can accommodate, it contains some elements that it cannot. In its effort to win the external competitions, the trailer and therefore the epic must compete with the very means that they deploy to these ends.[28] Some of these means are neutral, such as the witty citation of the Peugeot car commercial, when Hercules mechanically assembles himself to confront the mortal athlete.[29] But at least two means tell against this epic telling: one is the suggestive ethnicity of the athlete himself, along with his gesture of raising his arm; the other is Greek tragedy, emerging spectrally from the Greek apparatus invoked by the trailer.[30]

Let's take them in turn. By casting the athlete as Jesse Owens, the trailer poses him as a final solution to Fascism and then, in the combined gesture of the Olympic salutation/Black Power salute, seeks to de-activate him as a problem in his testimony to Western colonialism. But acknowledging Tommie Smith and John Carlos's gesture is not quite enough rhetorically to write colonialism, in Africa as elsewhere, out of the story of the West.[31] Whether acknowledged or not, colonialism is a principal condition, as well as cost, in that 'success' story. It is this contradiction within the epic, otherwise muted, that was amplified by Carl Lewis, the African-American four-times gold medallist, in his public statement about the Athens Olympics. This statement was a reaction to President George W. Bush's apparent attempt to use the presence of Iraqi and Afghan teams at the Athens Olympics to vindicate his foreign policy, during the 2004 presidential election campaign. Lewis challenged the President's argument that the American military presence in Iraq and Afghanistan enabled the sporting presence of Iraqis and Afghans in Athens. Said Lewis:

> 'I felt that was disingenuous. It is funny that we boycotted the 1980 Games [in Moscow] in support of Afghanistan, and now we're bombing Afghanistan...
> 'Of course, we've invaded Iraq and are in there and are using it for political gain. It bewilders me, and I understand why the Iraqi players are offended.
> 'To support the players or the community is fine, but for political gain I disagree.'[32]

Just as Smith and Carlos resisted any attempt to integrate their victory in the 200 metres race into a larger national narrative of the arms race, the space race and American foreign policy in Vietnam, so Lewis blocked the logic that would assimilate Iraqi soccer to an ongoing epic of Western values. As much as Smith and Carlos's gesture, Lewis's intervention is sensitive to a partly hidden and hypocritical colonialism.[33] Black bodies will not simply settle under the sign of 'black athleticism', since the minds within and behind those bodies know better, and what they know, quite often, is other worldviews. Discernible here is an African-American tradition, further empowered by the Black Consciousness Movement, of telling part of the African diaspora against an epic of the West composed of chiefly European and American components.[34]

Cognate with this African-American tradition was a larger Pan-African

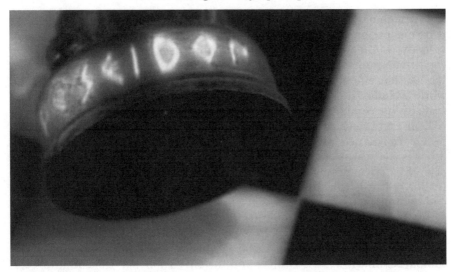

Fig. 10.4. Overturned chess piece on board.

tradition of contesting the complicity of international institutions, such as the Olympics, in their appropriation by apartheid South Africa, as it sought bilateral ties that worked to corrupt such larger institutions. I'm thinking here of the boycotting of the 1976 Montreal Olympics by most African nations, in protest against New Zealand's participation following its sporting links with South Africa. Almost as rehearsals for this action were the threatened boycott of the 1968 Olympics in Mexico City, also on the grounds of alleged Olympic complicity with the apartheid regime, and a similar campaign against the inclusion of Rhodesia in the Munich Games in 1972.[35] Though epic in its defiance, this tradition is tragic in mood, as it exposes the multiple tragedies that are spun off from the epic of Western values. In the terms of the chess game shown in the trailer, which is played exclusively on the white squares, black modernity insists on playing simultaneously on the black squares, thus conducting a parallel game, which enables it to strategise against the great game, and its own playing, on the white squares.[36] The perfect asymmetry between the two games means that a move in one is also a move in the other, to the advantage of a black double consciousness that is acutely aware of playing in both (Fig. 10.4).[37] In the alternative terms of the athletic competitions depicted in the long trailer, this Pan-African tradition is a refusal to take the baton, or torch, in the figurative relay of the history of the West. Or, to adjust the terms, if this baton is taken, it is brandished as a torch on a new course, which returns the Olympics to Greece only in the sense of illuminating modern shortcomings and hypocrisies, before this torch blazes a more independent trajectory.

The second resource within the trailer that contests this epic story, after the African or African-descended athlete, is the Greek apparatus itself as it furnishes the tragic genre in an unwelcome addition to the epic. Greek tragedy would certainly be a more appropriate genre in accounting the conditions and cost of Western values. There are several aspects of the trailer that cue a tragic dimension, even as the ideological thrust of the work occludes it. One is the homology between the Games and Greek tragedy as competitive events, such that the Festival of Dionysos in Athens and the Games at Olympia awarded almost the same prize for the best performance: an olive wreath and an ivy wreath, respectively. Another is the status of the trailer as a work of art. Starting with a pastiche of a Nike advertisement, in the opening shot of the athlete's shoes, the trailer gestures towards 'high' and 'low' cultural artifacts, such as video games and Homeric epic, which together promote it as a postmodern artwork; meanwhile, the breathtaking production values compound this aesthetic self-consciousness. Beyond this partly ironic, partly earnest self-assertion, however, there is a quality of the trailer, related to the comparison between the Games and the City Dionysia, that qualifies the postmodernity of this playful palette and recalls the dignity of tragedy: insistently resembling the Olympic opening ceremony, and replaying it ritually within the cycle of the BBC's daily programming, before and during the 2004 Games, the trailer itself assumes the aura of a ritual action. As well as being a kitsch artwork, it is also a ceremonial event, like an Athenian tragedy.

But what evokes this form most strenuously is, ironically enough, a strategic absence: aside from Hera, there are no women in the trailer. Despite the ethnic diversity figured by the black athlete, such diversity does not extend, from a white, male norm, to the realm of gender.[38] Sport, like war, is once again gendered as male.[39] Where women do exist in numbers, of course, is Greek tragedy, wherein they regularly represent the underside and aftermath of wars, interrogating the masculine heroism that generates those most spectacular of competitions. As in ancient Athens, so in Athens 2004, tragedy puts epic, and Olympia, to the question. But African, or black, modernity prevents this questioning from merely falling into line within a familiar classical tradition now recomposed around Greek tragedy, rather than Homeric epic. The 2004 Olympics is not allowed simply to return to origins, in Olympia 776 BCE and Athens 1896 CE, as a legitimation of a narrow and circular notion of civilisation. This questioning, springing from within what I have elsewhere called the Black Aegean, redirects global attention from the Olympic podium itself to peoples and communities, other than nations, who either get nowhere near it or whose bones go to build it.[40]

This questioning provokes a further question: Having interrogated the epic and exposed its wide cost, does tragedy then transcend this interrogation and its unsavoury answers by transfiguring the suffering that it discloses within a formal context of beauty? The answer to that question may very well depend on what we understand by tragedy.[41] As underdeveloped and overdeveloped nations convene for the London Games in 2012, amid economic distress caused by the latter group, new versions of old tragedies may be clearer and more clamorous against this Olympic epic. Legends may indeed be rewritten.

Notes

1. Nick Willing's TV movie, also called *Jason and the Argonauts*, but minus the chess game, appeared in 2000. *Harry Potter and the Philosopher's Stone*, in 2001 the first of the Harry Potter films, also featured a gigantic game of 'wizard chess'.

2. The song is 'Hate To Say I Told You So', by the Swedish band The Hives, known for dressing only in black and white.

3. IOC Marketing Report Athens 2004, section 4, 85, at http://www.olympic.org/Documents/Reports/EN/en_report_899.pdf. There is scope for studying such trailers: scholarly inquiry into media coverage of the Olympics has not much remarked such framing. For example, Moragas Spà et al. 1995 begin their own coverage with the commercial, legal and technological entry of broadcasting companies into the actual site of the Games; how the audience is conditioned and maintained, other than by actual coverage, is not treated.

4. This trailer was made for the BBC by Passion Pictures. See it at http://www.createascene.co.uk/commercials/bbc_olympics, along with an account of its staging and filming.

5. Furthermore, chess is recognised as a sport by the IOC, though not an Olympic one, and has its own biennial 'Olympiad'.

6. Wyke 1997: 1-13 examines the stakes in Hollywood's romance with the classics, especially as engendering 'Roman' epics. Nisbet 2006: 1-44 addresses the absence of Greece and presence of Rome in film. Winkler 2001 explores a wide range of cinematic receptions, as does Solomon 2001.

7. The NBC trailer in 2004 differed considerably from the BBC's. There was rapid intercutting between different athletes and sports, and barely any clear references to classical myth. An African-descended runner did appear intermittently, a rowing team may have been pulling between Scylla and Charybdis, and there were some classical ruins, but the format resembled a travel advertisement. NBC's coverage of the 2004 Olympics was the first to be broadcast in HD.

8. Tomlinson 1996 identifies the 1984 Los Angeles Olympics as a beginning here, discussing comparatively the BBC's coverage of several Olympic opening ceremonies.

9. Moragas Spà et al. 1995: 103 are sensitive to the matrix of narratives accruing to the modern Olympics.

10. At Beijing 2008, the ceremony dramatised Chinese civilisation, from ancient to modern times, minus the Revolution.

11. Bass 2002: XVI opines: 'the black athlete is a malleable and complex site, a place to look for discussions of race and nation in the most popular forms.' Hoberman 1997 substantiates this claim powerfully.

12. Owens won the 100 metres dash, the 200 metres dash, the 4 x 100 metres relay and the long jump.

13. See Large 2007 on the 1936 Games overall, and Wiggins and Miller 2003: 163-4 and 169-73 on Owens' achievement related to that of boxer Joe Louis against Max Schmeling in 1938.

14. See Pressly in the present volume for comparably allegorical reading.

15.Tr. Barbara Goff, in a private communication.

16. Coordinating geography and history thus, the trailer exemplifies the potentially global reach of Anderson's 1983 'homogeneous spacetime'.

17. Winkler 2009 explores the origin of Fascist and Nazi salutes, and the Roman connection, in film and theatre.

18. Bass 2002: 240.

19. Spivey 1985: 250.

20. They were powerfully supported, however, by Olympians past and present, including many team mates, and the Olympic Project for Human Rights. See Bass 2002: 233-90.

21. By far the best formal terms for understanding the trailer as frame are MacAloon's 1984. The BBC trailer would thus be 'spectacle', containing 'festival', 'ritual', 'game', and 'truth' in a concentric relay. Here, the frame markers are pointing to 'game'.

22. See also Tomlinson's formulation 1996: 589-90.

23. Giulianotti 2005 goes beyond Hargreaves' focus (2002) on the national, to consider the local as where globalisation is challenged but also implemented, in the process designated 'glocalisation'. See especially 190-209.

24. See Stocking in this volume.

25. Lowe 2009 discusses videogaming with classical figures and imagery.

26. In a speech at the Foreign Policy Centre, 21 March 2006 (http://fpc.org.uk/events/past/clash-about-civilisation accessed 29 October 2009). Blair has recycled the quoted phrases elsewhere.

27. This activity is still compatible with MacAloon's 'spectacle' 1984: 270.

28. See MacAloon 2006 on the limits of theory of the spectacle.

29. The wit herein is that the television commercial for Peugeot was not shown on the BBC.

30. See Simpson 2010 on a similar macro-cultural history which suppresses any significant internal contradiction.

31. Guttman 1992: 131 observes that 'Smith and Carlos were the most successful militants' but also recounts how the African-American athletes Lee Evans, Larry James and Ron Freeman wore black berets at the Victory ceremony for the 400m, just when Smith and Carlos were expelled from the Olympic village.

32. *The Observer*, 29 August 2004 (http://www.guardian.co.uk/world/2004/aug/29/usa.uselections2004 accessed 16 January 2011).

33. Lewis was, coincidentally, the first athlete to break Smith's record for the 200 metre dash, at the 1984 Los Angeles Games.

34. African Olympians other than those from the diaspora(s) have, of course, been politically vocal and active, especially in the boycotts aimed against South Africa and Rhodesia in 1968 and 1972, respectively. Abebe Bikila the great Ethiopian Marathon runner, whose crossing of the finish line in Rome 1960, after he had run barefoot, provided one of the first iconic television images of the Olympics, was one. See Ali 1976: 46. Bikila's triumph may be another citation in the athlete's spectacular arrival at the stadium in the long BBC trailer.

35. One of the biggest debates within sports studies concerns the impact of international and global sporting events on constituent national identities. See Hargreaves 2002. (Pan-)African nationalism productively complicates the polarity here. Of similar complexity, an inclusive Greek nationalism was almost cultural imperialism at the 2004 Olympics. See Hamilakis 2007: 1-7.

36. I separate 'black' modernity and 'Western' modernity only provisionally, since my argument assumes Gilroy's thesis 1993 that modernity itself is disproportionately a production of the Black Atlantic.

37. The notion of a black double consciousness was developed by W.E.B. Du Bois 1996 (1903).

38. My critical turn here reverses the turn in Carrington 2002: 291, where the feminist identification of sport as a patriarchal formation is contradicted, and the masculine subject is revealed as divided by racialised and hierarchical relations. Since the BBC trailer denies this reality by fusing these masculinities together within the athlete as an everyman, to the exclusion of women, the latter exclusion must be reckoned. Carrington makes a pertinent concession at 285.

39. Markula 2009: 5 argues that 'while women now have increased access to sport, the ideology of masculinity works in more subtle ways to exclude them'. This collection examines women athletes' presence and presentation at the 2004 Olympics.

40. See Goff and Simpson 2007: 38-51 and 258.

41. Hall 2010 gives a resounding answer apropos ancient tragedy. Now added to the specifically historical tragedies underwriting this epic of the West, which have been notably (post-)colonial, is the financial implosion and resulting social distress of modern Greece, among other nations. In an ironic sense, the BBC's trailer has been vindicated in its ideological privileging of Greece with a central role within liberal democracy and, by extension, within the economic system of capital that has come to be associated with it. But this is a tragic irony, since that system, and especially the globalisation of finance that it has promoted, have been found grievously wanting. There is thus a certain perverse ideological logic in modern Greece being a conspicuous economic casualty within the system that ancient Greece has been used to promote symbolically, when that system spectacularly malfunctions. The trailer is largely right about the importance of Greece within the epic, but wrong about the epic. Only tragic irony here, and the basis of political critique. Perhaps the latter will provide a Promethean illumining of a different globalisation.

Pindar at the Olympics: the Limits of Revivalism

Armand D'Angour

It is well known that the Olympic Games held in Athens in 1896 were the outcome of Pierre de Coubertin's vision for reviving a classical ideal of physical and sporting excellence. Less well known is the curious episode that took place at the closing ceremony of the Games, which de Coubertin briefly reported as follows in his account of the Games published in a New York quarterly magazine *The Century* (Coubertin (1897) 2000: 357-8):

> After the distribution of the prizes, the athletes formed for the traditional procession around the Stadion. Louës [the Greek runner Spiridon Louis], the victor of Marathon, came first, bearing the Greek flag; then the Americans, the Hungarians, the French, the Germans. The ceremony, moreover, was made more memorable by a charming incident. One of the contestants, Mr. Robertson, an Oxford student, recited an Ode which he had composed, in ancient Greek and in the Pindaric mode, in honor of the games. Music had opened them [the Olympic anthem by Spiridon Samaras and Kostis Palamas], and Poetry was present at their close; and thus was the bond once more renewed which in the past united the Muses with feats of physical strength, the mind with the well-trained body. The king [George I of Greece] announced that the first Olympiad was at an end [...]

Not everyone, perhaps, was as charmed by the incident as de Coubertin. The Oxford student in question was George Stuart Robertson, who shortly before his death (aged 94) in 1967, told Don Anthony, a former competitive hammer-thrower and historian of the Olympics, that 'local poets had been warned off such an activity, but a Royal Prince [George's son Constantine, President of the organising committee] made it clear to George that, when he gave a nod and a wink, the Ode could be presented' (Anthony 2005). The Ode, declaimed without amplification in the standard Victorian English pronunciation of ancient Greek, in front of a densely packed and patriotically charged audience in the Panathenaic stadium, will have been almost entirely incomprehensible even to those to whom it was audible. Yet such was the prestige of Oxford scholarship that Robertson had evidently succeeded in persuading the Games' hosts that an Oxford graduate and one-time winner of the Gaisford Greek Prize for Greek Verse was uniquely qualified to be the bearer of the Pindaric flame. It was the only success he was to achieve at the Games: the recipient of an Oxford Blue for hammer-throwing, he had travelled to Athens only to find that there was no hammer-throwing event, whereupon he entered for the shot put and discus, coming last in the latter with a distance of 25.2 metres – the worst Olympic result on record.

And what of Robertson's Ode? He took pains to make it authentically Pindaric, not least by modelling its metrical form exactly on that of Pindar's fifth Olympian Ode (three stanzas, with the first two metrically identical). Given the lack of individual winners to celebrate before the Games had been held, he makes the object of praise the host city Athens, home of Athena the Maiden goddess, and Mother of the Muses. The Ode begins with the poet sailing to Athens along with the army of other foreign athletes; the second stanza pays tribute to Athens' traditional hospitality to foreigners and highlights Greece's connections with England; the third makes honourable mention of other non-Greek nations and visitors present, as well as alluding to the Games' royal host, King George I of the Hellenes ('Father of the Country'). Since the text of the Ode is not widely available, I offer a literal translation here and reprint the Greek below in full.

FOR ATHENS

I shall sing of the swarm of foreign men coming from countries far,
I, who am myself participating in the strenuous toil of
the foreign expedition;
for with onrush of tireless-footed battle
I come, they come[1] – hurrah! – 5
hastening with passion for the Mother of fair-dancing skills,
and for the beauty of the Mother, the violet-crowned city,
Athens, and for glory.
Come, brethren, raise in song
the flower of praise-utterances. 10
Let (a) god[2] be for us, as we sail the sweet sea-swell,
an ocean-guide for our song,
for stricken with love of the fairest Maiden
we are now making our way across the sea.

Mother Athens, you are known for providing a welcome that is always 15
hospitable,
and to you bears witness the holy stalwart Orestes, he who fled the
goddesses,
to whom indeed you granted a cleansing of his blameless crime;[3]
now in turn, o illustrious one,
receive us with kindly intent and bring us near the victorious glories 20
of your Games, we who from afar come in quest of
your gracefulness and glory.
For massed from distant shores we now arrive,
including some from England

191

hastened by a proud desire to see the Land   25
where they themselves once fought for lovely
freedom, and in company with
the son of the Muses[4] risked their lives;

Some lords of the Games has blessed France provided,
and some I spy who possess the deep corn-meadow of Hungary   30
and of the Teutons,
nor is the host that the Land of America has sent forth
to the running-races a negligible one.
Now, at the wedding of Peleus and Thetis it is told that
a great palace was host to festivity for gods and heroes;   35
with you, o all-blessed one,
the Father of the Country is now present, beloved blood-relative
of my Queen;
and the glory of Muscovites is here, and the other
Alexander[5] exchanges his   40
country for yours. Rejoice, dearest land,
and receive a gift of minstrelsy.

ΑΘΗΝΑΙΣ

ἀνδρῶν τηλεδαπῶν ἑσμὸν ἀείσομαι βαρβάρων,
αὐτὸς συμπεδέχων κρατεροῦ πόνου, οὗ
βάρβαρον στράτευμα·
ἀκαμαντόποδος γὰρ ὁρμᾷ μάχας
ἦλθον, ἦλθον, ἰώ,   5
ματρός τ᾽ ἐσσυμένοι καλλιχόρων τεχνᾶν ἱμέρῳ,
κάλλους ματρός, ἰοστεφάνου πόλιος,
καὶ κλέους, ᾿Αθανᾶν.
ἴτ᾽ ἀδελφεοί, ὕμνῳ ὀρθώσατ᾽ ἐγ-
κωμίων ἄωτον·   10
ἔστω δ᾽ ἅμμι θεὸς γλυκὺ λαῖτμα πλέουσι
ναυσίπομπος αὐδᾶς,
πληχθέντες γὰρ ἔρωτ᾽ ἐρατεινοτάτας παρθένου
νῦν διαστείβομεν θάλασσαν.

μᾶτερ, δόξαν ἔχεις ξεινοσύνας ἀεὶ πανδόκου,   15
καί σοι μαρτυρέει μένος ἷρον ᾿Ορέσ-
του θεᾶς φυγόντος,
λύτρον ᾧ γ᾽ ἀβλαβοῦς ἔδωκας βλάβας·
ἄμμε δ᾽, ὦ κλεεννά,
εὔφρων δεξαμένα γ᾽ ἀγλαΐαισι νικαφόροις   20
ἄθλων σῶν πέλασον μεθέποντας ἑκὰς
σὴν χάριν κλέος τε.
ἄποθεν γὰρ ἐπερχόμεσθ᾽ ἀθρόοι,
τοὺς γὰρ ᾿Αγγλίαθεν
ἔσσευεν φιλότιμος ἔρως ἐφορᾶν χώ-   25
ραν, ὅθ᾽ ἀμφὶ καλᾷ
αὐτοὶ μαρνάμενοί ποτ᾽ ἐλευθερίᾳ, σὺν δὲ Μοι-
σᾶν τέκνον, τὸν βίον προῆκαν·

11. Pindar at the Olympics: the Limits of Revivalism

τοὺς δ᾽ ἄθλων μοι ἄνακτας πόρεν ὀλβία Γαλλία,
τοὺς δ᾽ ἀθρέω βαθὺ λήϊον Οὑγγαρίας   30
  Τευτόνων τ᾽ ἔχοντας,
στράτον οὐδ᾽ Ἀμέριστος αἵ ἐξέπεμ-
  ψεν δρόμοις ἀφαυρόν.
Πηλέος δὴ λέγεται καὶ Θέτιος γάμοισιν θεῶν
  ἡρώων τε χόρον μέγα δῶμα γερᾶ-   35
  ραι· σοί, ὦ πάνολβε,
πατρίδος πάρα νῦν Πατήρ, τῆς ἐμῆς
  προσφιλὴς ὅμαιμος·
Μοσκώων τε γάνος πάρα, χἄτερος αἶαν
  πατρίαν Ἀλέξαν-   40
δρος τῆς σῆς πεδαμείβει. ἀγάλλεο δ᾽, ὦ φιλτάτα,
  καὶ δέκευ δωρεὰν ἀοιδᾶς.

Robertson employs recognisably Pindaric elements such as dialectal word-forms, descriptive epithets, and first-person self-promotion, and he introduces appropriate mythical allusions: Orestes was someone to whom Athens had offered generous refuge, and the wedding of Peleus and Thetis occasioned an ingathering of heroes from far and wide. Some inevitable elements of pastiche are evident: the fourth line, for example, begins with *akamantopodos* 'tireless-footed' (as found in the same place in *Olympian* 5), and the final phrase 'receive (*dekeu*) this gift of song' varies Pindar's 'receive (*dekeu*) the gifts' (line 3). Robertson's wish to include contemporary allusions create some almost self-parodic passages, such as *tous d'athreô bathu lêïon Oungarias Teutonôn t' echontas*, 'and some I spy who possess the deep corn-meadow of Hungary and of the Teutons' (lines 30-1), and *Moskôôn te ganos para*, 'the glory of Muscovites is here' (39). But there is also genuine enthusiasm and warmth of sentiment, and it is clear that Robertson approached the Ode's composition with intelligence and scholarly commitment.

The Ode was accompanied by an English version by E.D. Moreshead entitled 'The Parthenon', i.e. the home of Athena 'the Maiden'. Moreshead takes a number of liberties in translation: he excludes the anachronistic place-names, omits the allusions to Peleus and Thetis, King George I of Greece, Queen Victoria ('my Queen'), Tsar Alexander, and Lord Byron ('the son of the Muses'), and adds the coda contrasting the current friendly expedition to Greece with the hostile Persian incursions of the fifth century BCE. His version, liberally sprinkled with exclamation marks, captures the Victorian heartiness and proud Hellenism of the original:

THE PARTHENON

I too, who sing hereof,
I too, in strenuous sport, with sons of Hellas strove.
"All hail!" we cry, "All hail!"

Fair mother of the Arts! O violet-crowned,
Home of Athena! Glory's sacred ground!
Onward, in love of thee, we spread our eager sail!

Up comrades! Let your voices raise
The flower of song, the blossom of her praise –
And, as we fleet across a halcyon sea,
May the god gently waft our song to thee!
Love-smitten for the Maid, the loveliest birth
That Heaven e'er gave to earth
We come, her grace to gain –
Ploughing with pinnace fair the bright auspicious main!

O mother Athens! ever from old time
The homeless wanderer found a home with thee –
Bear witness Agamemnon's son, thy guest,
Whom awful Furies drove o'er land and sea
In stern requital of his glorious crime,
Till Athens gave him rest!
Now unto us, O Land of fame divine,
Stretch forth thy hand in welcome! from afar
Let glory of the strife that is not war
Commend us to thy shrine!

Lo, from the wide world manifold we come –
From England's hearths and homes draw hither some,
Children of sires who, in the days gone by,
Warred for thy liberty.

Up, my song!
An alien crowd, we come
To this Athenian home –
Yet not like Persian plunderers of old,
But in frank love and generous friendship bold.

What led Robertson to compose his Ode? The idea of a Pindaric Ode would have sprung immediately to the mind of any highly-educated Hellenist of the time – and there were many more then than now – in relation to the revival of the ancient Olympics. Not only was Pindar considered to be, in his own times and beyond, the foremost lyric poet of the nation that had founded the Games and celebrated them over the course of around a thousand years; but by an accident of textual selection and transmission, while only few and fragmentary texts represent the huge range of poetic genres in which Pindar composed, all his Victory Odes (*epinikia*), 44 in total, celebrating winners at the four main locations of Games in the ancient world – Olympia, Delphi (the Pythian Games), Nemea, and at the Isthmus of Corinth – have miraculously survived into modern times. They remain something of a challenge and a mystery to students of ancient Greek, who after toiling away at translation and interpretation can come

194

to find their rhythms and poetic intricacies uniquely seductive (but it should not be forgotten that, apart from rhythm, the music itself – the melodic, instrumental and choral accompaniment that made the original performances of the Odes memorable events in their own right – is entirely lost). Secondly, to win a prize for Greek verse composition at Oxford was (and to some extent still is) an achievement held in the highest regard in academic circles. Robertson will have enjoyed both the reputation and the financial rewards (around £250 for the Gaisford, a significant sum of money in the 1890s) consequent on his successful versification. It would therefore have been inevitable that someone like Robertson should attempt to compose a Pindaric Ode in honour of the revived Games, and it would only be worth doing if the result could be assured to display genuine scholarly accuracy. Few could claim to have the requisite knowledge and skill to emulate an ancient poet notorious for his unusual dialect, idiosyncratic expression, and poetic complexity; but Robertson could. Even if he was to fail wholesale in his athletic endeavours, he could at least bank on upholding his country's honour and receiving a wreath for his poetic efforts.

The genre of Victory Odes was developed in the late sixth and early fifth centuries BCE by celebrated poets such as Simonides and Bacchylides. Some of the latter's *epinikia* survive intact, and are considerably less complicated in style and structure than Pindar's. Pindar, however, was acknowledged (not just in his own eyes) as the master of the genre. But over the centuries, his surviving oeuvre has met with a mixed and sometimes negative response (the latter in particular from poets and general readers rather than from classical scholars).[6] The sheer difficulty of understanding and appreciating his poetry, with its abstruse verbal and metrical features and obscurities of style and expression, was already a feature of its reception in antiquity: a generation after the poet's death in the mid-fifth century BCE, the comic playwright Aristophanes parodies Pindaric poetry with some semi-nonsensical oracular-sounding verses in his comedy *The Birds* (lines 904f.). Subsequently, the Odes have often been dismissed as wilfully impenetrable compositions, such as when Voltaire addresses the poet's shade with the scathing lines (which I translate below):

Sors du tombeau, divin Pindare,
toi qui célébras autrefois
les chevaux de quelques bourgeois
ou de Corinthe ou de Mégare;
toi qui possédas le talent
de parler beaucoup sans rien dire;
toi qui modulas savamment
des vers que personne n'entend
et qu'il faut toujours qu'on admire.

Emerge from your grave, divine Pindar,
you who in olden times used to celebrate
the horses of some good citizens,
whether from Corinth or Megara;
you who possessed the talent
of speaking much without saying anything;
you who skilfully modulated
verses that no one understands
and which one must always admire.

The ancient Greek victory odes were created in honour of individual,
mainly aristocratic, athletes, who commissioned them both to establish
their local and Hellenic reputations and to ensure posthumous fame. They
ceased to be composed after the death of Pindar, so his *epinikia* represent
both the epitome and the final flourish of the genre; this may have
reinforced the sense that his poetic style was inimitable. While Roman
poets of the first century BCE, Horace and Ovid, make references to some
brave attempts to compose Latin verse in Pindaric style, Horace's own
opinion on the matter is clear: the second Ode of his fourth Book, addressed to the nobleman and poet Iullus Antonius, is a tribute to the
matchless grandeur of Pindar's poetry. The first three of its fifteen stanzas
(translated below by Colin Sydenham) are as follows:[7]

> *Pindarum quisquis studet aemulari,*
> *Iulle, ceratis ope Daedalea*
> *nititur pennis, vitreo daturus*
> > *nomine ponto.*
>
> *monte decurrens velut amnis, imbres*
> *quem super notas aluere ripas,*
> *fervet immensusque ruit profundo*
> > *Pindarus ore,*
>
> *laurea donandus Apollinari,*
> *seu per audaces nova dithyrambos*
> *verba devolvit numerisque fertur*
> > *lege solutis.*

Whoever seeks to soar like Pindar risks
the fate of Icarus; his only fame,
Iullus, will be to leave to some marine
    expanse his name.

For Pindar is Apollo's laureate,
and like a mountain stream that bursts its bounds
and seethes and swirls storm-swollen, he deep-throat-
    edly resounds

in mighty onrush irresistible:
sometimes new-minted words he will unfold,
in daring dithyrambs transported, by
    no law controlled [...]

In this Ode, whose long periods and breathless enjambement bid to indicate something of the style of Pindar himself, Horace characterises the poet more as a force of nature than a literary artist. The thrust of his depiction is technical: where Horace himself only uses predetermined, regularly-repeated stanzaic structures such as the Sapphic stanzas of this ode, Pindar composed his Odes using complex patterns of metre that make each of them metrically distinct and individual.

Most of Pindar's *epinikia*, including the fifth Olympian Ode on which Robertson modelled his, conform to a characteristic three-part (triadic) structure. The way this operated is that the poet first created the individual metrical pattern of the first stanza or *strophe* (usually a verse of between three and ten lines), and then repeated the metre identically in a second stanza (*antistrophe*), before going on to compose a third stanza (*epode*) with metrical patterns and line lengths independent from the earlier two. The resulting triad might comprise a complete Ode; but more often than not, Pindar embarks on a second triad or a third, or in fact as many as (in the most extended instance, his fourth Pythian Ode) thirteen repetitions of triads, each demonstrating exactly the same sequence of metrical patterns as the first. This is a highly skilled and complicated procedure, particularly given the need to pursue a coherent train of thought or intelligible narrative while preserving poetic integrity and avoiding undue artificiality of expression (though exasperated critics have claimed that Pindar did not succeed in the latter respect).

Of all the Games, those that took place at Olympia held by far the highest prestige. 'The best thing, they say, is water', begins the famously extravagant preamble of Pindar's First Olympian Ode, 'and gold shines out like gleaming fire in night-time, the highest form of wealth'. He goes on to insert a characteristic self-address, of the kind imitated by Robertson:

But if, my soul, you want to speak of athletic contests,
look no further than the sun for the hottest
    of shining stars in the empty sky,
nor let us speak of any Games greater than those of Olympia.[8]

The revived Olympics were not in fact held at the site of Olympia, nor have they been since. In this as in other respects, to compose a Pindaric Ode for the modern Olympics could only be an artificial exercise. An Ode composed before the Games had actually taken place could not be a true Victory Ode since there would be no victory as yet to celebrate; nor could it be written to be performed, as were Pindar's own Odes, by choruses more or less at home with his linguistic, melodic and rhythmical forms. But of all Olympic Games of modern times at which such an exercise might seem appropriate, even irresistible, those held in Athens in 1896 and then for a second time in 2004 seemed the obvious occasions to revive the ancient Greek genre in some form.

In early 2004, in the frenetic run-up to the second Athens Olympics, the above-mentioned Don Anthony alerted Dame Mary Glen-Haig, an energetic former Olympic fencer and (at the age of 85) the most long-standing member of the International Olympic Committee, to the precedent set by Robertson of an Englishman's composing and reciting a Pindaric-style Ode at the first Games' closing ceremony. Dame Mary was determined to repeat the event in some form, and persuaded IOC President Jacques Rogge to consent that, in honour of her seniority, she might herself recite such an Ode in English at the closing session of the Committee on the final day of the Games. She immediately approached a senior member of the Classics Faculty at Oxford (Professor Michael Vickers) to see if there might be anyone suitably qualified to compose a new Ode. It was not a request to which a scholar could readily accede: Horace's assertion that the emulator of Pindar is destined, like Icarus, to plummet to a watery grave, is bound to ring in the ears of any classicist as a grim warning against making the attempt. But the tradition of composing Greek and Latin verses in English public schools and in universities such as Oxford, a practice that had given Robertson the confidence and skill to make his bid for Olympic laurels, is still not entirely defunct. Although I had no intention of composing such an Ode, an aerial image of the newly-built Olympic Stadium brought to my mind the Greek words *deut' es omphalon*, 'Come to the Hearth of the World'; the *Omphalos* or 'Navel' of ancient Greece was thought to be Apollo's temple at Delphi, but Pindar himself uses the word (in a dithyramb composed for the Athenians) with reference to Athens. The phrase happened to fit into one of Pindar's favoured metres, dactylo-epitrite; and after other similar units of verse began to assemble themselves in my mind, I accepted the commission and proceeded to compose a 25-line Ode consisting of three stanzas (8+8+9 lines) in that metre.

The dactylo-epitrite pattern may be represented by the image of a necklace studded with jewels, the former representing lines of verse and the latter represent repeated syllabic patterns within the line. Some of the jewels are large and some small; they are either strung directly together, or joined by a connecting link that might be either a long (–) or a short (v) syllable. The two main types of jewel are the dactylic pattern – v v – v v – (technically notated 'D') and the epitrite – v – (notated 'e'). Without having seen Robertson's Ode (he had chosen another favoured Pindaric metrical form, Aeolic verse), I similarly recognised that such an Ode could only be dedicated to Athens itself. Like Robertson, I felt that such a composition should as far as possible be accessible to a contemporary audience while remaining authentically Pindaric in terms of metre, dialect and style.

The following is my 'Ode to Athens for the Olympics 2004':

τᾶς Ἀθάνας γᾶς ἱερὸν τέμενος
    καὶ πόλιν ἀθάνατον Θησέος καὶ Ἐρεχθεῖδᾶν
ὑμνήσομεν ἔνθεν Ἀθαναῖοι παλαιοί
    καί ποθ᾽ ἥρωες πρὸς ἀγῶνα μόλον
    τᾶς Ὀλυμπίας φαεννᾶς·   5
νῦν τάδ᾽ ἄεθλα χρόνῳ δευτέρῳ σὺν τύχᾳ
    αὖθί σε δεξαμέναν
ἀγλαΐζωμεν μέλει σὺν Πινδαρείῳ.

δεῦτ᾽ ἐς ὀμφαλόν, νέοι ἠδὲ κόραι,
    τηλόθεν ἐρχόμενοι χωρῶν ἀπὸ μυριάδων,   10
ἀλκᾷ μὲν ἀγαλλόμενοι γνώμᾳ τε πιστοί
    ἀμφὶ νίκας, ἡσυχίας τε χάριν
    ἀντιαζέμεν πρόθυμοι.
τοῖς γὰρ ἀεθλοφόροις ἔσσεται μὲν χάρις
    ἀμφ᾽ ἀρεταῖς μεγάλαις,   15
νῦν δ᾽ ἀώτῳ μουσικᾶς σφε κωμάσωμεν.

ἄλλοτε δ᾽ ἄλλῳ ἐπέσθω φίλον εὐτυχίας
    δῶρον Ὀλυμπιονίκαις, δίδωσι γὰρ θεός
    οἷς θέμις καὶ καιρὸς ἔπεστι λαχεῖν.
ἀλλὰ σὺν θεῷ γε λάμποι φάος ἀθάνατον καὶ τᾷ πόλει,   20
τᾶς ξενίας ἕνεκεν τᾶς τε φιλοφροσύνας.
ὦ ματρόπολις σοφίας ἐξαίρετος καθ᾽ Ἑλλάδα,
    νῦν ἀσμένως δέξαι τόδ᾽ ἄγαλμα λόγων
    ἀρχαΐῳ τετελεσμένον τρόπῳ,
τέλος δὲ καὶ φωνᾷ μεγάλᾳ μακαρίζωμεν σ᾽ ἀκμάζοισαν ὄλβῳ.   25

1 Παλλάδος γαίας Henry   4 ἀγῶν᾽ ἔμολον Willink   5 τᾶς κλυτᾶς Ὀλυΐμας Henry
10 χωρῶν Willink (χώρων MS)   11 χερσίν μεν … ποσίν τε κραιπνοῖς Henry
24 ἀρχαίῳ *sine diaerisi* Henry

The following translation sets out to mimic precisely the syllabic rhythm of the Greek:

Blesséd Athens, land of Athena divine,
    city eternal of Theseus and the Erechtheïd line,
of you will we sing, whence Athenians and heroes
    once of old set forth to contend in the Games
    of Olympia the shining.   5
Now as good luck has decreed that you welcome the games
    here on your soil once again,
let us hail your glory with Pindaric music.

Men and women, come to the hearth of the world,
    gathering here from afar, from nations and lands beyond count,   10

exultant in strength and physique, steadfast in purpose
  to prevail, and keen in the service of peace
  to compete with one another.
There will be grateful reward for the ones who excel
  thanks to their marvellous skills,   15
and with finest music let us sing their praises.

May the sweet gift of success fall to each victor in turn,
  joy to the winners to whom God decrees it is their due –
  timely grace for victory justly attained.
But, with God's assent, may there shine on the city as well   20
  undying light,
due to her welcoming gifts and her benevolent grace.
Now, O mother-city of wisdom, famed throughout the length of Greece,
receive with gladness this precious offering of words
  carefully wrought in the style of ancient times;
and in finale, come let us hail you, with voices raised, at your height of   25
fortune.

The Ode in Greek is closely imitative of Pindar's language and style; for
instance, the literary dialect of Pindar uses long *alpha* instead of *êta* (so
Athena is *Athânâ*) and *â* rather than *ô* in the genitive plurals (as in
Erechtheïdân); and the poet often draws on Homeric forms and features,
as with the unaugmented aorist *molon* (line 4) and the future *essetai* (14).
In fact, nearly every word in the Ode may be found somewhere in Pindar's
own poetry, and some phrases are taken directly from or closely modelled
on those used by his Odes (e.g. line 16 *en d'aôtôi mousikâs* simply trans-
poses the words *mousikâs en aôtôi* at *Olympian* 1.15). The thematic
features are notably Pindaric e.g. praise of the city for its divine patron
Athena, its most famous hero Theseus, its ancestry (the Athenians were
the descendants of the legendary Erechtheus), its deeds (sending heroes
to the Games, twice hosting the Olympics) and its qualities (wisdom,
brilliance, hospitality). The city's success is linked to the splendour of the
Games and (typically) to the skill of the poet himself. Some wordplay, as
often to be found in Pindar, is evident: thus *Athânâ* (line 1) is picked up by
âthanaton (2, 20); *charin* (12) by *charis* (14); *tetelesmenon* (24) by *telos* (25),
and so on. On the whole, however, these aural echoes were not consciously
intended (a cautionary message for the literary critic who is apt to find
deliberate artifice in such aspects of a literary composition); nor was the
supposed pun on *alla* ('but', line 20) followed by the words 'with God' (*sun
theôi*), for which I was commended by a zealous reader.

Classical scholars were bound to scrutinise my text for errors and
infelicities; but the main scholarly criticism I received was, in fact, the
somewhat rueful observation that the style of my piece, unlike that of
Pindar's Odes, was too easy to read and understand. Two metrical experts,
Dr Ben Henry and Sir Charles Willink, suggested variations to my text for
purposes of enhancing its accuracy or authenticity.[9] These are selectively

presented (in light-hearted imitation of the layout of an Oxford Classical Text) in the 'critical apparatus' printed below my text. The metrical structure of the Ode may be given as follows, using the technical notation using the symbols D, e, —, v, as explained above. The metrical analysis of each line is laid out on different levels, so that the double strings of strophe/antistrophe visually indicate something of the necklace effect suggested by the repetitive pattern of jewels and links:

Strophe/antistrophe:

```
  e — D
       D — D                                          e — e — e —
            — D — e —                            D
                 e — D           D e e
                      e v e —
  e v D
       D — D                                          e — e v e —
            — D — e —                            D
                 e — D           D e e
                      e v e —
```

Epode:

```
D D                                                      v e — D — e e —
   D e v e                                          D v e
        e — D
             e — e D — e        — D — e v e
                         D D
```

What sort of statement about the world's cultural connectedness to the classical past is made by the commissioning of a Pindaric Ode for a modern staging of the revived Olympics? One cannot expect a contemporary audience to appreciate the long-deceased tradition of poetic celebration of victory. Only a tiny proportion of the millions of people around the globe who have viewed the Olympics in recent times, whether in person or on screen, will have heard of Pindar's name, and even fewer will have any idea of what lies behind the name. Choral praise poetry is not a conspicuous element of the modern sports scene, though perhaps some approximation to it survives in the popular songs and chants heard at UK soccer tournaments and in the cheerleading squads conspicuous at American football and basketball matches.

The general lack of interest in such an Ode among Greeks themselves is a more complex phenomenon. On the one hand, Pindar is a proud part of the Hellenic heritage; on the other, few Greeks today are equipped to read and understand Pindar in the original Greek, and fewer would be able to compose an Ode in authentically Pindaric style. Political factors contribute to an obscure sense of discomfort that some Greeks today might still feel at the sight or sound of an Ode composed in ancient style and language. In the twentieth century, bitter political conflicts in Greek society were reflected in linguistic contestations. In 1967, after the coup that led to the overthrow of the Greek monarchy, the military junta forcefully reintroduced the official use of *katharevousa* ('purifying' Greek), a form of the language based on ancient Greek and largely divorced from vernacular speech. This policy was decisively reversed after the fall of the

Colonels, but partly as a result the sound of ancient Greek words is for some unfortunately redolent of the dictates of the shortlived fascist regime. Yet more strange is the fact that even well-educated Greeks are often keenly prepared to contest the supposition that classical Greek was pronounced in a form different from its modern pronunciation. It is almost a matter of national pride to decry 'Erasmian' pronunciation, even though the scholarly consensus is unshakeable, and the modern Greek stress-accent (which replaced the pitch accent used in ancient Greece) clearly violates the glorious rhythms of ancient verse.[10]

Largely thanks to the efforts of veteran *Times* journalist Philip Howard, a keen former classicist (educated, as it happens, at Eton and Oxford), the *Times* of 31 July 2004 gave a full page covering the Ode to Athens, printing it in its entirety both in Greek and English, accompanied by detailed exposition of Pindaric style and of the circumstances of its commissioning (Howard 2004). The story was subsequently picked up by the *Guardian*, the *Independent*, the BBC, and even the *Boston Globe*. These notices were overlooked by the Greek press; but a week after the Games had finished, an article appeared in the Greek daily *Kathimerini* in which a journalist patriotically lamented the absence of Pindar from the Games.[11] The surprisingly widespread publicity given to the Ode, a welcome boost to the profile of the Classics, was largely a quirk of chance and of the vagaries of the Press's 'silly season' (the politically quiet summer months when newspapers are inclined to print frivolous items). Evidently, however, those to whom the composition of such an Ode will most appeal are classicists who are *au fait* with or at least curious about ancient traditions of verbal and poetic skill – traditions now barely preserved and appreciated outside elite academic environments. It is, therefore, an ironic stroke of fortune that the man with overall responsibility for the organisation of the forthcoming London Olympics in 2012, Mayor of London Boris Johnson, is a former classicist (educated, as it happens, at Eton and Oxford). On a number of occasions, the Mayor has insisted that the London Olympics should avail themselves of a Pindaric laureate, or at least a Horatian one.[12] One can never be sure when Classical revivalism has reached its limits.

Notes

1. The Greek verb *êlthon* may in this context equally mean 'I come' and 'they come'; the ambiguity was surely intended, since not until the following line is it clear that the subject must be plural.

2. Robertson's use of *theos* allows for the sense 'a god' but may also be interpreted not to offend the Christian sensibilities of his audience as 'God'.

3. As dramatised in Aeschylus' tragic trilogy, the *Oresteia*, Orestes was required by the god Apollo to kill his mother Clytemnestra in requital of her killing his father Agamemnon. This act led to his being pursued by the Erinyes, goddesses of the Underworld and spirits of vengeance. He fled to Athens, where he was tried and acquitted partly on the grounds that he had acted under a god's compulsion

(hence his 'blameless crime'), whereupon the Erinyes became objects of worship under their new name *Eumenides* ('Kindly Ones').

4. An allusion to Lord Byron, who died in 1824 after travelling to help the Greeks fighting for independence from the Turks, and subsequently became a Greek national hero.

5. Alexander III, Emperor of Russia from 1881 to 1894.

6. For an account of responses to Pindar from Aristophanes to Hölderlin see Hamilton 2003.

7. Sydenham 2005: 193. I am grateful to the author and publisher for permission to use the translation.

8. My translation. In the opening line I translate the particle *men* as 'they say' to bring out the force of Pindar's citation of the commonplace Greek sentiment that 'the best thing is water'.

9. W. Ben Henry, a brilliant scholar of Pindar, made some crucial corrections and improvements before I submitted the Ode to the IOC. In the end I chose not to adopt the particular suggestions indicated in the apparatus, though they would no doubt have been closer to genuine Pindaric expressions (e.g. in line 11, Pindar is more likely to have said 'exulting in their swift hands and feet' than my more abstract expression 'exultant in strength and physique'). The late Sir Charles Willink made his suggestions for emending word-division and accentuation after the Ode's publication.

10. For a balanced historical discussion of the issue, and a defence of Erasmus' real intentions, see Dillon 2001.

11. Pantelis Boukalas, *Kathimerini* 7 September 2004. Subsequently a correspondent to the paper, Nikolaos Pilavachis, drew attention to the fact that a Pindaric Ode had indeed been written for the Games (*Kathimerini* 15 September 2004).

12. Horace composed an Ode in Sapphic metre at the behest of the emperor Augustus for the Secular Games celebrated in Rome in 17 BCE. Performed to music by a band of boys and girls, it arguably provides a more suitable and accessible model for a celebratory Ode destined for a modern, mainly English-speaking, audience (cf. the anniversary Ode in Sapphics commissioned for the Roman Society in 2010 and printed with translation in the *Times Literary Supplement* of 28 May 2010).

Afterword

Tessa Jowell

With a worldwide audience of billions, the modern Olympics have a global reach and significance that could barely have been dreamt about in classical times. While the first Games lasted for a single day and welcomed only Greek-speaking participants, the London 2012 Olympic and Paralympic Games will be a 60-day celebration, with more than 200 countries involved.

However, while the Games themselves may have altered dramatically, many of the values and ideals that underpin the Olympic movement have remained unchanged. The Olympic Truce, for example, which in classical times allowed athletes to travel safely to the Games, is still upheld today in the form of a United Nations resolution.

Pierre de Coubertin, the father of the modern Games, had a vision of an Olympics that, as well as helping to promote peace, would bring the full power of sport to bear on educational and cultural development. It is a vision that is very much at the heart of our ambition for London 2012.

London's promise to host a Games that would create a lasting legacy of benefits for the whole of the UK was what set our bid apart. It is a promise that captures the true spirit of the Games, and will ensure that the Olympic flame will continue to burn brightly in East London long after the Games are over.

Bibliography

'2008 Summer Olympics', *Wikipedia*, http://en.wikipedia.org/wiki/2008_Summer_Olympics

'Crystal Palace', *Pall Mall Gazette*, 11 July 1866 (Issue 443)

'Crystal Palace', *The Times*, 14 June 1866 (Issue 25524), 9 col. C

'Fascist Symbols Go for Rome Olympics', *New York Times*, 9 August 1960

'Hall des sports de Vienne', *Architecture d'Aujourd'hui* (1954) July-August, v. 25, 72-5

'Juvenile Olympic Festival', *North Wales Chronicle* (Bangor Wales), 28 July 1866, Issue 2071

'National Olympian Association', *The Morning Post*, 2 August 1866 (Issue 28905), 3

'National Olympic Festival', *Penny Illustrated Paper* (London), 11 August 1866 (Issue 254), 81

'Nervi's Views on Architecture, Education, and Structure', *Architectural Record* (1958) December, 118

Adak, M., N. Tüner Önen, and S. Şahin (2005) 'Neue Inschriften aus Phaselis I', *Gephyra* 2: 6-8

Albersmeier, S. (ed.) (2009) *Heroes, Mortals and Myths in Ancient Greece* (Baltimore: Walters Art Museum)

Ali, Ramadhan (1976) *Africa at the Olympics* (London: Africa Books)

Aloni, Antonio (2009) 'Elegy', in Budelmann (ed.) 2009: 168-88

Anderson, Benedict (1983) *Imagined Communities* (London: Verso)

Anderson M.J. (2009) 'Heroes as Moral Agents and Moral Examples,' in Albersmeier (ed.) 2009: 144-73

Anthony, Don (2004) 'Letters Pierre De Coubertin – William Penny Brookes', *Journal of Olympic History* 12: 61-4

Anthony, Don (2005) 'Celebration by Replication: Athens 2004, the Road of the Ode', *Journal of Olympic History* 13.2: 58-63

Ashrafian, H. (2005) 'William Penny Brookes (1809-1895): Forgotten Olympic Lord of the Rings', *British Journal of Sports Medicine* 39: 969

Athens Committee for the Olympic Games (2004) *Official Report of the Games of the XXVIIIth Olympiad,* http://www.la84foundation.org, accessed April 2010

Atlanta Committee for the Olympic Games (1996) *Official Report of the Centennial Games*, http://www.la84foundation.org, accessed April 2010

Baretti, Joseph (1779) *The Introduction to the Carmen Seculare* (London)

Barney, Robert Knight, Stephen R. Wenn, and Scott G. Martyn (2002) *Selling the Five Rings: The International Olympic Committee and the Rise of Olympic Commercialism* (Salt Lake City, UT: University of Utah Press)

Barry, James (1783) *An Account of a Series of Pictures, in the Great Room of the Society of Arts, Manufactures, and Commerce, at the Adelphi* (London: Printed for the Author by William Adlard, Printer to the Society)

Bibliography

Bass, Amy (2002) *Not the Triumph but the Struggle: The 1968 Olympics and the Making of the Black Athlete* (Minneapolis, MN: University of Minnesota Press)

Bataille, Georges (1970) *Oeuvres Complètes II* (Paris: Gallimard)

Bataille, Georges (1976) *Oeuvres Complètes VII* (Paris: Gallimard)

Bataille, Georges (1985a) 'The Labyrinth', in Stoekl (ed.) 1985

Bataille, Georges (1985b) 'The Notion of Expenditure', in Stoekl (ed.) 1985

Bataille, Georges (1985c) 'The Use Value of D.A.F. de Sade', in Stoekl (ed.) 1985

Bataille, Georges (1988) *Inner Experience*, tr. Leslie Anne Boldt (Albany: State University of New York Press)

Bataille, Georges (1991) *The Accursed Share: An Essay on General Economy*, vol. 1: *Consumption*, tr. Robert Hurley (New York: Zone Books)

Bataille, Georges (1998) *On Nietzsche* (Minnesota: Paragon House)

BBC Olympics trailer (2004) dir. Camille Bovier-Lapierre (Passion Pictures)

Beijing Olympic Games Official Website, 8-24 August 2008, http://en.beijing2008.cn/

Bentz, M. (1998) *Panathenäische Preisamphoren* (Basel: Vereinigung der Freunde Antiker Kunst)

Benveniste, Emile (1973) *Indo-European Language and Society,* tr. Elizabeth Palmer (London: Faber and Faber)

Bernand, É. (1969) *Inscriptions métriques de l'Égypte gréco-romaine. Recherches sur la poésie épigrammatique des Grecs en Égypte* (Paris: Les Belles Lettres)

Biddiss, Michael (1999) 'The invention of modern Olympic tradition', in Biddiss and Wyke 1999: 125-44

Biddiss, Michael and Maria Wyke (eds) (1999) *The Uses and Abuses of Antiquity* (Bern: Peter Lang)

Blass, F. (1887) *Die Attische Beredsamkeit* Zweite Auflage (Leipzig: Teubner)

Bohringer, F. (1979) 'Cultes d'athlètes en Grèce classique', *Revue des Études Anciennes* 81: 5-18

Booth, J., J. Macartney, C. Ayres (2008) 'IOC May Scrap Beijing Olympic Torch Relay over Protests', *Sunday Times*, 8 April

Bowie, A.M. (1997) 'Thinking with Drinking: Wine and the Symposium in Aristophanes', *Journal of Hellenic Studies* 117: 1-21

Brauer, Fae (2008) 'Introduction. Making Eugenic Bodies Delectable: Art, "Biopower" and "Scientia Sexualis"', in Brauer and Callen (eds) 2008: 1-34

Brauer, Fae (2008a) 'Eroticizing Lamarckian Eugenics: The Body Stripped Bare during French Sexual Neoregulation', in Brauer and Callen 2008: 97-138

Brauer, Fae and Anthea Callen (eds) (2008) *Art, Sex and Eugenics* (Aldershot: Ashgate)

Brophy, R.H. (1978) 'Deaths in the Pan-Hellenic Games: Arrachion and Creugas', *American Journal of Philology* 99: 363-90

Brophy, R.H. and M. Brophy (1985) 'Deaths in the Pan-Hellenic Games II: All Combative Sports', *American Journal of Philology* 106: 171-98

Broudehoux, Anne-Marie (2007) 'Delirious Beijing: Euphoria and Despair in the Olympic Metropolis', in Mike Davis and Daniel Bertrand Monk (eds) *Evil Paradises: Dreamworlds of Neoliberalism* (New York: The New Press) 87-101

Brunet, S. (2010) 'Winning the Olympics without Taking a Fall, Getting Caught in a Waistlock, or Sitting out a Round', *Zeitschrift für Papyrologie und Epigrafik* 172: 115-24

Budelmann, Felix (ed.) (2009) *The Cambridge Companion to Greek Lyric* (Cambridge: Cambridge University Press)

Bibliography

Buford, Kate (2010) *Native American Son: The Life and Sporting Legend of Jim Thorpe* (New York: Alfred A. Knopf)

Bulman, Patricia (1992) *Phthonos in Pindar* (Berkeley: University of California Press)

Burnet, J. (1920) *Early Greek Philosophy*, 3rd edn (London: A&C Black)

Buzard, James (2005) *Disorientating Fiction: The Autoethnographic Work of Nineteenth-century British Novels* (Princeton: Princeton University Press)

Callen, Anthea (2008) 'Man or Machine: Ideals of the Labouring Male Body and the Aesthetics of Industrial Production in Early Twentieth-century Europe', in Brauer and Callen 2008: 139-61

Carcopino, J. (1926) *La basilique pythagoricienne de la Porte Majeure* (Paris: L'artisan du livre)

Carey, C. (2005) 'Propaganda and Competition in Athenian Oratory', in K. Eenenkel and Il. Pfeijffer (eds) *The Manipulative Mode: Political Propaganda in Antiquity. A Collection of Case Studies* (Leiden: Brill) 65-99

Carey, C. (2007a) 'Epideictic Oratory', in Worthington 2007: 236-52

Carey, C. (ed.) (2007b) *Lysiae Orationes cum Fragmentis* (Oxford: Clarendon)

Carrington, Ben (2002) 'Sport, Masculinity and Black Cultural Resistance', in J. Sugden and A. Tomlinson (eds) *Power Games: A Critical Sociology of Sport* (London: Routledge) 267-91

Carter, J.M., and A. Krüger (1990) *Ritual and Record: Sports Records and Quantification in Pre-modern Societies* (New York: Greenwood Press)

Catling, R.W.V. and N. Kanavou (2007) 'Hermesianax the Olympic Victor and Goneus the Ambassador: a Late Classical-Early Hellenistic Family from Kolophon', *Epigraphica Anatolica* 40: 59-66

Cerchiai, L. (1982) 'Sesso e classi di età nelle necropolis greche di Locri Epizefiri', in G. Gnoli and J-P. Vernant (eds) *La mort, les morts dans les sociétés anciennes* (Cambridge: Cambridge University Press) 289-98

Chariots of Fire (1981) dir. Hugh Hudson (Twentieth Century Fox)

Chelsea School of Art, 'The Life Room: press release', 03/11/2009, http://www.chelseaspace.org/archive/theliferoom-pr.html, accessed 15/08/2010

Christesen, P. (2007a) *Olympic Victor Lists and Ancient Greek History* (Cambridge: Cambridge University Press)

Christesen, P. (2007b) 'The Transformation of Athletics in Sixth-Century Greece', in Schaus and Wenn 2007: 59-68

Christesen, P. (2010) 'Kings Playing Politics: The Heroization of Chionis of Sparta', *Historia* 59: 26-73

Clark, G. (1989) *Iamblichus: On the Pythagorean Life* (Liverpool: Liverpool University Press)

Clarke, G.W. (1989) *Rediscovering Hellenism: The Hellenic Inheritance and the English Imagination* (Cambridge and New York: Cambridge University Press)

Clay, Jenny Strauss (1999) 'Pindar's Sympotic Epinicia', *Quaderni Urbinati di Cultura Classica*, new series, vol. 62, no. 2

Coe, Sebastian (2007) 'A cultural fit', *Daily Telegraph*, 23 May

Collins, Wilkie (1995) *Man and Wife* (Oxford: Oxford University Press)

Comes, Natalis (1567) *Mythologiae* (Venetiis: Comin da Trino)

Cook, Matt (2003) *London and the Culture of Homosexuality 1885-1914* (Cambridge: Cambridge University Press)

Coonan, Clifford (2008) 'Opening Ceremony: The Meaning Behind the Spectacle', *Independent*, 9 August

Coubertin, Pierre de (1888) *L'Éducation en Angleterre* (Paris: Hachette), in Coubertin 2000: 51-9

Bibliography

Coubertin, Pierre de (1889) 'L'Éducation Athletique', *Compte rendu de la 18e session, Association pour l'Avancement des Sciences* (Paris: Masson), in Coubertin 2000: 121-33

Coubertin, Pierre de (1890) 'Les Jeux Olympiques à Much Wenlock', *La Revue Athlétique* 1.25: 705-13, in Coubertin 2000: 281-6

Coubertin, Pierre de (1892) 'Conference faite à la Sorbonne au Jubilée de l'U.S.F.S.A.', in Coubertin 2000: 287-97

Coubertin, Pierre de (1894) 'Le caractère de notre enterprise', *Bulletin du Comité International des Jeux Olympiques*, vol 1.2: 1, in Coubertin 2000: 660-3

Coubertin, Pierre de (1894b) 'The Celebrations of the Congress', *Bulletin du Comité International des Jeux Olympiques*, vol 1:3, in Coubertin 2000: 531-2

Coubertin, Pierre de (1894c) 'Le Néo-olympisme', *Le Messager d'Athènes* 39: 287-8, in Coubertin 2000: 533-41

Coubertin, Pierre de (1896) 'The Modern Olympic Games', in *The Olympic Games BC 776-AD 1896: Official Report* (Athens and London: Ch. Beck), in Coubertin 2000: 308-11

Coubertin, Pierre de (1896b) *Lettre Olympique, 12 Avril, Journal des Débats, Politiques et Litteraires*, in Coubertin 2000: 338-40

Coubertin, Pierre de (1896c) 'Lettre Olympique, Athènes, 31 Mars', *Journal des Debats, Politiques et Litteraires*, in Coubertin 2000: 336-8

Coubertin, Pierre de (1897) 'The Olympic Games of 1896', *The Century Illustrated Monthly Magazine* LIII n.s. XXXI November 1896-April 1897, 39-53, in Coubertin 2000: 350-60

Coubertin, Pierre de (1906) 'Le devoir d'un philhellène', *Revue Olympique* April, 64, in Coubertin 2000: 250

Coubertin, Pierre de (1908) 'Why I Revived the Olympic Games', *Fortnightly Review* 84: 110-15, in Coubertin 2000: 542-6

Coubertin, Pierre de (1909-10) 'A Modern Olympia', *Revue Olympique*, in Coubertin 2000: 256-68

Coubertin, Pierre de (1909b) *A Twenty-Year Campaign* (Paris: Librairie de l'Éducation physique), in Coubertin 2000: 343-9

Coubertin, Pierre de (1910) 'Le Sport et la Morale', *Revue Olympique*, February: 20-2, in Coubertin 2000: 167-9

Coubertin, Pierre de (1918) 'Ce que nous pouvons maintenant demander au Sport', *Conférence faite a l'Association des Hellènes Libéraux de Lausanne* (Lausanne), in Coubertin 2000: 269-77

Coubertin, Pierre de (1918b) 'Lettre Olympique V', *La Gazette de Lausanne* 325: 1-2, in Coubertin 2000: 217

Coubertin, Pierre de (1919) 'Lettre Olympique XI', *La Gazette de Lausanne*, no. 12, 13 January, in Coubertin 2000: 172-3

Coubertin, Pierre de (1919b) 'Lettre à Messieurs les membres du CIO', *Archives of the IOC*, in Coubertin 2000: 737-41

Coubertin, Pierre de (1920) 'Lettre no. 3 à Messieurs les membres du Comité Internationale Olympique', *Archives of the IOC*, in Coubertin 2000: 672-4

Coubertin, Pierre de (1920b) 'Sport is King', Address delivered at the Opening Meeting of the 18th Plenary Session of the IOC, in Coubertin 2000: 222-6

Coubertin, Pierre de (1922) 'Entre deux batailles: de l'Olympisme à l'Université ouvrière', *La Revue de la Semaine* 3.1: 299-310, in Coubertin 2000: 203-9

Coubertin, Pierre de (1927) 'Les nouvelles Panathénées', *Bulletin Officiel du CIO*, September: 5-6, in Coubertin 2000: 279-81

Bibliography

Coubertin, Pierre de (1927b) 'La verité sportive', *Le Figaro* 73: 3, in Coubertin 2000: 235-6

Coubertin, Pierre de (1927c) 'De la transformation et de la diffusion des études historiques: caractère et conséquences', Communication faite à l'Académie d'Athènes à la séance du jeudi 14 avril 1927, in Coubertin 2000: 227-34

Coubertin, Pierre de (1928) 'L'utilisation pédagogique de l'activité sportive', *Le Sport Suisse* 1074: 1

Coubertin, Pierre de (1932) *Olympic Memoirs* (Lausanne B.I.P.S.), in Coubertin 2000: 313-33, 369-72,403-9

Coubertin, Pierre de (1938) 'The Origins and Limits of Athletic Progress', *Olympic Review* 1.2: 1-2, in Coubertin 2000: 195-202

Coubertin, Pierre de (2000) *Olympism: Selected Writings* (Lausanne: International Olympic Committee)

Cromarty, Helen Clare (2004) *Oxford Dictionary of National Biography*, 'Brookes, William Penny', online edn, Oxford University Press, September 2004 http://www.oxforddnb.com/view/article/39187, accessed 31 July 2010

Crotty, Kevin (1982) *Song and Action: The Victory Odes of Pindar* (Baltimore: Johns Hopkins University Press)

Crowther, Nigel (2007) 'The Ancient Olympics and their Ideals', in Schaus and Wenn 2007: 69-80

'Crystal Palace', *Pall Mall Gazette*, 11 July 1866 (Issue 443)

Cujàs, Romà (1992) *Official Report of the Games of the XXVth Olympiad*, http://www.la84foundation.org, accessed April 2010

Currie, B. (2002) 'Euthymos of Locri: A Case Study in Heroization in the Classical Period', *Journal of the Hellenic Society* 122: 24-44

Currie, B. (2005) *Pindar and the Cult of Heroes* (Oxford: Oxford University Press)

Daily Mail (2008) 'Olympic Drug Inquiry Launched after 300 Tests from Beijing go Missing', 16 October

Daley, R. (1959) 'Roman Splendor Will Mark Olympics of 1960', *New York Times* 29 March, S3

D'Amore, L. (2007) *Iscrizioni greche d'Italia: Reggio Calabria* (Rome: Quasar)

Daux, G. (1968) *Guide de Thasos*, École Française d'Athènes (Paris: E. de Boccard)

De Juliis, E. and D. Loiacono (1988) *Taranto: Il Museo Archeologico* (Taranto: Mandese Editore)

Decker, Wolfgang (2008) 'Eine Reminiszenz an die Olympischen Spiele im Byzanz des 14. Jahrhunderts', *Nikephoros* 7-13

Delatte, A. (1922) *La Vie de Pythagore de Diogène Laërce* (Brussels: Lamertin)

Delorme, J. (1960) *Gymnasion* (Paris: Boccard)

Demick, B. (2008) 'Beijing Goes to Extremes for its Olympic Face-lift', *Los Angeles Times*, 22 July.

Dillon J. and J. Hershbell (1991) *On the Pythagorean Way of Life* (Atlanta, GA: Scholars Press)

Dillon, M. (2001) 'The Erasmian Pronunciation of Greek: A New Perspective,' *Classical World* 94.2: 1-12.

Disraeli, Benjamin (1881) *Lothair* (London: Longmans & Co)

Downing, Taylor (1992) *Olympia*, BFI Film Classics (London: British Film Institute)

Drury, P.M.E. (2007-8) 'From Much Wenlock to Athens: A Life of Dr William Penny Brookes', *Medical Historian. Bulletin of Liverpool Medical Historical Society* 2007-2008 Session, 23-8

Du Bois, W.E.B. (1996) (1903) *The Souls of Black Folk* (New York: Penguin)

Bibliography

Dunbabin, T.J. (1948) *The Western Greeks* (Oxford: Clarendon Press)

Dunne, Tom (ed.) (2005-6) *James Barry, 1741-1806: The Great Historical Painter* (Cork, Crawford Art Gallery)

Dyreson, Mark (2007) ' "To Construct a Better and More Peaceful World" or "War Minus the Shooting": The Olympic Movement's Second Century', in Schaus and Wenn 2007: 335-49

Dyreson, Mark (2008) *Crafting Patriotism for Global Dominance: America at the Olympics* (New York: Routledge)

Ebert, J. (1998) 'Zur neuen Bronzeplatte mit Siegerinschriften aus Olympia', *Stadion* 24: 137-49

Ekroth, G. (2009) 'The Cult of Heroes', in Albersmeier 2009: 120-39

Epstein, David (2008) 'Catching up with Frank Shorter', *Sports Illustrated on-line*, 5 August

ESPN Track and Field, Associated Press (2008) 'IOC Votes to Strip Jones' Teammates of Medals from 2000 Games', 10 April

Faber, Petrus (1592) *Agonisticon* (Lugduni: F. Fabrum)

Fagiolo dell'Arco, Maurizio (1997) *La Festa Barocca* (Rome: De Luca)

Farnell, Lewis Richard (1921) *Greek Hero Cults and Ideas of Immortality* (Oxford: Oxford University Press)

Fasick, Laura (1994) 'Charles Kingsley's Scientific Treatment of Gender', in Hall (ed.) 1994: 91-113

Felson, Nancy (1999) 'Vicarious Transport: Fictive Deixis in Pindar's Pythian Four', *Harvard Studies in Classical Philology* 99: 1-31

ffrench, Patrick (2007) *After Bataille: Sacrifice, Exposure, Community* (London: Legenda)

Fischer-Lichte, Erika (2005) *Theatre, Sacrifice, Ritual: Exploring Forms of Political Theatre* (London and New York: Routledge)

Fischer-Lichte, Erika (2008) 'Resurrecting Ancient Greece in Nazi Germany: The *Oresteia* as Part of the Olympic Games in 1936', in Martin Revermann and Peter Wilson (eds) *Performance, Iconography, Reception: Studies in Honour of Oliver Taplin* (Oxford: Oxford University Press) 481-96

Fitzpatrick, F. (2009) 'An Upbeat Jones Opens Up in Talk', *Philadelphia Inquirer*, 24 April

Flesca, C. (2004-05) 'Mosaico agonistico severiano a Regium Iulium (con una nota epigrafica di Felice Costabile)', *MEP* 7-8: 329, 346, repr. 2008 in F. Costabile (ed.) *Enigmi dell Civiltà antiche dal Mediterraneo al Nilo* II (Regio Calabria) 642-56

Fontenrose, J. (1968) 'The Hero as Athlete', *California Studies in Classical Antiquity*, 1: 73-104

Forbes, C.A. (1939) '*Hoi aph'Herakleous* in Epictetus and Lucian', *American Journal of Philology* 60: 473-4

Francis, Revd. Mr Philip (1749) *A Poetical Translation of the Works of Horace with the Original Text*, tr. into English with notes, 3rd edn, 2 vols (London: printed for A. Miller)

Frisch, P. (1991) 'Der erste vollkommene Periodonike', *Epigraphica Anatolica* 18: 71-3

Fryer, Edward (1809) *The Works of James Barry*, 2 vols (London: T. Cadell and W. Davies)

Fukuyama, Francis (1989) 'The End of History?', *The National Interest* 15: 3-18

Furbank, M., H. Cromarty, G. McDonald and Chris Cannon (2007) *William Penny Brookes and the Olympic Connection* (Much Wenlock: Wenlock Olympian Society)

Bibliography

Galton, Francis (1869) *Hereditary Genius: An Inquiry into Its Laws and Conse-quences* (London: Macmillan)

Garcia, Beatriz (2000) 'Sydney Olympic Arts Festivals and the Visual Arts', *Culture@ the Olympics* 2.1: 1-4

Garcia, Beatriz (2008) 'Beijing Cultural Festivals ... Bigger but not always Better', in 'Beijing 2008 Olympic Games: Academics' views of the event', Centre d' Estudis Olímpics, Universitat Autònoma de Barcelona. http://olympicstudies.uab.es/beijing08/eng/index.asp, accessed July 2009

Gardiner, E.N. (1910) *Greek Athletic Sports and Festivals* (London: Macmillan)

Gardiner, E.N. (1925) *Olympia. Its History and Remains* (Oxford: Clarendon Press)

Gardiner, E.N. (1930) *Athletics of the Ancient World* (Oxford: Clarendon Press)

Garms, Jörg (1995) *Vedute di Roma dal Medioevo all'Ottocento* (Naples: Electa Napoli)

Gebhard, E.R. and M.W. Dickie (1989) 'Melikertes-Palaimon, Hero of the Isthmian Games', in R. Hägg (ed.) *Proceedings of the Fifth International Seminar on Ancient Greek Cult* (Stockholm: Svenska Institutet i Athen) 159-65

Giacomini, R. (1960) *The Games of the XVII Olympiad, Rome 1960: Official Report of the Organizing Committee*, vol. 1 (Rome: Organizing Committee of the Games of the XVII Olympiad)

Giangiulio, M (1989) *Ricerche su Crotone arcaica* (Pisa: Scuola normale superiore)

Gilroy, Paul (1993) *The Black Atlantic: Modernity and Double Consciousness* (London and New York: Verso)

Giulianotti, R (2004) *Sport: A Critical Sociology* (Oxford: Polity Press)

Glubok, S. and A. Tamarin (1976) *Olympic Games in Ancient Greece* (New York: Harper & Row)

Goff, Barbara and Michael Simpson (2007) *Crossroads in the Black Aegean: Oedipus, Antigone, and Dramas of the African Diaspora* (Oxford: Oxford University Press)

Gold, J.R. and M.M. Gold (2007) *Olympic Cities: City Agendas, Planning, and the World's Games, 1896-2012* (London: Routledge)

Gold, J.R. and M.M. Gold (eds) (2005) *Cities of Culture: Staging International Festivals and the Urban Agenda, 1851-2000* (Aldershot: Ashgate)

Golden, Mark (2008) *Greek Sport and Social Status. Fordyce W. Mitchel Memorial Lecture Series* (Austin TX: University of Texas Press)

Gordon, Barclay F. (1983) *Olympic Architecture: Building for the Summer Games* (New York: John Wiley & Sons)

Gössel, P. and G. Leuthäuser (1991) *Architecture in the Twentieth Century* (Köln: Benedikt Taschen)

Grant, Jarvie, Dong-Jhy Hwang and Mel Brennan (2008) *Sport, Revolution, and the Beijing Olympics* (Oxford: Berg Publishers)

Grossardt, P. (2002) 'Der Ringer Maron und der Pankratiast "Halter" in epi-graphischen und literarischen Quellen (*SEG* 41, 1407 A und B bzw. Philostr. *Gym.* 36 und *Her.* 14-15)', *Epigraphica Anatolica* 34: 170-2

Guttmann, Allen (2002) *The Olympics: A History of the Modern Games*, 2nd edn (Chicago: University of Illinois Press)

Hagel, S.and K. Tomaschitz (1998) *Repertorium der westkilikischen Inschriften: nach den Scheden der Kleinasiatischen Kommission der Österreichischen Akademie der Wissenschaften* (Vienna: Verlag der Österreichischen Akademie der Wissenschaften)

Bibliography

Hall, Donald E. (ed.) (1994) *Muscular Christianity. Embodying the Victorian Age* (Cambridge: Cambridge University Press)

Hall, Edith (2010) *Greek Tragedy: Suffering under the Sun* (Oxford: Oxford University Press)

Hamilakis, Yannis (2007) *The Nation and its Ruins: Antiquity, Archaeology and National Imagination in Greece* (Oxford: Oxford University Press)

Hamilton, J.T. (2003) *Soliciting Darkness: Pindar, Obscurity and the Classical Tradition* (Cambridge, MA: Harvard University Press)

Hampton, Janie (2008) *When the Games Came to London in 1948* (London: Aurum)

Hargreaves, John (2002) 'Globalisation: Sport, Nations, Nationalism', in John Sugden and Alan Tomlinson (eds) *Power Games: A Critical Sociology of Sport* (London and New York: Routledge)

Harris, H.A. (1962) 'Notes on Three Athletic Inscriptions', *Journal of Hellenic Studies*: 19-24

Harris, H.A. (1968a) 'An Athletic *hapax legomenon*', *Journal of Hellenic Studies* 88: 138-9

Harris, H.A. (1968b) *Greek Athletes and Athletics* (Bloomington and London: Indiana University Press)

Harris, H.A. (1972) *Sport in Greece and Rome* (London and Southampton: The Camelot Press Ltd.)

Harry Potter and the Philosopher's Stone (2001) dir. Chris Columbus (Warner Bros.)

Haskins, E.V. (2004) *Logos and Power in Isocrates and Aristotle* (Columbia, SC: University of South Carolina Press)

Heath, Malcolm (1988) 'Receiving the *kômos*: The Context and Performance of Epinician', *American Journal of Philology*, vol. 109, no. 2: 180-95

Herman, J. (2004) *Athenian Funeral Orations* (Newburyport, MA: Focus Philosophical Library)

Hersh, P. (2010) 'Jones' Relay Teammates Get to Keep Medals,' *Chicago Tribune*, 16 July.

Herz, P. (1996) 'Seltsame Kaisergentilizien: Beobachtungen zur kaiserzeitlichen Nomenklatur', in F. Blakolmer et al. (eds) *Fremde Zeiten: Festschrift für Jürgen Borchhardt zum 60. Geburtstag am 25. Februar 1996* (Vienna: Phoibos-Verlag) 253-9

Hill, Christopher R. (1992) *Olympic Politics* (Manchester: Manchester University Press)

Hoberman, John (1997) *Darwin's Athletes: how sport has damaged black America and preserved the myth of race* (New York: Houghton Mifflin)

Hogan, Jackie (2009) *Gender, Race and National Identity: nations of flesh and blood* (London: Routledge)

Hornblower, Simon and Catherine Morgan (eds) (2007) *Pindar's Poetry, Patrons, and Festivals: From Archaic Greece to the Roman Empire* (New York: Oxford University Press)

Hornblower, Simon (1991) *The Greek World 479-232 BC* (London: Routledge)

Howard, Philip and Alan Hamilton (2004) 'Olympics Ring to Sound of Winning British Ode', *The Times*, 31 July

Huffman, C.A. (2005) *Archytas of Tarentum: Pythagorean, Philosopher and Mathematician King* (Cambridge: Cambridge University Press)

Hulley, Ray (n.d.) *John Hulley* (www.johnhulley-olympics.co.uk) (accessed August 2010)

Bibliography

Hunter, R.L. (1983) *Eubulus: The Fragments* (Cambridge: Cambridge University Press)

Huxtable, A.L. (1960) *Pier Luigi Nervi* (New York: George Braziller)

Imizcoz, J.M.F. (2000) *Discursos xxvi-xxxv. Fragmentos*, vol. III (Madrid Consejo Superior de Investigaciones Científicas)

International Olympic Committee (2004) IOC Marketing Report, Athens 2004 http://www.olympic.org/Documents/Reports/EN/en_report_899.pdf, accessed November 2010

Jameson, Fredric (1981) *The Political Unconscious: Narrative as a Socially Symbolic Act* (London: Methuen)

Janson, H.W. (1995) *History of Art* (New York: Harry N. Abrams)

Jason and the Argonauts (1963) dir. Don Chaffey (Columbia Pictures)

Jason and the Argonauts (2000) dir. Nick Willing (Hallmark Entertainment)

Jenkins, Rebecca (2008) *The First London Olympics, 1908* (London: Piatkus)

Jenkyns, Richard (1980) *The Victorians and Ancient Greece* (Oxford: Blackwell)

Jin Yuanpu (2004) 'Quintessence of Oriental Wisdom: What does China Seal- the Emblem of 2008 Olympic Games Speak to Us?' http://www.c2008.org/rendanews/english_te.asp?id=733, accessed July 2009

Johnson, Samuel (1968) *Lives of the English Poets*, vol. 3, ed. G. Birkbeck Hill (Hildesheim: G. Olms) reprografischer Nachdruck der Ausgabe (Oxford: Clarendon Press, 1905)

Jones, Maggie (2010) 'What Makes Marion Jones Run?' *New York Times Magazine*, 2 May: 32-7

Jones, Marion (2010) *On the Right Track* (New York: Howard Books)

Judah, T. (2008) 'The Glory Trail', *The Guardian* Weekend section, 26 July: 46

Jüthner, J. (1909) *Philostratos über Gymnastik* (Leipzig: Teubner)

Kang Shin Pyo (2005) 'The Seoul Olympic Games and Dae-Dae Cultural Grammar', http://www.c2008.org/rendanews/english_te.asp?id=1809, accessed July 2009

Kanin, David B. (1981) *A Political History of the Olympic Games* (Boulder, CO: Westview Press)

Kassel, R. (1991) 'Korrekturen zu Epigraphica Anatolica 17 (1991)', *Epigraphica Anatolica* 18: 74

Kennedy, G.A. (1994) *A New History of Classical Rhetoric* (Princeton, NJ: Princeton University Press)

Kennell, N.M. (1988) 'Nerôn Periodonikês', *American Journal of Philology* 109: 239-51

Kent, Graeme (2008) *Olympic Follies: The Madness and Mayhem of the 1908 London Games* (London: JR Books)

Kidder Smith, G.E. (1955) *Italy Builds: Its Modern Architecture and Native Inheritance* (New York: Reinhold)

Kindscher, F. (1845) 'Die herakleischen Doppelsieger zu Olympia', *Neue Jahrbücher für das klassische Altertum* 11: 392-411

Kingsley, Charles (1874) 'Nausicaa in London: Or, The Lower Education of Woman', in *Health and Education* (New York: D. Appleton and Company) 69-88

Kingsley, Charles (1880) *Sanitary and Social Lectures and Essays* (London: Macmillan)

Kingsley, Charles (1901) *Two Years Ago*, vol. 1 (London: Macmillan)

Kingsley, Charles (1983) *Alton Locke* (Oxford: Oxford University Press)

Kingsley, F.E. (1877) *Charles Kingsley. His Letters and Memories of his Life*, vol. 2 (London: Henry S. King and Co)

Bibliography

Kirk, T. (2005) *The Architecture of Modern Italy*, vol. 2: *Visions of Utopia, 1900-Present* (New York: Princeton Architectural Press)

Knox, Robert (1852) *A Manual of Artistic Anatomy for the Use of Sculptors, Painters and Amateurs* (London: Henry Renshaw)

Kontorini, V. (1989) *Anekdotes epigraphes Rhodou* II (Athens: Kardamitsa)

Krause, J.H. (1835) *Theagenes* (Halle)

Krause, J.H. (1838) *Olympia* (Wien: Fr. Beck's Universität's Buchhandlung)

Krause, J.H. (1841a) *Die Pythien, Nemeen und Isthmien* (Leipzig: J.A. Barth)

Krause, J.H. (1841b) *Die Gymnastik und Agonistik der Hellenen.* (Leipzig: J.A. Barth)

Kurke, L. (1991) *The Traffic In Praise: Pindar and the Poetics of Social Economy* (Ithaca, NY: Cornell University Press)

Kurke, L. (1993) 'The Economy of *Kudos*', in C. Dougherty and L. Kurke (eds) *Cultural Poetics in Archaic Greece* (Cambridge: Cambridge University Press) 131-63

Kyle, Donald G. (1987) *Athletics in Ancient Athens* (Leiden: Brill)

Kyle, Donald G. (1990) 'Norman Gardiner and the Decline of Greek Sport', in Allen Guttman, Donald G. Kyle, and Gary D. Stark (eds) *Essays on Sport History and Sport Mythology* (College Station TX: Texas A & M Press) 7-43

Kyle, Donald G. (2007) *Sport and Spectacle in the Ancient World* (Malden, MA: Blackwell)

La Regina, A. (ed.) (2003) *Nike* (Rome: Electa)

Large, David Clay (2007) *Nazi Games: The Olympics of 1936* (New York and London: W. W. Norton and Co.)

Lee, Hugh M. (2001) *The Program and Schedule of the Ancient Olympic Games* (Hildesheim: Weidmann)

Lee, Hugh M. (2003a) 'Galen, J.H. Krause, and the Olympic Myth of Greek Amateur Athletics', *Stadion* 29: 11-20

Lee, Hugh M. (2003b) 'Politics, Society, and Greek Athletics: Views from the Twenty-first Century,' *Journal of Sport History*, 167-71

Lee, Hugh M. (2004) 'Gilbert West and the Revival of the Olympic Ideal', in E. Albanidis (ed.) *Ancient and Modern Olympic Games: Their Political and Cultural Dimensions, 25-28 September 2003, Ancient Olympia, Greece* (Komotini) 237-40

Lefkowitz, Mary R. (1976) *The Victory Ode: An Introduction* (Park Ridge: Noyes Press)

Lennartz, Karl (1974) *Kenntnisse und Vorstellungen von Olympia und den Olympischen Spielen in der Zeit von 393-1896* (Schorndorf: Karl Hofmann)

Lenskyj, Helen (2008) *Olympic Industry Resistance* (Albany, State University of New York Press)

Leoussi, Athena S. (1999) 'Nationalism and the Antique in Nineteenth-century English and French Art', 79-106 in Biddiss and Wyke

Lichfield, J. (2008) 'France Debates Beijing Boycott as Olympic Torch Reaches London', *Independent*, 6 April

Litsky, F. (2007) 'Al Oerter, Olympic Discus Champion is Dead at 71', *New York Times*, 1 October

Lo Porto, F.G. (1967) 'Tombe di atleti tarentini', *Atti e Memorie della Società di Magna Grecia* 8: 33-84

Longman, J. (1998) 'US Seeks Redress for 1976 Doping in Olympics', *New York Times*, 25 October

Bibliography

Longman, J. (2008) 'As Records Fall, Suspicions of Doping Linger', *New York Times*, 22 August

Longrigg, J. (1993) *Greek Rational Medicine* (London: Routledge)

Loraux, N. (2008 tr.; originally 1981 Paris) *The Invention of Athens: The Funeral Oration in the Classical City* (New York: Zone Books)

Lorimer, Douglas A. (1978) *Colour, Class and the Victorians: English Attitudes to the Negro in the Mid-nineteenth Century* (Leicester: Leicester University Press)

Los Angeles Olympic Organising Committee (1984) *Official Report of the Games of the XXIIIrd Olympiad, Los Angeles*, http://www.la84foundation.org, accessed April 2010

Lowe, Dunstan (2009) 'Playing with Antiquity: Videogame Receptions of the Classical World', in Dunstan Lowe and Kim Shahabudin (eds) *Classics For All: Re-Working Antiquity in Mass Cultural Media* (Cambridge: Cambridge Scholars Publishing) 62-88

Lucas, John J. (1988) 'The Genesis of the Modern Olympic Games', in J. Segrave and D. Chu (eds) *The Olympic Games in Transition* (Champaign: Human Kinetics Books)

MacAloon, John J. (1984) *Rite, Drama, Festival, Spectacle: Rehearsals Toward a Theory of Cultural Performance* (Philadelphia, PA: Institute for the Study of Human Issues)

MacAloon, John J. (1987) *The Great Symbol: Pierre de Coubertin and the Origins of the Modern Olympic Games* (Chicago and London: University of Chicago Press)

MacAloon, John J. (1996) 'Olympic Ceremonies as a Setting for Intercultural Exchange', in Moragas Spà et al. 1996: 29-43

MacAloon, John J. (2006) 'The Theory of Spectacle: Reviewing Olympic Ethnography', in Alan Tomlinson and Christopher Young (eds) *National Identity and Global Sports Events: Culture, Politics, and Spectacle in the Olympics and the Football World Cup* (Albany, NY: SUNY Press) 15-20

MacKay, D. (2003) 'Lewis: Who Cares I Failed Drug Test?' *Guardian*, 24 April

Mackenzie, Michael (2003) 'From Athens to Berlin: the 1936 Berlin Olympics and Leni Riefenstahl's Olympia', *Critical Inquiry* 29.2: 302-36.

MacLachlan, Bonnie (1993) *The Age of Grace: Charis in Early Greek Poetry* (Princeton: Princeton University Press)

MacMullen, R. (1982) 'The Epigraphic Habit in the Roman Empire', *American Journal of Philology* 103: 233-46

Macur, J. (2008) 'Olympic Blood Samples to be Retested,' *New York Times*, 9 October

Maddock, Alfred Beaumont (1860) *On Sydenham: Its Climate and Palace* (London: Simpkin, Marshall & Co)

Mandell, Richard D. (1971) *The Nazi Olympics* (London: Souvenir Press)

Mann, C. (1998) 'Krieg, Sport und Adelskultur. Zur Entstehung des griechischen Gymnasions', *Klio* 80: 7-21.

Manuel, Frank E. (1963) *Isaac Newton Historian* (Cambridge MA: Belknap Press of Harvard University Press)

Maraniss, David (2008) *Rome 1960: The Olympics that Changed the World* (New York: Simon and Schuster)

Markula, Pirkko (ed.) (2009) *Olympic Women and the Media: International Perspectives* (New York: Palgrave Macmillan)

Maróti, E. (2004-05) 'Gab es Doping im altgriechischen Sportleben?', *Acta Classica Universitatis Debreceniensis* 40-1: 65-71

Bibliography

Masson, O. (1994) 'À propos de Théagénès, athlète et héros thasien', *Revue des études greques* 107: 694-7

Matheson, S. (1989) 'Panathenaic Amphorae by the Kleophrades Painter', in *Greek Vases in the J. Paul Getty Museum*, vol. 4 (Malibu: The Getty Museum) 111-12

Matthews, V. (1979) 'Sulla and the Games of the 175th Olympiad (80 BC)', *Stadion* 5: 239-43

Matthews, V. (2007) 'Olympic Losers: Why Athletes who did not Win at Olympia are Remembered', in Schaus and Wenn 2007: 81-93

Medda, E. (1995) *Lisia Orazioni (xvi-xxxiv) introduzione, traduzione e note* (Milan: I Classici della BUR)

Mercuriale, Girolamo (2008) *De Arte Gymnastica: The Art of Gymnastics*, ed. Concetta Pennuto, tr. Vivian Nutton (Firenze: Leo S. Olschki)

Merkelbach, R. (2003) 'Corrigendum zu Ep. Anat. 34, 170 (Der Ringer Maron)', *Epigraphica Anatolica* 35: 54

Meyer, E. (1990) 'Explaining the Epigraphic Habit in the Roman Empire: The Evidence of Epitaphs', *Journal of Roman Studies* 80: 74-96

Meyer-Künzel, Monika (2007) 'Berlin 1936', in Gold and Gold 2007: 165-82

Miller, Stephen G. (2004a). *Arete: Greek Sports from Ancient Sources* (Berkeley, CA: University of California Press)

Miller, Stephen G. (2004b) *Ancient Greek Athletics* (New Haven, CT: Yale University Press)

Moragas Spà, Miquel de, and Nancy K. Rivenburgh (1996) 'Television and Olympic Ceremonies', in Moragas Spà et al. 1996: 309-32

Moragas Spà, Miquel de, John MacAloon and Montserrat Llinés (eds) (1996) *Olympic Ceremonies: Historical Continuity and Cultural Exchange* (Lausanne: International Olympic Committee)

Moragas Spà, Miquel de, Nancy K. Rivenburgh and James F. Larson (eds) (1995) *Television in the Olympics* (London: John Libbey)

Moretti, L. (1953) *Iscrizioni agonistiche greche* (Rome: A. Signorelli)

Moretti, L. (1957) *Olympionikai. I vincitori negli antichi agoni olimpic* (Rome: Accademia Nazionale dei Lincei) with 'Nuovo supplemento al catalogo degli olympionikai', *MGR* 12 (1987): 67-91, supplement reprinted 1992 in W. Coulson and H. Kyrieleis (eds) *Proceedings of an International Symposium on the Olympic Games* (Athens): 119-28

Moretti, L. (1968-90) *Inscriptiones Graecae urbis Romae* (Rome: Istituto italiano per la storia antica)

Moretti, L. (1970) 'Supplemento al catalogo degli Olympionikai', *Klio* 52: 205-13

Morgan, C. (1990) *Athletes and Oracles: The Transformation of Olympia and Delphi in the Eighth Century BC* (Cambridge: Cambridge University Press)

Morgan, Kathryn A. (1993) 'Pindar the Professional and the Rhetoric of the ΚΩΜΟΣ', *Classical Philology* 88.1: 1-15.

Mullen, William (1982) *Choreia: Pindar and Dance* (Princeton: Princeton University Press)

Müller, Norbert (2000) 'Coubertin's Olympism', in Coubertin 2000: 33-48

Murray, Oswyn (1990) 'The Affair of the Mysteries: Democracy and the Drinking Group', in *Sympotica: A Symposium on the Symposium* (Oxford: Clarendon)

Nagy, G. (1990) *Pindar's Homer: The Lyric Possession of an Epic Past* (Baltimore: Johns Hopkins University Press)

Nagy, G. (1994) 'Genre and Occasion', *Mètis. Anthropologie des mondes grecs anciens*, vol. 9: 11-25

Nancy, Jean-Luc (1991) *The Inoperative Community,* tr. Peter Connor, Lisa Garbus, Michael Holland and Simona Sawhney (Minneapolis and London: University of Minnesota Press)

Nervi, P.L. (1956) *Structures* (New York: F.W. Dodge Corp)

Neumüller, Benno (1985) *Die Geschichte der Much Wenlock Games 1850-1895*, diploma thesis (Cologne)

Newton, Sir Isaac (1728) *The Chronology of Ancient Kingdoms Amended. To which is Prefix'd, A Short Chronicle from the First Memory of Things in Europe, to the Conquest of Persia by Alexander the Great* (London)

Nicholson, Nigel (2005) *Aristocracy and Athletics in Archaic and Classical Greece* (Cambridge, Cambridge University Press)

Nielsen Wire (2008) 'Beijing Games Most Watched Olympics Ever,' 25 August

Nisbet, Gideon (2006) *Ancient Greece in Film and Popular Culture* (Exeter: Bristol Phoenix Press)

Novikov, I. (1980) *Official Report of the Games of the XXII Olympiad, Moscow*, http://www.la84foundation.org, accessed April 2010

O'Keefe, M. (2007) 'Marion Jones Gives Back Medals', *New York Daily News*, 9 October

Olympic Museum Lausanne (2002) *Visitor's Guide* (Lausanne: Olympic Museum)

Panagiotopoulou, Roy (2008) 'The Beijing 2008 Olympic Games from the Greek side of view: first impressions', 'Beijing 2008 Olympic Games: Academics' views of the event' (Centre d' Estudis Olímpics, Universitat Autònoma de Barcelona), http://olympicstudies.uab.es/beijing08/eng/index.asp, accessed July 2009

Pelliccia, Hayden (2009) 'Simonides, Pindar, and Bacchylides', in Budelmann 2009

Peter, J. (2000) *The Oral History of Modern Architecture* (New York: Harry N. Abrams)

Petzl, G. (1982-90) *Die Inschriften von Smyrna I-II, Inschriften griechischer Städte aus Kleinasien* 23-4 (Bonn: R. Habelt)

Pfeijffer, Ilja Leonard (1999) *Three Aeginetan Odes of Pindar. A Commentary on Nemean V, Nemean III, and Pythian VIII* (Leiden: Brill)

Philip, J.A. (1966) *Pythagoras and Early Pythagoreanism* (Toronto: University of Toronto Press)

Phillips, Samuel (1854) *The Palace and Park: Its Natural History and its Portrait Gallery Together with a Description of the Pompeian Court* (London: Crystal Palace Library)

Pick, Daniel (1989) *Faces of Degeneration: A European Disorder c. 1848-c. 1918* (Cambridge: Cambridge University Press)

Poliakoff, M. (1986) 'Deaths in the Pan-Hellenic Games: Addenda et Corrigenda', *American Journal of Philology* 107: 400-2

Poljakov, F.B. (1989) *Die Inschriften von Tralleis und Nysa 1, Inschriften griechischer Städte aus Kleinasien* 36 (Bonn: R. Habelt)

Pollitt, J.J. (1995) 'The Canon of Polykleitos and Other Canons', in W.G. Moon (ed.) *Polykleitos, the Doryphoros, and Tradition* (Madison, WI: University of Wisconsin Press) 19-24

Potter, John (1706) *Archaeologia Graeca, or, The Antiquities of Greece*. 2nd edn, 2 vols (London)

Pouilloux, J. (1994) 'Théogénès de Thasos ... quarante ans après', *Bulletin de Correspondance Hellénique* 118: 199-206

Powell, D. (2008) 'The Top 50 Olympic Athletes', *The Times* and *The Sunday Times*, 8 January

Pressly, William (2010) '*Crowning the Victors at Olympia*: The Great Room's

Primary Focus', in Tom Dunne and William L. Pressly (eds) *James Barry, 1741-1806: History Painter* (Farnham, Surrey: Ashgate) 189-210

Pro Sport München (1982). *Official Report of the Games of the XXth Olympiad, Munich*, http://www.la84foundation.org, accessed April 2010

Race, William H. (1990) *Style and Rhetoric in Pindar's Odes* (Atlanta: Scholars Press)

Race, William H. (1997a) *Pindar: Olympian Odes, Pythian Odes* (Cambridge: Harvard University Press)

Race, William H. (1997b) *Pindar: Nemean Odes, Isthmian Odes, Fragments* (Cambridge: Harvard University Press)

Ramba, D. (1990) 'Recordmania in Sports in Ancient Greece and Rome', in Carter and Krüger 1990: 31-9

Raven, J.E. (1951) 'Polyclitus and Pythagoreanism', *Classical Quarterly* n.s. 1: 147-52

Rehm, A. (1958) *Die Inschriften von Albert Rehm; Didyma 2* (Mainz: Verlag Philipp von Zabern)

Renfrew, C. (1988) 'The Minoan-Mycenaean Origins of the Panhellenic Games', in W. Raschke (ed.) *The Archaeology of the Olympics* (Madison, WI: University of Wisconsin Press) 13-25

Rhoden, W.C. (2010) 'Bonds is Still the King of the City', *New York Times*, 21 October

Richman, Michele H. (1982) *Reading Georges Bataille* (Baltimore: Johns Hopkins University Press)

Rioux, G. (2000) 'Pierre de Coubertin's Revelation', in Coubertin 2000: 23-32

Rivenbergh, Nancy K. (2003) 'The Olympic Games: Twenty-first-century Challenges as a Global Media Event', in Alma Bernstein and Neil Blain (eds) *Sport, Media, Culture: Global and Local Dimensions* (London: Frank Cass) 31-50

Rizzo, Betty (ed.) (2003) *The Early Journals and Letters of Fanny Burney* (Montreal: McGill-Queen's University Press)

Robert, L. (1949) 'Un athlète milésien', *Hellenica* 7: 117-25

Robert, L. (1968) 'Les épigrammes satiriques de Lucillius sur les athlètes: parodie et réalités', *Entretiens Hardt* 14: 181-295

Rollin, Charles (1774) *The Ancient History of the Egyptians, Carthaginians, Assyrians, Babylonians, Medes and Persians, Macedonians, and Grecians*, 6th edn (London)

Romano, D.G. (1996) 'The Real Story of the Ancient Olympic Games', http://www.penn.museum/sites/olympics/olympicintro.shtml

Romano, D.G. (2004) 'Multiple Victors at Olympia', in M. Kaila, G. Thill, H. Theodoropoulou, Y. Xantacou (eds) *The Olympic Games in Antiquity* (Athens: Atrapos Press) 95-133

Romano, D.G. (2007) 'Judges and Judging at the Ancient Olympic Games', in Schaus and Wenn 2007: 95-113

Romano, F. (2006) *Giamblico: Summa Pitagorica* (Milan: Biblioteca Universale Rizzoli)

Roueché, C. (1993) *Performers and Partisans at Aphrodisias in the Roman and Late Roman Periods* (London: Society for the Promotion of Roman Studies)

Ruehl, Joachim K. (1975) *Die 'Olympischen Spiele' Robert Dovers* (Heidelberg: Carl Winter)

Ruehl, Joachim K. (2004) 'Olympic Games before Coubertin', in John E. Findling and Kimberly D. Pelle (eds) *Encyclopedia of the Modern Olympic Movement* (Westport, CT: Greenwood Press) 3-16

Sacchi, L. (2004) *Tokyo: City and Architecture* (New York: Universe)

Bibliography

Sadie, Stanley (1992) (ed.) *The New Grove Dictionary of the Opera* (New York: Macmillan Press)

Şahin, S. (1991) 'Inschriften aus Seleukia am Kalykadnos (Silifke)', *Epigraphica Anatolica* 17: 139-66

Şahin, S. (2004) *Die Inschriften von Perge 2, Inschriften griechischer Städte aus Kleinasien* 61 (Bonn: R. Habelt)

Sandys, John Edwin (1964) *A History of Classical Scholarship*, vol. 2 (New York: Hafner Pub. Co) (repr. 2003, Mansfield Centre, CT: Martino Publishing)

Sansone, David (1988) *Greek Athletics and the Genesis of Sport* (Berkeley: University of California Press)

Sayar, M.H. (2000) *Die Inschriften von Anazarbos und Umgebung 1, Inschriften griechischer Städte aus Kleinasien* 56 (Bonn: R. Habelt)

Scanlon, Thomas F. (2002) *Eros and Greek Athletics* (New York: Oxford University Press)

Schaffer, Kay and Smith, Sidonie (2000) *The Olympics at the Millennium: Power, Politics, and the Games* (New Brunswick and London: Rutgers University Press)

Schaus, Gerald, and Stephen Wenn (eds) (2007) *Onward to the Olympics: Historical Perspectives on the Olympic Games* (Waterloo, Ontario: Wilfrid Laurier Press)

Schmidt, M.S. and L. Zinser (2007) 'Jones Pleads Guilty to Lying about Drugs', *New York Times*, 5 October

Scott, M. (2010) *Delphi and Olympia: The Spatial Politics of Panhellenism in the Archaic and Classical Periods* (Cambridge: Cambridge University Press)

Segal, Charles (1998) *Aglaia: The Poetry of Alcman, Sappho, Pindar, Bacchylides, and Corinna* (New York: Rowman & Littlefield Publishers, Inc.)

Segrave, Jeffrey O. (2005) 'Pietro Metastasio's L'Olimpiade and the Survival of the Olympic Idea in 18th Century Europe', *Olympika: The International Journal of Olympic Studies* XIV: 1-28

Segrave, Jeffrey O. (2010) 'Music as Sport History: The Special Case of Pietro Metastasio's *L'Olimpiade* and the Story of the Olympic Games', in Anthony Bateman and John Bale (eds) *Sporting Sounds: Relationships Between Sport and Music* (London and New York: Routledge)

Senn, Alfred E. (1999) *Power, Politics, and the Olympic Games* (Champaign, IL: Human Kinetics)

Sennott, R.S. (ed.) (2004) 'Exhibition Hall, Turin', in *Encyclopedia of Twentieth Century Architecture* (New York: Fitzroy Dearborn)

Seoul Olympic Organising Committee (1988) *Official Report of the Games of the XXIVth Olympiad,* http://www.la84foundation.org, accessed April 2010

Serwint, Nancy (1993) 'The Female Athletic Costume at the Heraia and Prenuptial Initiation Rites', *American Journal of Archaeology* 97: 403-22

Shaw, Christopher A. (2008) *Five Ring Circus: Myths and Realities of the Olympic Games* (Gabriola Island, BC: New Society Publishers)

Shulman, C. (2008) 'Top 100 Olympic Athletes', *The Times* and *The Sunday Times*, 30 July.

Silk, Michael (2007) 'Pindar's Poetry as Poetry: A Literary Commentary on Olympian 12,' in Hornblower and Morgan 2007

Simpson, Michael (2011) 'Oedipus, Suez, and Hungary: T.S. Eliot's Tradition and *The Elder Statesman*', *Comparative Drama*, 44.4 and 45.1: 509-28

Sinn, U. (2000) *Olympia, Cult Sport and Ancient Festival* (Princeton: Markus Wiener Publishers)

219

Bibliography

Smith, Michael Llewellyn (2004) *Olympics in Athens 1896: The Invention of the Modern Olympic Games* (London: Profile Books)

Snell, F.J. (1987) *Lysias Epitaphios*, edited with introduction and notes (Oxford: Oxford University Press)

Soldatow, Sasha (1980) *Politics of the Olympics* (North Ryde, NSW: Cassell)

Sokolove, Michael (2010) 'Epic Confusion', *New York Times*, 8 August, Week in Review

Solomon, Jon (2001) *The Ancient World in the Cinema*, revised and expanded edition (New Haven: Yale University Press)

Spivey, Donald (1985) 'Black Consciousness and the Olympic Protest Movement, 1964-1980' , in Donald Spivey (ed.), *Sport in America: New Historical Perspectives* (Westport, CT: Greenwood Press) 239-62

Spivey, Nigel (1997) 'Art and the Olympics', *Apollo* (July), vol. CXLVI, no. 25: 3-6

Spivey, Nigel (2004) *The Ancient Olympics* (Oxford: Oxford University Press)

Steiner, Deborah (1986) *The Crown of Song* (New York: Oxford University Press)

Stevenson, Jane (2005) 'Nacktleblen', in Dominic Montserrat (ed.), *Changing Bodies, Changing Meanings: Studies on the Human Body in Antiquity* (London: Routledge) 198-211

Stoekl, Allan (ed.) (1985) *Georges Bataille: Visions of Excess: Selected Writings, 1927-1939*, tr. Allan Stoekl with Carl R. Lovitt and Donald M. Leslie, Jr. (Minneapolis: University of Minnesota Press)

Strasser, J. (2003) 'La carrière du pancratiaste Markos Aurèlios Dèmostratos Damas', *Bulletin de Correspondance Hellénique* 127: 251-99

Strasser, J. (2004-05) 'Les Olympia d'Alexandrie et le pancratiaste M. Aur. Asklèpiadès', *Bulletin de Correspondance Hellénique* 128-9: 421-68

Strasser, J. (2004a) 'Sur une inscription rhodienne pour un héraut sacré (Suppl. Epig. Rh. 67)', *Klio* 86 (1): 141-64

Strasser, J. (2004b) 'Une inscription de Kéramos, le coureur Politès et la Carie "Trachée"', *Revue des Études Anciennes* 106: 547-68

Swaddling, J. (1980) *The Ancient Olympic Games* (Austin: University of Texas Press)

Swift, E. (1996) 'See y'all in Sydney', *Sports Illustrated*, 12 August

Sydenham, C. (2005) *Horace: The Odes* (London: Duckworth)

Taines, Richard (2005) *Sporting London: A Race through Time* (London: Historical Publications Ltd)

Teja, A. (1994) 'Gymnasium Scenes in the Stuccoes of the Underground Basilica di Porta Maggiore', *International Journal of the History of Sport* 11: 86-96

Teja, A. and S. Mariano (eds) (2004) *Agonistica in Magna Grecia: La scuola atletica di Crotone* (Calopezzati: Edizioni Studium)

Thomas, Rosalind (2007) 'Fame, Memorial, and Choral Poetry: The Origins of Epinikian Poetry – an Historical Study', in Hornblower and Morgan 2007: 141-67

Timmers, Margaret (2008) *A Century of Olympic Posters* (London: V&A Publishing)

Tod, M.N. (1949) 'Greek Record-Keeping and Record-Breaking', *Classical Quarterly* 43: 105-12

Todd, S C. (2000) *Lysias Translated by S.C. Todd*, The Oratory of Classical Greece, vol. 2 (Austin TX: University of Texas Press)

Todd, S.C. (2007) *A Commentary on Lysias, Speeches 1-11* (Oxford: Oxford University Press)

Bibliography

Tomlinson, Alan (1996) 'Olympic Spectacle: Opening Ceremonies and Some Paradoxes of Globalisation', *Media, Culture and Society* 18: 583-602

Toohey, K. and A.J. Veal (2007) *The Olympic Games: A Social Science Perspective*, 2nd edn (Wallingford and Cambridge MA: CAB International)

Trollope, Anthony (1985) *Orley Farm* (Oxford: Oxford University Press)

Turner, Frank M (1981) *The Greek Heritage in Victorian Britain* (New Haven and London: Yale University Press)

USATF Hall of Fame, http://www.usatf.org/halloffame/TF/showBio.asp?HOFIDs=124

Usher, S. (1990) *Isocrates Panegyrius and To Nicocles*, Greek Orators, vol. III (Warminster: Aris & Phillips)

Usher, S. (1999) *Greek Oratory: Tradition and Originality* (Oxford: Oxford University Press)

Usher, S. (2007) 'Symbouleutic Oratory', in Worthington 2007: 220-35

Usher, S. and Najock, D. (1982) 'A Statistical Study of Authorship in the Corpus Lysiacum', *Computers and the Humanities* 16: 85-105

Valavanis, Panos (2004) *Games and Sanctuaries in Ancient Greece: Olympia, Delphi, Isthmia, Nemea, Athens*, tr. Dr. David Hardy (Los Angeles: Getty Publications)

Van Alfen, Peter (2004) *A Simple Souvenir: Coins and Medals of the Olympic Games* (New York: American Numismatic Society)

van Nijf, O. (1999) 'Athletics, Festivals, and Greek Identity in the Roman East', *Proceedings of the Cambridge Philological Society* 45: 176-200

van Nijf, O. (2001) 'Local Heroes: Athletics, Festivals, and Elite Self-fashioning in the Roman East', in S. Goldhill (ed.) *Being Greek under Rome: Cultural Identity, the Second Sophistic and the Development of Empire* (Cambridge: Cambridge University Press) 306-34

van Nijf, O. (2004) 'Athletics and Paideia: Festivals and Physical Education in the World of the Second Sophistic', in B.E. Borg (ed.) *Paideia. The World of the Second Sophistic* (Berlin: De Gruyter) 203-27

van Nijf, O. (2005) '"Aristos Hellenôn": succès sportif et identité grecque dans la Grèce romaine', *Mètis* n.s. 3: 271-94

van Nijf, O. (forthcoming) 'Athletes, Artists and Citizens in the Imperial Greek City', in A. Heller and A. Pont (eds) *Patrie d'origine et patries électives: les citoyennetés multiples dans le monde grec d'époque romain*

Vance, Norman (1985) *The Sinews of the Spirit: The Ideal of Christian Manliness in Victorian Literature and Religious Thought* (Cambridge: Cambridge University Press)

Vance, Norman (2004) 'Kingsley, Charles (1819-1875)', *Oxford Dictionary of National Biography* (Oxford: Oxford University Press, online edn May 2006), www.oxforddnb.com/view/article/15617, accessed 10 April 2008.

Versnel, H.S. (1974) 'A Parody on Hymns in Martial V 24 and Some Trinitarian Problems', *Mnemosyne* 27: 365-405

von Albrecht, M. et al. (2002) *Jamblich. Pythagoras: Legende-Lehre-Lebensgestaltung* (Darmstadt: Wissenschaftliche Buchgesellschaft)

von Fritz, K. (1940) *Pythagorean Politics in Southern Italy: An Analysis of the Sources* (Columbia: Columbia University Press)

Walbancke, Matthew (1636) *Annalia Dubrensia* (London: Robert Raworth), repr. as *Dover's Annalia Dubrensia*, ed. E.R. Vyvyan (Cheltenham: Williams & Son, 1878)

Washington, Robert and David Karen (eds) (2010) *Sport, Power, and Society: Institution and Practices: A Reader* (Boulder, CO: Westview Press)

Bibliography

Wee, C.J.W.-L.b (1994) 'Christian Manliness and National Identity: The Problematic Construction of a Racially "Pure" Nation', 66-88 in Hall (ed.) 1994

West, Gilbert (1749) *Odes of Pindar, With several other Pieces in Prose and Verse, Translated from the Greek. To which is prefixed a Dissertation on the Olympick Games* (London: R. Dodsley)

Whitfield, Christopher (1962) *Robert Dover and the Cotswold Games* (Evesham: The Journal Press)

Wiggins, David K. and Patrick B. Miller (2003) *The Unlevel Playing Field: A Documentary History of the African-American Experience in Sport* (Chicago: University of Illinois Press)

Wilson, Penelope, *Oxford Dictionary of National Biography*, 'West, Gilbert', online edn, May 2005, http://www.oxforddnb.com/view/article/29084, accessed 31 July 2010

Winkelmann, J.J. [Winckelmann] (1765) *Reflections on the Painting and Sculpture of the Greeks*, tr. from the German edition of 1755 by Henry Fusseli [Fuseli] (London: Printed for the Translator, and sold by A. Millar)

Winkler, Martin (2001) *Classical Myth and Culture in the Cinema* (Oxford: Oxford University Press)

Winkler, Martin (2009) *The Roman Salute* (Columbus, OH: Ohio State University Press)

Woolf, G. (1996) 'Monumental Writing and the Expansion of Roman Society in the Early Empire', *Journal of Roman Studies* 86: 22-39

Worthington, Ian (ed.) (2007) *A Companion to Greek Rhetoric* (Malden: Blackwell Publishing)

Wyke, Maria (1997) *Projecting the Past: Ancient Rome, Cinema and History* (London: Routledge)

Young, D.C. (1984) *The Olympic Myth of Greek Amateur Athletics* (Chicago: Ares Publishers, Inc)

Young, D.C. (1996a) *The Modern Olympics: A Struggle for Revival* (Baltimore: Johns Hopkins University Press)

Young, D.C. (1996b) 'First with the Most: Greek Athletic Records and "Specialization"', *Nikephoros* 9: 175-97

Young, D.C. (2004) *A Brief History of the Olympic Games* (Oxford: Blackwell Publishing)

Zaidman, L.B. and P.S. Pantel (1992) *Religion in the Ancient Greek City* (Cambridge: Cambridge University Press)

Zinser, L. (2009) 'Jones's Gold in 100 Meters Won't go to Greek Sprinter', *New York Times*, 10 December

Index

Index

Chess, 172, 174, 177, 182, 185, 187n.5
Chionis, 98, 99
Christesen, P., 98
City Dionysia, 186
Civil rights, 180, 181
Classical reception studies, 1, 173
Coe, Sebastian, 18n.11, 42
Cold War, 3, 174, 177, 182, 183
Collins, Wilkie, 147
Colonels' coup, 201-2
Colonialism, 184
Communism, 174, 177
Competition, 80, 81, 129, 138, 146,
      147, 177, 178, 179, 181, 182, 186
Computer games, 182, 186
Cook, Matt, 145
Corinthian War, 83, 87n.26
Coubertin, Pierre de, 1-8, 9, 10, 15,
      16, 38, 68, 74n.19, 76, 110, 113,
      118, 119n.8, 141, 146, 156, 190,
      204
Croton, 25-7, 29-30, 36
Crotty, Kevin, 57
Crystal Palace Olympics 1866, 142-5,
      149, 153
Cultural Olympiad, 8

Dactylo-epitrite, *see* Metre
Damas, Demostratos, 90, 91, 102-3,
      104, 105n.1, 107n.17
Delphi, 37, 49, 115
Democracy, 15, 177, 178, 179, 189n.41
Diagoras of Rhodes, 124-7, 135-6, 138
Diem, Carl, 10
Dionysides, 96, 107n.17
Dionysios of Sicily, 78, 82, 83, 84
Disraeli, Benjamin, 147, 148
Doping, 42-4, 54, 55n.18
Dover, Robert, 109-10, 117, 119n.5
Du Bois, W.E.B., 189n.37

Epic, 174, 175, 177-87
Epideictic oratory, 79, 85-6, 86n.12,
      88n.35

Faber, Petrus, 112, 114, 116, 117, 133
Fascism, 159, 160, 163, 170n.5, 176,
      177, 179, 180, 184; *see also*
      Colonels' coup
Felson, Nancy, 72
Fukuyama, Francis, 181, 183

Galen, 111, 116
Gardiner, Norman, 110
Gender, *see* Athlete, Body
Glen-Haig, Dame Mary, 198
Globalisation, 173, 174, 179, 181-2,
      189n.41
Gordon, Barclay, 164, 165
Gordon Riots, 138
Gorgias, 78, 81
Great Exhibition, 3, 143
Guttman, Allen, 74n.19, 107n.16,
      170n.1, 188n.31
Gymnasium, 7-8, 23, 24, 27, 33, 111,
      152-3

Hagia Sophia, 165, 167
Hangars, 161
Harris, H.A., 99, 100, 103, 104,
      107n.14, 110
*Harry Potter and the Philosopher's
      Stone*, 187
Hellenism, 5, 8, 9, 142, 145, 193
Henry, Ben, 200-1, 203n.9
Hera, 25, 45, 46, 52, 172, 174, 175,
      177, 186
Herakles, 13, 24, 28, 29, 30, 44-5, 51,
      52, 53, 84, 90, 172, 175, 177,
      178, 184
Hermes, 172, 175, 178
Herodotus, 29, 30
Hollywood, 22, 174, 175, 187n.6
Homer, *Iliad* and *Odyssey*, 21-3, 28,
      37, 150, 178, 186, 200
Horace, 130-2, 196-7, 198, 203n.12
Hulley, John, 110, 143
Human rights, 14, 188n.20
Huxtable, Ada Louise, 162, 164, 168

Ideal, of Ancient Greece, 1-2, 4-6, 11,
      14, 15, 127, 141-2, 146, 147-50,
      152, 174, 177, 190; *see also*
      Olympic ideals
Ideology, 23, 37, 61, 62, 68, 73n.10,
      76, 129
Industrialisation, 4, 5
International Olympics Committee, 3,
      9, 12, 14, 18n.6, 43, 51, 52, 156,
      157
Isokrates, 78, 79, 80, 81
Isthmian Games, 25, 55n.32, 56n.49,
      86n.3, 99, 100, 101, 129, 194

224

225